The Hamilton Kerr Institute

Bulletin number 1 *The first ten years*

The examination and conservation of paintings 1977 to 1987

The Bulletin of
The Hamilton Kerr Institute
Number 1: 1988

Editor Ian McClure

Published by the Hamilton Kerr Institute of the Fitzwilliam Museum, University of Cambridge

ISBN 0 904454 23 1

Photography, radiography and reflectography by Christopher Hurst

Additional photography by:
Staff and students of
The Hamilton Kerr Institute
Ashmolean Museum, Oxford
A. C. Cooper Ltd
Central Office of Information
Fitzwilliam Museum, Cambridge
D. W. Gardiner
Westfälisches Landesmuseum für Künst und Kulturgeschichte, Münster

Designed by Sally Jeffery
Typesetting by Goodfellow & Egan, Cambridge
Printed in England by Balding + Mansell, Wisbech

Cover: Paint cross-section made from a sample taken from the counterpane of Titian's *Tarquin and Lucretia* (Fitzwilliam Museum) × 720

Contents

Preface

This is the first issue of the Hamilton Kerr Institute Bulletin. Its publication coincides with the exhibition held in the Fitzwilliam Museum from 12 January to 20 March 1988, to mark the first ten years of the Institute's activity. A bulletin reporting the Institute's work has been considered for some time. Now, through the great generosity of two individuals, who wish to remain anonymous, and of two Foundations, the Calouste Gulbenkian and the Samuel J. Kress, the production costs of this first issue have been met. Its sales will finance the next issue, to be published in 1990.

Our first Bulletin is divided into two sections. The first section covers the first part of the exhibition. The articles and shorter entries in this section represent the anticipated format of subsequent issues. The second section, with shorter entries, catalogues the second part of the exhibition. Together the two sections survey the work of the Institute to the present.

The texts of the Bulletin and of the display materials in the exhibition have been prepared by staff and students, past and present, of the Institute and the Institute's London studio. I am grateful for the time they have so willingly given, in addition to their other commitments, to meet deadlines that seemed impossible. David Scrase provided material for the catalogue entries, as well as valuable advice. The Institute secretary, Valerie Birkett, has typed (and retyped) many illegible drafts. Particular thanks are due to Christopher Hurst, who has taken, prepared and mounted the photographs for the display boards and Bulletin, and to Sally Jeffery who designed both. Without them the exhibition and Bulletin might still be at the planning stage. The illustrations of works from the Royal Collection are reproduced by gracious permission of Her Majesty the Queen; the illustration of Ben Nicholson's *Still Life with Knife and Lemon* by permission of Angela Verren-Taunt.

The exhibition has been most generously supported by Ciba-Geigy UK Limited. The Institute is particularly indebted to Sean Hudson and David Glass of Ciba-Geigy Plastics Division, Duxford, whose enthusiasm and support made this possible. The Institute is grateful also to Laporte Industries and Lloyds Bank (Cambridge) for additional support.

I would also like to thank Professor Michael Jaffé for his support of this project. Frances Hazelhurst has ably overseen the complex administration of the exhibition.

Finally, I would like to express our gratitude to those owners and curators who have lent to this exhibition and who have supported (and provided) the Institute's work, in particular, Sir Oliver Millar, Mrs P. A. Tritton, Mr St J. Gore, Dr Christopher White, Dr Nicholas Penny and Mr Alastair Laing.

Ian McClure
Director

Introduction

Michael Jaffé

The Hamilton Kerr Institute, declared open by The Prince of Wales on 2 June 1978, was founded in the University of Cambridge as a Sub-department of the Fitzwilliam, on the Council of the Senate's recommendation of 10 November 1975. The foundation so recommended, 'as an important and desirable step in enabling the Fitzwilliam Museum to contribute yet more fully to the artistic culture of this country', was to be the University's response to the Report, published in 1972 by the Calouste Gulbenkian Foundation (U.K. & Commonwealth Branch), of which the short title was 'Training for the conservation of paintings'. The terms of reference for the committee of enquiry set up by the Calouste Gulbenkian Foundation in concert with the Standing Commission on Museums & Galleries early in 1969, under the chairmanship of Sir Colin Anderson, were:

To consider the desirability of establishing in the United Kingdom an institute for training in the conservation of paintings and drawings and the objects, size, organization, location and financial requirements of such an institute; and to make recommendations.

The Gulbenkian Report, most persuasively written, had envisaged a metropolitan institute on an ambitious scale; '15,000 square feet of well-lit accommodation in Central London, comparable, perhaps, to a house in Carlton House Terrace', costly in rates and services above the prime costs of purchase and installation; a full-time staff of twenty six (ranging from a director and deputy director to a night watchman and three cleaners), also an unspecified number of part-time staff, all at a cost estimated sixteen years ago of £70,000 p.a.; *plus*, more modestly, £5,000 p.a. to meet the cost of materials, library, photographic and documentation archives on top of £100,000 laid out on equipment and materials. To launch such a project required Government grant-in-aid. To meet recurrent costs there would be income earned 'from the restoration of paintings and drawings; and from investigation and research undertaken, and advice given on their conservation', from tuition fees, and from 'private benefactors towards the endowment of scholarships and for other purposes'.

In the event no lead came from Government, unprepared even to take the hint about Carlton House Terrace. The Gulbenkian Foundation's offer of £150,000 attracted no further generous proposals from private benefactors. The scheme for several years kept barely afloat in the doldrums. This country continued to be without properly organized and supervised training for would-be conservators of paintings, experiencing at first hand works of art of serious consideration; and, outside the National Gallery, without sufficient records, let alone generally available documentation of work done. Nor had even the leading private restorers any laboratory backing at hand for testing or experiment.

Then a fresh breeze blew from Cambridge. The Council of the Senate had reported to the University in October 1972, referring to 'the very generous benefaction by Sir Hamilton Kerr of the Mill House, Whittlesford, and of a substantial sum to maintain that house as an extension of the Fitzwilliam Museum.' Sir Hamilton's gift had been in 1970, it being agreed that he should occupy for life the house which he had converted. During Sir David Piper's directorship of the Museum a variety of eventual uses for the benefaction were mooted: a sculpture park (rather near the Cam); a relocation of some part of the Fitzwilliam's collections (rather far, 7¼ miles, from the Museum's buildings on Trumpington Street); an elegant lodging for successive Slade Professors of Fine Art or for Museum guests (rather an extravagance for such sporadic occupation). Then, from October 1973 until Sir Hamilton's death on 27 December 1974, serious discussion began, seeking his reaction to a conservation institute being established by the Fitzwilliam on the Mill House property. He at once welcomed the idea, suggesting that a start could be made without delay in the extensive but unused outbuildings. After due consultation with the Standing Commission, an institute for conserving textiles was first considered: but the much needed working space for textile conservation could be found better in 'grace and favour' apartments at Hampton Court; and investigation revealed that the Mill House outbuildings were liable every fifteen years or so to be flooded by the Cam. Happily some months before he died Sir Hamilton, himself an amateur painter, was gratified by the news that the Gulbenkian Foundation would consider reviving their 1972 offer, provided that Cambridge could offer, with certain guarantees, a feasible scheme for an institute devoted to scientifically backed training and research in the conservation of easel paintings.

The proposal put forward by the Fitzwilliam

Museum Syndicate, which had by then noted also the 1975 Report of the International Institute for Conservation – U.K. Group ('Conservation in Museums and Galleries'), was the basis of the Council's Report to the University on 10 November 1975. The Council could announce the Syndicate's commitment of income from the Sir Hamilton Kerr Trust Fund to the support of the institute proposed in his name; the agreement of the Gulbenkian Foundation to make £110,000 available, to be used over five years on revenue costs; and of additional offer of £40,000 from the Monument Trust and of £10,000 from the Baring Trust. There were soon to be further benefactions from the Wolfson Foundation, the Pilgrim Trust and, in support of the Institute's Library, the Esmée Fairbairn Trust. The recommendations, which were accepted without demur, provided the Institute with its own advisory council, including at least two persons without official connection with the University. The Fitzwilliam's new Sub-department should be regularly advised by persons of international standing and understanding of its management and aims.

The recommendations specified the appointment of Herbert Lank from 1 January 1976 as the Institute's first Director. The choice for that key office was not wide. Had Mr Lank not been ready to relinquish his flourishing practice in London as a leading restorer, and to come to Whittlesford in order to use his skill and experience to prepare the Institute and to set it on the right course for the tasks ahead, we could not have ventured responsibly upon so hazardous an undertaking. We shall never cease to be grateful to him for his initial lead of the work and training; and to Joyce Plesters of the scientific department of the National Gallery who helped invaluably by her care of planning the laboratories in the Mill House for teaching as well as research, and by instructing the Institute's first chemist, Pamela England, with her own new assistant at the National Gallery. Staff and students of the Hamilton Kerr Institute have continual reason to be glad of the foresight which went into the plans for converting and equipping the spaces of a private house to provide beside the laboratories two large well-lit studios, workshops for lining, panel work and photography, and a library/lecture room. We have been delighted by the visits of Joyce Plesters as one of the distinguished series of specialist lecturers before, during and after the period of her husband, Norman Brommelle's directorship of the Institute (September 1978 – July 1982).

The first meeting of the Advisory Council was held in the Director's Office, formerly Sir Hamilton's dining-room, on 20 April 1976, with the Chairman of the Fitzwilliam Museum Syndicate, Mrs Peter Floud, Principal of Newnham, in the chair. The members have been happy with her genial guidance and that of her successor, Professor Bernard Williams, Provost of King's. On this body have always served representatives of the two chief clients apart from museums, that is the Royal Collection and the National Trust; the Principal Scientific Officers of the National Gallery, first Garry Thomson and, since his retirement in 1987, John Mills; scientists with special interest in the work of the Institute, the late Sir Gordon Sutherland, formerly Chairman of the Honorary Scientific Advisory Committee of the National Gallery, his successor Professor E. T. Hall, founder of Oxford's Laboratory for Archaelogical Research, and Professor Raphael, Professor of Chemistry in the University of Cambridge; John Brealey, Chairman of paintings Conservation in the Metropolitan Museum, New York; in addition to the University's Treasurer, the Head of the History of Art Department and *ex officiis* the Chairman of the Syndicate and the Director of the Fitzwilliam Museum. In September 1976 the first Assistant to the Director was appointed, Alec Cobbe; and in 1977, with a Scientific Research Council grant for three years in support of a research chemist, Mrs England was appointed.

With these appointments the work of the Institute got under way: but from 1976 onwards it was bound to feel financial pressures from the world energy crisis and the consequent inflation of salaries and all other costs. Nevertheless the Institute, while not forgetful of its primary commitment to work for public or publicly shown collections in the U.K., did not turn inward. The Advisory Council Meeting in October 1976 agreed the desirability of accepting foreign students as well as those to whom the Department of Education and Science could, having accepted the Institute's education criteria, award bursaries. We take the best students, one, two or three a year, regardless of nationality; and in return we place suitable students, who have successfully completed their years in the Institute and gained their Certificates, for a fourth year in institutions abroad as widespread as the Vienna Akademie and the J. Paul Getty Museum at Malibu.

We have had J. Paul Getty Foundation support from 1984 onwards: for a student grant, for funding an internship at the Institute, and for funding advanced internships for our own students.

We have had also from 1984 invaluable support from the S. H. Kress Foundation both for equipment and for the support of publication in *The Burlington Magazine* of a series of joint articles by art historians and our own conservators on the problems and lessons of particular masterpieces treated at the Institute. Inside Britain we have had excellent support of our sorely stretched endowment in establishing the essential post of Research Chemist; and we have especially to thank the Rayne Foundation, the Esmée Fairbairn Trust, the Monument Trust, the Baring

Trust and ICI. Thanks to a grant from the Silver Jubilee Trust our first student whose education authority was Scottish was enabled to complete his final year.

The international reputation of the Institute received an accolade in the Introduction to the catalogue of *The Treasure Houses of Britain* exhibition at the National Gallery of Art in Washington. J. Carter Brown wrote of 'the distinguished Conservation Panel . . . Norman Brommelle . . .; Herbert Lank, formerly director of the Hamilton Kerr Institute at Whittlesford; and David Winfield . . . Much additional help came from Dr Ian McClure, the present director of the Hamilton Kerr Institute, and his staff, who undertook much of the work on the pictures and braved fog, snow, ice and numbing cold on their rounds of inspection'. Mr McClure, Director of the Institute since October 1983, has indeed an excellent staff: Renate Keller and Ann Massing appointed Assistants to the Director in 1978 and Karin Groen appointed Research Chemist from 1981. With Herbert Lank, still our Chief Restorer, and his staff, we jointly keep an Ebury Street studio with a workshop for Simon Bobak to work on canvas linings and panels. Each Hamilton Kerr student in turn has a period of training with these experts in London. Paintings of outstanding interest for special scientific investigation or demonstration may be transferred with their owners' permission for part of their time in treatment to Whittlesford. The London studio relies on the research laboratory at Whittlesford for the analysis of pigments and media in paint samples, a service which is also available to other institutions.

We still need that equivalent of a full-time post for the teaching of theory to replace the invaluable work of Norman Brommelle, now in retirement; also more funds for maintaining the archive and library and research projects. One thrust of this research will be into the archive of Charles Roberson, nineteenth century colourman in London, of which the derelict condition was noticed by Alec Cobbe. This unexplored resource was deposited at the Institute on loan in 1978, and in 1986 presented after Roberson went into voluntary liquidation.

Nevertheless we hope in 1988 that we are fulfilling the essential hopes of the Calouste Gulbenkian Report of 1972. The Institute functions as a much appreciated part of a great university museum with an old established and gradually growing collection of paintings, from which each student selects one to copy using materials matched to those of the artist, and for which each monitors conditions in the public galleries as part of his or her course experience. These exercises reinforcing instruction and individual supervision in the treatment of paintings can be achieved at Whittlesford and in Pimlico without the benefit of what would have been an indubitably grander affair overlooking St James's Park.

The Hamilton Kerr Institute of the Fitzwilliam Museum is not only one of the most remarkable developments in the University of Cambridge since the second World War, but also an outstanding contribution to the improvement world-wide of understanding and action in the conservation of paintings.

The training programme

Ian McClure

The Report published by the Calouste Gulbenkian Foundation in 1972 on *Training in the Conservation of Paintings* recommended that a national centre for conservation be set up which would provide conservation services complementary to conservation departments in public museums and galleries. In this framework a training programme could be established which would also undertake and publish research. The Hamilton Kerr Institute was founded in response to these recommendations and, as the Report envisaged, such an establishment is in a position to provide a training that combines the varied practical experience of an apprenticeship to an established restorer, with a more formally organised programme, which when taught in larger groups can leave less opportunity for studio work and the chance to observe and assist in treatment of works of high quality.

The three year certificate course in the conservation of easel paintings, which has now run for just over ten years, has been successful in producing students of high potential. A great deal depends on the selection of the right student as the course demands considerable self-discipline and motivation. The applicants selected are now invariably graduates of Art History, Fine Art or the Sciences. On average two students are selected each year, which in practice gives a staff: student ratio of 2:3. Numbers greater than this would unacceptably reduce the degree of supervision in the studio (fig. 1). An average of sixty candidates apply for a place each year, of whom about sixteen are interviewed. Each interview lasts half a day, and through tests, a formal interview with presentation of a portfolio of work and less formal discussions in the laboratory and studio, an attempt is made to select candidates with the best potential, given that some applicants might have some experience of conservation and others virtually none through lack of opportunity. It is unusual for candidates to have had a rounded education with sufficient background in both arts and sciences – a result of a too early specialization in schools. In many cases, part of the first year is spent in an attempt to redress this imbalance.

Over three years the content of the Certificate Course is approximately 75% practical work and

Fig. 1

25% theoretical. A greater proportion, about 40%, of the first year is spent out of the studio attending seminars, lectures and instruction in the laboratory, and in practical exercises in photography. At the end of the first year, qualifying examinations are set consisting of written papers in practical conservation, the theory of conservation and the science of materials. In addition, three practical examinations are set: the preparation of an examination report on a painting before treatment; the identification of pigments, media and supports and the production of a portfolio of photographs for conservation records.

The results of these examinations are assessed together with the student's performance in the studio. The student is expected to pass easily in all subjects, although written examinations may be taken again. These results determine whether the student should complete the course.

In the second year students devote more time to the studio and the problems encountered generate much of the teaching material: where possible students pursue the required research. On completion of the course students are expected to be able to prepare paint samples, examine cross-sections and carry out micro-chemical tests. They should also know what further results can be obtained from other analytical techniques, such as gas chromatography, infrared spectrometry and the electron-microprobe. In addition, six essays, critical reviews of the literature on given subjects, are set. These essays are assessed at the end of the third year. They replaced the final written examinations in 1984.

In the third year the student is required to make a copy of a painting from the Fitzwilliam Museum and present a project on an agreed topic.

In making the copy the student must examine the condition and technique of the original work, carry out necessary conservation work and undertake, where possible, sufficient scientific analysis to determine the artists' materials. The copy is, therefore, a reconstruction of the original rather than an imitation of the present surface appearance, and gives insight into the artists' working methods and materials and often demonstrates the degree of change that occurs both through changes to the original materials and as a result of restoration treatment in the past. For example, a copy made by Mary Allden, a student at the Institute from 1977 to 1980, of *The Adoration of the Kings* from the studio of Joos van Cleve[1] provided an opportunity to study mixed media in paintings of this period (plate 1, p. 37). The copy (plate 2, p. 37) shows the preparation of the oak panel, the underdrawing of the whole work and parts of the copy completed to different stages in the paint layer structure. Analysis had shown that different media were present, but as the tests could not identify the medium of each paint layer, experiments in different media were carried out. The landscape section was painted in linseed oil; the figures of Joseph and the King were painted in egg tempera in the underlayers with oil in the upper layers and oil and resin in the King's robe. The section along the bottom was completed in an emulsion medium of Venice turpentine, linseed oil and egg yolk. It was found that oil did not provide sufficient opacity in smooth thin layers. The emulsion proved difficult to handle. The oil and resin mixture worked well over tempera underlayers. This type of copy is a valuable teaching aid, particularly if the original is of sufficient technical complexity. For this reason most copies tend to be of fifteenth and sixteenth century panels, although a copy of a seventeenth century flower painting by Balthasar van der Ast yielded considerable technical information.

The project, of about 15,000 words, is expected to include original research, into source material on artists' techniques and materials, the examination of a particular painting or a group of related works, and into conservation techniques and materials. Recent subjects have included an examination of the technique of a group of paintings by George Stubbs, a study of Sir Peter Lely's technique compared to that of his studio and a study of the drying properties of different varnishes.[2] The written work of the second year, the project and the copy are assessed with the studio work at the end of the third year by staff and an external examiner.

Throughout the course the studio work depends on the work load of the Institute and its commitment to its clients. While this ensures the students will observe treatments undertaken on many different works from all periods, the pressure to complete work exerts a discipline of its own.

As students become proficient in skills their contribution becomes valuable. On large projects, particularly with very large paintings, a close-knit team of staff and assistants enables the Institute to undertake work beyond the scope of most studios. On the other hand the temptation to exploit particularly gifted students at the expense of their own development as conservators must be resisted. It is important to ensure that no student becomes involved with a single project for too large a part of their training.

Students work in the studio with a member of staff on a particular project, moving to the point where students working under close supervision can undertake most of the conservation treatment themselves. A limitation of any course is that it is impossible to provide sufficient experience in lining and in panel work in the time available. It is often only possible to engender a critical eye and a clear understanding of what is possible. Emphasis is placed on hand-lining techniques as well as mechanical methods such as hot-table and cold-table techniques (fig. 2).

In addition to lectures and seminars by staff

members, guest lecturers visit on average once a month. Subjects either cover a specialised field or give an introduction to other areas of conservation, for example, the role of the conservation scientist in the museum and the conservation of textiles and libraries. Visits are arranged to other conservation departments and time is allotted to visit exhibitions and permanent collections regularly.

On the completion of the third year and the award of the Certificate, students are expected to seek a further internship for at least one year in a conservation department either in Britain or abroad. It is considered essential that students should have experience of different approaches to conservation problems. Students have gained fellowships to study in the USA, Austria and Holland. The completion of at least a year of internship leads to the award of the Diploma.

The Institute has increasingly accepted interns for periods of up to a year. Students who have completed a recognized training programme are eligible. Interns to date have come from Austria, Canada and the USA as well as this country. As well as those in the conservation of paintings, an internship supported by the J. Paul Getty Trust, specialising in the scientific examination and analysis of painting materials and artists' techniques, has been advertised and filled.

In 1978 the Institute's London Studio was established. Under the direction of Mr. Herbert Lank, students work on attachment during the Certificate course and have the opportunity to work for longer periods during and after their fourth year.

Notes

1 Fitzwilliam Museum, 1784 Studio of Joos van Cleve *Adoration of the Kings*, Catalogue of Paintings I, pp 21–22.

2 A list of student projects is printed in 'Theses and Dissertations' *Conservation News* no. 30, July 1986, p. 18.

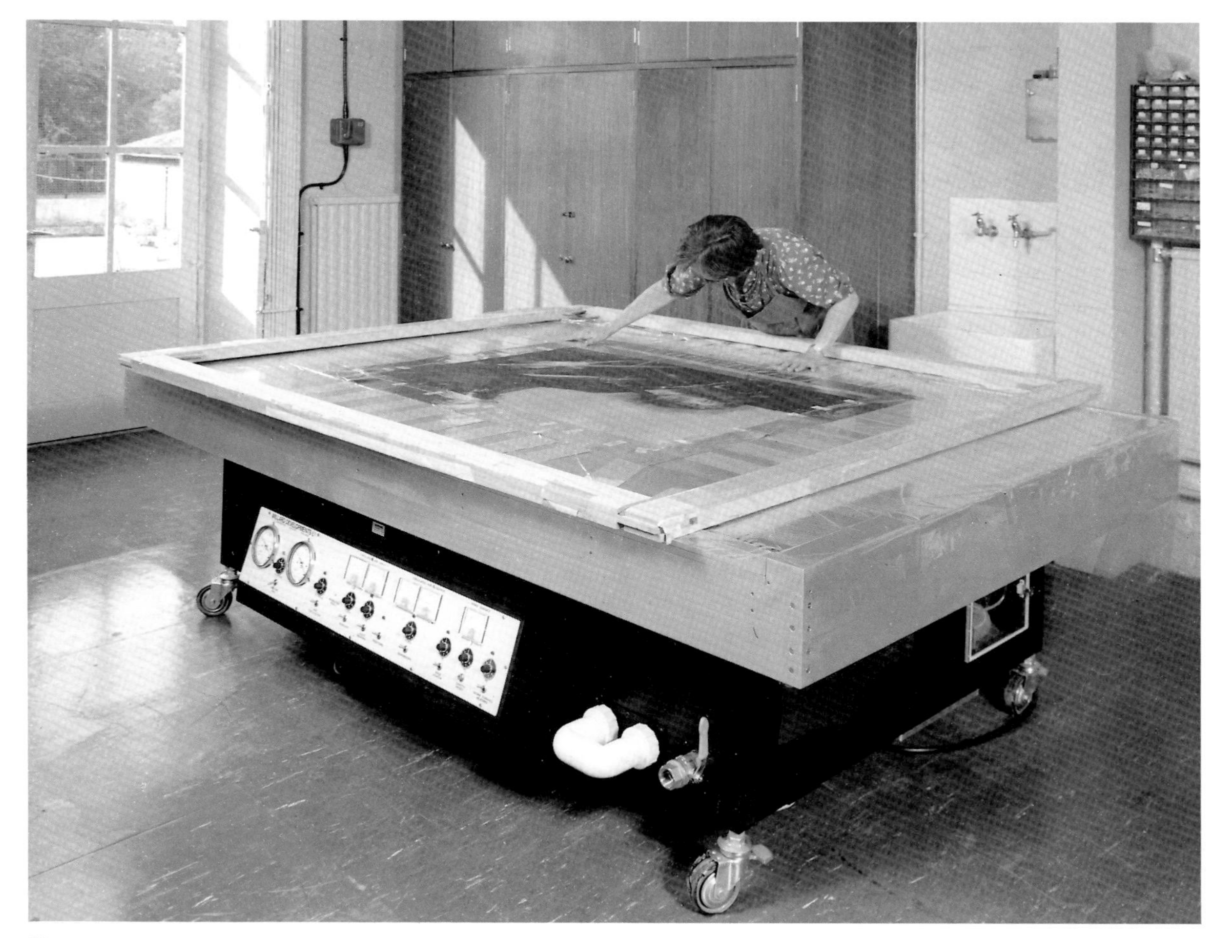

Fig. 2

Aims and achievements

Herbert Lank

An institution devoted to the training of painting conservators must fulfil several related functions in order to achieve its goal. The teaching being largely practical requires a source of quality paintings. It is essential that students are in the presence of good paintings from the beginning. It is of little help to learn from second-rate inadequately painted objects. As well as these, there is the need for a technical back-up system consisting of the relevant analytic tools. Additionally, and equally important, is access to comparative paintings and documentation. Finally, such an institution should be in a position to test and improve upon present methods and materials, enabling it to have a questioning and flexible response to all aspects of the profession.

The Institute was fortunate in that the bequest made by Sir Hamilton Kerr to the Fitzwilliam Museum consisted of premises suitable for conversion into two studios, workshops, laboratories, lecture room and library (figs. 1 and 2).[1] Further space remains available for future expansion. The vision and driving energy of Professor Jaffé and the devoted attention of the then Treasurer of the University, Trevor Gardner, enabled a start to be made in 1975 under the skilled chairmanship of Jean Floud, at that time Principal of Newnham College.

The limited funds available allowed only for a director, one studio assistant, a part-time secretary and a caretaker. In 1977 it was found possible to appoint a Research Chemist. Three students started the three year course in January 1977. Another three students came in September that year. It is indicative of the difficulties encountered in selecting suitable candidates and of fulfilling their expectations, that one of these dropped out at the end of the first year.

In the ten years, 13 students have been awarded the Certificate in the Conservation of Easel Paintings, after successful completion of the three years' basic course. Nine of them were also awarded the Diploma at the end of a fourth year of study as interns in a museum conservation department, or in a similarly practising institution. Up to this year 15 students have received Department of Education and Science post-graduate grants, while four overseas students were funded from other sources.

In recent years, it has been possible to find room for five interns from other countries; coming to the Institute, one at a time, for periods varying from six months to a year. This innovation has proved to be particularly fruitful in that everyone gains from the presence of trained students, coming to the work with differing techniques and attitudes.

In 1979 it became possible to appoint a second studio assistant, as well as a full-time secretary.

In addition, the Hamilton Kerr Institute's London studio continues the practical work beyond the time limit of the course. Seven former students have been accommodated at these premises, some for several years.

How far then have staff, past and present students been able to fulfil the desired aims? In a course of practical training in the art and technique of easel painting conservation lasting, initially, for a period of 135 weeks, it is not possible to instil a mastery of all possible ways of interpreting and of achieving desirable results. It is, however, essential that methods taught can be used with confidence by students and that these can be shown to fall within internationally accepted museum practice.

Underlying the day to day work, which for the students amounts to an apprenticeship by the side of experienced practitioners, are basic principles which should not be transgressed. These start with the tenet that a painting is a work of art and not an object to be treated mechanistically. Each treatment will involve adaptation and sympathetic handling. It is to be hoped that the paintings in the present exhibition will show that this has been achieved.

The workshops are in a calm environment but that does not mean that the work can proceed without the considerable pressures that arise in any institution. It has often been difficult to maintain the set objective with limited staff and the constant need to double annual endowment income with income from conservation work. At the same time it has been essential to have that variety of paintings which will give students an overview of some of the many problems which can arise.

Up to a point these pressures prove a useful challenge and indicative of difficulties to be experienced in their later careers. Beyond that point, as in politics, the underlying philosophy will tend to be lost in the daily battle. At the same time that the financial hazards had to be faced, the supporting services essential to the teaching have had to be built up from scratch.

Fig. 1 The Mill before conversion

Fig. 2 Studio 1 during conversion

The library needs to contain not only technical literature and all relevant journals but also general books on art history and monographs on the painters. This is supplemented by the libraries of the University and of the Fitzwilliam Museum.

Written and photographic records have been kept of the 1360 paintings with which the Institute has been involved over the last ten years. These, together with the slide collection and the results of the laboratory analysis, now require to be coordinated into a suitable computer system, which can also be made available to other conservation workers.

The laboratories are equipped to carry out analysis on pigments, media and the physical construction of paintings. There is, however, one aspect, originally envisaged as an essential part of the duties of the Hamilton Kerr Institute, in which owing to financial constraints little progress has been possible. That is to make a significant contribution to the improvement of methods and materials used in conservation. As the department forms part of a scientifically well equipped University it would be well placed to play its part in this vital research and development.

These seemingly disparate elements of the restorer's task must focus, in practice, on presenting paintings of the past in a manner which is coherent, aesthetically satisfying, and true to the artist's intent within the limitations created by time and other adverse factors. It has to be achieved with a clear understanding of the history of painting and the policies of those museums and art galleries which it serves.

The present exhibition shows that conservation and restoration of paintings is not carried out in an arbitrary manner; that the purpose is not to 'make the painting as new', or 'as it left the artist's studio'. Conservation implies the preservation of the object for the maximum possible period of time, without further treatment. Restoration is the filling-in of disturbing losses in such a manner that the artist's intention is best served, within the natural ageing process.

Staff apart, and the Institute's staff is expected to cover the whole of the syllabus, the choice of students remains a crucial factor. Students should eventually surpass their mentors in skill and knowledge.

Up to this year, there have been around 60 applicants annually for places on the three year course. These were from graduates in science and the humanities aged mainly between 20 and 28. At the opening of the Institute, 30 of them were interviewed. Since then 16 are seen for the annual intake of one to three students. In some years three suitable candidates have been found; in others two or only one. One year no suitable candidate came forward. There are, therefore, no signs of potential talent being widely available. Twelve students who have completed the full four years, to be awarded the Diploma, can be considered capable of reaching the top ranks of the profession.

That the students at the Institute at any one time are small in number is not surprising. It is first of all essential that the student ratio remains as close to 1:1 as possible. Students are not let loose on the fine paintings that surround them but act strictly as assistants under close staff supervision. Secondly, these small numbers remain adequate for the limited opportunities available in the U.K.

What then are the qualifications likely to produce a suitable painting conservator at the end of the course, followed by at least three further years of supervised work? Despite the fact that each student will eventually be expected to be able to carry out a work of conservation in all its aspects and to be fully conversant with the supporting analytical and examination methods, it is in many ways a team enterprise in which all are dependent on the view and advice of co-workers. The prudent restorer does not work in isolation, nor consider himself omnipotent. There is, therefore, some latitude in the choice of applicants. Several factors emerge as essential. Prior disciplined study, allowing for an analytical approach, coupled with artistic sensitivity and an ability to appreciate the subtle overtones of a work of art, which is expressed in the relationship of colour and form. Therefore, a blend of manual skills, basic science and art history is especially welcome.

The education systems of most European countries seldom provide a training both in science and in the humanities. They will, therefore, produce graduates of whom a few will be uneasy with this polarised education. It is amongst these that painting conservators are often to be found. It is nevertheless preferable for a student to have some in-depth knowledge, even if not strictly relevant to the professed intention to become a painting conservator, than to have had a smattering of superficial education in many subjects.

The restorers who have completed the full course are now playing a useful part in the preservation of paintings, both in this country and abroad. The paintings exhibited here show not only the results of staff work with student assistance but also what has been achieved by those former students who have become skilled practitioners themselves.

While endeavouring to train conservators to the best of its ability and resources, the Hamilton Kerr Institute is aware that the true goal is to preserve paintings for the enjoyment and instruction of all.

Reference

1. H. Lank, 'The Hamilton Kerr Institute Converted Premises for the Training of Painting Conservators', *International Journal of Museum Management and Curatorship*, ii, 1983, pp. 71–78; H. Lank, 'A Vertically Mounted X-ray Installation', *Studies in Conservation*, xxiii no. 1, 1978, pp. 42–44.

The examination and restoration of *Henry, Prince of Wales on Horseback* by Robert Peake

A description of the painting: its composition and technique and subsequent history

Renate Woudhuysen-Keller, Sally Thirkettle and Ian McClure

Robert Peake the elder c. 1551–1619
Henry, Prince of Wales, on horseback
Oil on canvas 231 × 219.5 cm
Collection: Mrs P. A. Tritton

The Institute acknowledges gratefully Mrs Tritton's support and enthusiasm for this project.

The portrait of Henry, Prince of Wales was cleaned and restored in preparation for the *Treasure Houses of Britain* Exhibition held in Washington in 1985. It was then that the landscape surrounding the Prince was found to be later overpaint (plate 3, p. 38). Cleaning revealed the dramatically different setting for the portrait. Accompanied by the naked figure of Father Time, Henry is riding in front of a red brick wall, with an arched opening on the left giving a view of a landscape with pollarded trees, a foot-bridge and a stream in the foreground (plate 4, p. 38).

The eldest son of James I, Henry was born in 1594 and died of typhoid fever in 1612. Created Prince of Wales in 1610, for a brief period he created a court noted for its brilliance, vying with courts of Europe in the patronage of art and literature.[1] Robert Peake was the Prince's picture maker. He painted a large number of formal portraits apart from three less conventional images of the Prince: in the hunting field, with particular friends and as a warrior. The inclusion of this equestrian portrait within his 'oeuvre' is, therefore, of particular interest.

The young Prince in splendid armour is riding a heavy white tilting horse. The horse's tail has been dyed with the Prince's colours. On his skirt and saddle-cloth emblems are displayed: hands emerging from the grass, holding anchors, with a rising sun on the horizon. Two marble plaques on the red brick wall in the background display his insignia as Prince of Wales. Behind the Prince walks the winged naked figure of an old man with a white beard. Father Time bears the Prince's lance and his helmet with sumptuous plumes in the Prince's colours, red, blue and white. He is tied by his forelock to the Prince's three-coloured favour. To the left of the wall the view of a distant landscape with trees opens through an arch. Above the wall the green foliage of the nearer trees is visible.

The support of the original painting

The sizes in the following sections are given in inches, as they fit more comfortably with the original measurements of the painting and stretcher. The painted canvas measures 91″ × 86½″. The painting is relined and mounted on a modern stretcher, 92¼″ × 87¾″, which has an inscription dated 1902. The stretcher is quite a bit larger than the painting in order to accommodate a considerable distortion. The painting has been pulled out of true by 1½″ at the top. The original canvas, which is of fine weave, was made up of two lengths of canvas sewn together to provide the required width. The left part is 46″ wide, the right one only 40½″. At the top a strip of canvas has been trimmed off, and later another strip added. The addition is about 3½″ wide. The size of the remaining original canvas is therefore 87½″ × 86½″. Traces of original green leaves surviving along the top of the wall, immediately before the joint of the addition, prove that the painting must have continued above the wall.

The original canvas is supported by three relining canvases, which in turn were strengthened by a strip-lining during the restoration of 1985.

The original size of the painting

The painting poses questions as to its original size, since there is the later addition along the top and possible trimming of the right side as one of the wings of Father Time is cut by the right edge. No cusping is visible along the edges. The only indication of an original edge is in the top half of the left edge. There one can see, about an inch from the edge, a vertical mark. During cleaning the paint to the left of the mark proved to be much softer, as if it had been protected by a frame.

The vertical mark meets the edge of the painting just below the middle, because the left edge had not been cut straight. Towards the left of the bottom edge there is a similar mark, although not as clear as the vertical one. The edge is quite damaged and frayed and, again, cut slightly askew.

Closer inspection revealed diagonal stretcher marks in the corners and horizontal lines of stretcher bars through Father Time's shoulder, through the horse's rump, and below the foot of

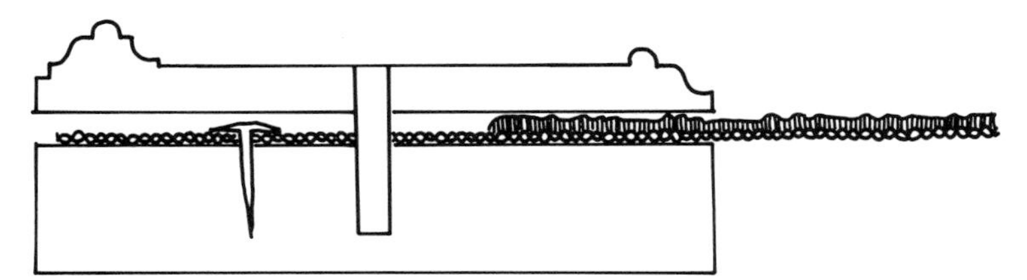

Fig. 1 Conjectural mounting of painting

Fig. 2 Reconstruction of earlier stretcher

Fig. 3 Suggested grid for the composition

the wall. There are also diagonal marks near the line of the grass.

As parts of the diagonal marks at the top of the painting were removed at the time it was trimmed, the reconstruction of the full size of the triangles in the corners has made it possible to determine the original height of the painting. The lack of stretcher marks near the edges is noticeable. If the reinforcing bars show marks, then the inside edges of the outer stretcher bars should show in the same way. There are two possible explanations for this: (a) the painting was trimmed by the width of the stretcher bar, at least 1½″ all round; (b) the painting did not extend beyond the inner edge of the stretcher bars. The second possibility is related to a common seventeenth-century practice of mounting paintings. The painted canvas was not stretched round the stretcher bars and nailed to the sides as has been the custom since the eighteenth century. Instead, the painting was mounted to the front of the stretcher which at the same time served as support for the frame. Usually it was nailed to the stretcher, sometimes also glued to it, which blocks the cusping of the canvas. This method does not produce stretcher marks near the edges (fig. 1).

It is important therefore to keep in mind that the relevant measurements with this type of mounting are those of the inner edge, the *sight size*. The sight size corresponds to the size of the composition visible through the frame.

Reconstruction of the earlier stretcher

The stretcher which left the marks in the painting has been reconstructed as follows (fig. 2):

a. it consisted of two parts: the main one 79″ × 86½″, and a short addition at the bottom, 13″ × 86½″, forming an all-over size of 92″ × 86½″;
b. the main part had diagonal slats fitted to prevent warping. These slats were 1½″ wide and were positioned at a distance of 13¾″ from the corners, forming 45° angles. The stretcher-bars must have been 1½″ to 1¾″ wide, as the marks of the bottom bar suggest;
c. the top bar of the addition left marks 1½″ to 1¾″ apart, matching the width of the bars of the main upper part. The diagonal slats however were slightly narrower, c. 1¼″, and they were fixed at an odd angle, probably due to lack of space within the addition;
d. to reinforce the large main part, two horizontal cross-bars were fitted. The lower one was 1¼″ to 1½″ wide and fitted 27″ above the inner edge of the bottom stretcher-bar. The upper one was 2½″ wide and fitted 24″ below the inner edge of the top stretcher-bar. It would seem that the cross-bars were intended to divide the space into roughly three equal parts;
e. the outer size of the stretcher can be calculated by adding the width of the stretcher-bars to the sight size: 95″/95½″ × 89½″/90″;

f. however, assuming that the painting was mounted onto the front of the stretcher, the sight size would equal the original composition: 92″ × 86½″.

It would seem therefore that the larger part of this stretcher was made up from an existing one, *narrower* than the painting, with an addition at the bottom to accommodate the height of the painting.

If the height of the painting at the time was 92″, and the seam joining the two widths of canvas runs 46″ from the left of the painting, we can reasonably assume that the right half of the painting canvas was 46″ wide as well, giving a square canvas 92″ × 92″.

Whether the painting was trimmed by 5½″ along the right edge to fit the existing main part of the stretcher, or whether it had been trimmed even earlier, is a matter for debate. However, it would have necessitated considerable labour to add 5½″ to the side of an existing stretcher, and it might well have seemed easier to trim the painting. The right edge of the painting was the only one that could be trimmed without losing essential parts of the composition. On the left the horse's plumes would have been lost, as would part of the landscape, whereas losing the tip of Father Time's wing would be more acceptable.

Assuming that the painting was originally 92″ square, it would have been made of two lengths of canvas, each 48″ wide. Sewn together they would have provided a support of 96″ × 96″.

Aiming for a composition of 92″ × 92″ the painter would have painted about one inch beyond the intended size to allow for distortion of the painted edge during mounting. Outside the painted area of 94″ × 94″ there would have been an inch or so of bare canvas to spare to fix it to the stretcher.

The composition

If the painting was originally square and the seam ran through the middle, there must be elements in the painting which are symmetric to the seam.

Indeed, the position of the marble slabs is symmetric to the centre of the painting. The horse also is placed in the middle; its forehead has the same distance to the seam as the fetlock of the left hind leg. In addition there are regular repetitions of measurements in the proportions of the composition: the grey foreground is twice as wide as the distance between the wall and the left edge, which is repeated in the distance between the row of ornamental bricks of the wall and its top. There is reason to assume that some sort of square grid had served as an aid to composition.

Experiments to divide the square of 92″ into a grid produced 16 × 16 subdivisions of squares measuring 5¾″. These divide the height of the wall into 11 units, the neck of the horse is two units below the row of ornamental bricks, its rump is two units further down again. Even the horizontal grouting lines of the brick wall correspond to the grid, four bricks to a square, which seems to confirm the theory.

Whereas single measurements seem to correspond to the grid, the overall composition is strongly governed by the 45° diagonals of the square and the steeper diagonals of its halves. (fig. 3).

The position of the Prince on his horse suggests diagonals rising at a ratio of 2:1. It seems that the triangle formed by the diagonals of the two halves of the square played an important part in the composition. The angle of the Prince's leg and body fits on the rising diagonal of half the inner square formed by subdivision of the painting into 4 × 4 squares. The echo of the diagonals recurs in the horse's mane, the angle of its left hind leg, and the smaller shape of its raised right hind leg. The Prince's right arm suggests this rhythm and it can be felt in the fall of the plumes of the helmet into the wings of Father Time. It is striking that the line of the grass, dividing foreground from background, three units from the bottom of the painting, coincides with the proportions of the Golden Section. The same is true for the top of the wall with the arch in the background.[2]

The level of the Prince's eyes, two units below the top edge of the painting, coincides with the top of an equilateral triangle based on the bottom of the square. This is an old motif to indicate the superior status of a figure. The numerical system of a grid of 16 × 16 units happens to coincide very closely with these geometric divisions.[3] It would be interesting to study contemporary documents connected with Prince Henry's court reflecting current art theory relevant to this composition.

Painting technique

When examining the painting technique the opportunity was taken to compare the results with the recommendations of contemporary authors.

For English paintings of the seventeenth century Richard Haydocke's English translation of Lomazzo's *Trattato dell'arte della pittura* . . . of 1598 is very important, as are Henry Peacham's treatises *The Compleat Gentleman* of 1612 and *The Gentleman's Exercise* of 1634.[4] Theodore Turquet de Mayerne, physician of James I, who came to England in 1610, kept a note-book on his observations on painting technique. He knew Van Dyck and Rubens and his book is an extremely valuable source for the reconstruction of seventeenth century painting materials and techniques.[5]

The following account of the processes involved in the making of this painting is an abbreviated version of Sally Thirkettle's final-year project at the Institute[6] whilst a student.

The stretched canvas was sized, then the two layers of ground, first a red one containing yellow ochre, red ochre and quartz, then a very light grey one made of lead-white, ochre and black, were applied. The texture of the ground is quite gritty and it must have been fairly paste-like to have been spread out with a priming knife, as the ridges visible on the X-radiograph suggest.

Gritty particles of quartz in the lower red layer can be seen in thinly painted areas like the foreground.[7]

There is hardly any underdrawing visible. The few dark lines that can be detected with infra-red reflectography, for example in the horse's right front leg, seem to have more to do with dark outlines painted during the first blocking-in of colours. This means that the under-drawing was made with a material which does not absorb infra-red light such as red chalk or umber.

Fig. 4 First stage in the composition

Fig. 5 Subsequent stage in composition

The painter then proceeded to block in the main areas with paint, as can be reconstructed by the sequence of the paint-layers where adjoining areas overlap. One has to keep in mind that oil-paint, depending on the pigment used, needed at least two or three days to dry sufficiently for the next layer to be painted on top.

The painter started with the figure of the Prince and the horse, laying in the Prince's face with a rather pinkish colour, his armour and saddle-cloth with a metallic blue-grey layer of smalt and black in a lot of medium (fig. 4). With azurite and white he laid in the sky and hills of the landscape. Then he painted the horse with broad brush-strokes. The fine, sharp impasto can still be seen in the tail, where the top layer is slightly abraded. Then the wall was painted round the horse and the Prince, as small gaps of light grey ground along the outlines show. The foreground was given a thin light greyish-brown layer. Whereas the figure of the Prince had been taken into account when the first red layer of the wall was painted, the figure of Father Time is painted on top of the wall and the grey foreground (fig. 5). This is the reason why his legs look greyish compared with his arms and chest, and why the red of the wall shines through his wings. It is tempting to draw conclusions from the fact that Father Time only appeared after the first blocking-in of colours. Without him the painting would have been an ordinary equestrian portrait. The presence of the allegorical figure of Time being tied to the Prince and carrying his lance and helmet elevates the portrait to a pictorial symbol of the promise of success and greatness during Prince Henry's forthcoming reign. This was a decisive change in the character of the commission to the painter.

Subsequently the painter made corrections, mainly to the horse. The legs were shortened, the outline of the rump lowered, and the arch of the horse's neck made higher. The position of the horse at the first stage, and the first version of Father Time's wings (see below), has become visible again as the top paint layer lost some of its covering power with age and due to a certain amount of abrasion. The plumes of the helmet were painted, the Prince's face received finer modelling, the ornaments and *imprese* of the armour and saddle-cloth were painted in, the trees in the landscape and the grass in the foreground received their green leaves. A second layer of a bright red rather transparent iron-oxide pigment was used on the wall to define the new outlines. During painting the second red layer of the brick wall the painter changed the position of Father Time's wings. In the first version the tip of the light grey wing overlapped the horse's rump, as if spread in a protective gesture. When the painter lowered the outline of the horse's rump, he did not lower the wing as well, but instead lifted and enlarged it, so that Father Time is now clearly walking in the second plane of the picture, behind the horse. At a final stage all the highlights and the decorative white grouting lines of the wall were put in (fig. 6).

The painting technique observed in this painting corresponds very closely to the recommendations given by Peacham.[8] There are precise instructions on how to paint ruffs, velvet, jewels, trees, landscapes. This extract from Peacham on how to paint a landscape well matches what is found in this painting: 'For Skie and Landscaps. For a Sky or Landscaps that seeme a great way off take Oyle Smalt, or Bice if you will, and with Linseed Oyle onely temper it on your pallet (for in grinding Smalt or Bice, they utterly lose their colour) with white Lead, and where it looketh redde as the morning, use Lake &c.'[9]

Fig. 6 Final stage in composition

Fig. 7 During cleaning, showing first restoration

The painting, having been mounted on a temporary loom during the painting process, was then stretched to its permanent stretcher, ready for the frame-moulding to be fitted in front. It was during this final mounting that straight lines near the edges could become distorted. To get parallel lines exactly straight is very difficult, because the tension required increases towards the corners. This might be the reason for the slight sloping movement of the wall on the right.

Previous restorations

Five earlier restorations were discovered during cleaning. From the various layers of retouchings and putties a relative chronology could be established.

The first restoration identified by putties and retouches directly on the original paint-layer involved turning the red brick wall into a grey wall of large rectangular blocks of stone and the ornamental row of bricks into a dark shadow (fig. 7). The putties below this grey layer looked yellowish-white and slightly transparent, with a fine-grain whitish top layer. On top of this the retouchings had been applied (plates 5 and 6, p. 39). Most of the damages were paint losses due to creases in the canvas; for example, the repeating series of losses in the horse's neck (plate 7, p. 39) and in Father Time's head, chest and shoulder. Minor damages in the Prince's face contained the same putty. It is possible that at some stage the painting was removed from its original stretcher and stored rolled up. This might explain the matter of the peculiar later stretcher. The original paint-layer must have reached a certain state of brittleness judging by the losses where the canvas had creased. This dates the first restoration to about fifty years after the original painting was finished.

The restorer also made quite a number of retouchings in the armour. The original paint is very abraded in the dark areas, and the shadows were reinforced at this stage. The restorer also made the Prince's chest look larger by adding a triangular piece to the front of the armour. From the functional point of view this made no sense at all. The new grey wall colour was painted round the alteration in the armour. Probably the made-up stretcher belongs to this first restoration. Its marks are very definitely established and the paint

Fig. 8 Detail showing alteration to armour and addition of stone wall

of the next restoration is found in the cracks (fig. 8). It would have been at this stage that the painting was trimmed by 5½″. There was a thick layer of dark brown varnish between this and the next restoration.

The second restoration brought the change from grey stone wall to distant landscape. Father Time disappeared under a bright blue sky painted with indigo and lead-white. From the right of the painting a tree stretched its branches across to provide support for the marble plaque on the left.

The plaque had been kept from the original composition and was made to look as if it was hanging from the end of the branch by a piece of string. The horse was turned into a slender Arab with a black mane; the muscles were emphasised with strong contrasts in the modelling.

The main feature of the painting technique of the overpaint is the strong impasto. The Prince remained unaltered, except for retouchings and strengthening of highlights in his skirt and saddle-cloth. The blades of grass behind the horse were changed into distant trees, and a strip of orange sky to the left of the horse's raised leg probably indicates a sunrise as in the *imprese* on the Prince's skirt. This second restoration involved mending a number of tears and holes. Some of the very hard, dense yellowish-white putty of this restoration is found on damages that had already been dealt with during the first restoration and obviously needed repair again; for example, the damage in Father Time's chest.

It is interesting that the sky is painted with indigo. In 1724 the method of making prussian blue was published in England by Woodward, and by the second quarter of the eighteenth century it was in general use.[10] Assuming that the restorer would have used prussian blue if it had been available to him, then the blue sky cannot have been painted much later than c. 1725.

The fact that the retouchings in Father Time's chest had developed cracks into which the indigo overpaint had penetrated proves that there must have been a considerable time between the first and the second restoration (plates 5 and 6). The painting of the landscape therefore must have been carried out towards the end of the seventeenth century at the earliest.

It was probably during the second restoration that the top of the painting was trimmed by 4½″ in order to make the painting as square as possible. The remaining original canvas measures 87½″ × 86½″.

The third restoration added 3½ to 4″ to the top of the painting, which restored it to almost its original height. The painting still had its original height at the time of the first restoration as is proved by the stretcher marks. The strip at the top must have been added during the third restoration, because prussian blue was used in painting the sky on it. In order to be able to add the strip the painting was relined with two layers of canvas. The pressure applied during this relining pressed the impasto of the landscape paint-layer down into the original paint-layer. The impressions of the shapes of the leaves are now, after the removal of the overpainted landscape, visible in the brick wall, and the impasto of the thick white brush-strokes on the horse's rump and neck is noticeable as slight dents in the surface.

The gap between the original and the addition was filled with grey putty. The entire strip received a coat of brown colour and was then painted out with prussian blue, lead-white and black to match the by then considerably darkened landscape. Grey putty and, for lighter areas, pinkish white putty, both very gritty, filled losses along the edges and in the horse. The retouching covered a broad strip along all four edges, going beyond the puttied areas. Nail-holes on all four edges indicate that there must have been another stretcher before the present one.

The fourth restoration is dated 1902 by an inscription in pencil on the present stretcher.[11]

The painting was relined again, but the double relining canvas was left in place. Cracks along the joint of the addition at the top and the nail-holes along the edges from the earlier stretcher were filled with white putty. The retouchings were brownish and very oily. The present stretcher measures 92¼″ × 87¾″ and has one vertical and two horizontal cross-bars.

That a fifth restoration must have taken place is indicated by the presence of reinforcements on the back of the stretcher and from the fact that there is a series of nail-holes in the canvas and the stretcher which does not continue in the reinforcements. The painting must have been removed from the stretcher, the repairs to the stretcher carried out, and the painting mounted on the stretcher again. The cleaning test to the left of the horse's left front leg which was discovered during the present restoration could have taken place on this occasion. The area was covered again by retouching.

The varnishes of the third to fifth restorations had combined to a thick brown layer, turning the sky greenish and very dark. The horse must have been partially cleaned before, because the varnish there had not yellowed to quite the same extent.

The 1985–86 restoration at the Hamilton Kerr Institute

The decision to remove the landscape

During removal of the layers of brown varnish from the landscape the old cleaning test to the left of the horse's left leg appeared. A different composition was clearly visible underneath (plate 8, p. 39). When the painting was scanned by infrared reflectography, the trees to the left and the small bridge could be recognised. The area behind the Prince remained confused. To obtain a better idea of what might lie underneath that area X-radiographs were taken. They showed an old man with a white beard, carrying a lance. The X-radiograph also showed very localised damages (fig. 9).

After the owner had been consulted, it was decided to carry out cleaning tests to establish whether the underlying paint-layers were sufficiently well-preserved to justify revealing them (plate 10, p. 39). There was the possibility that the original paint might have been roughened to provide a key for the overpaint; or that the very bad state of the original painting had been the reason for overpainting it. However, the

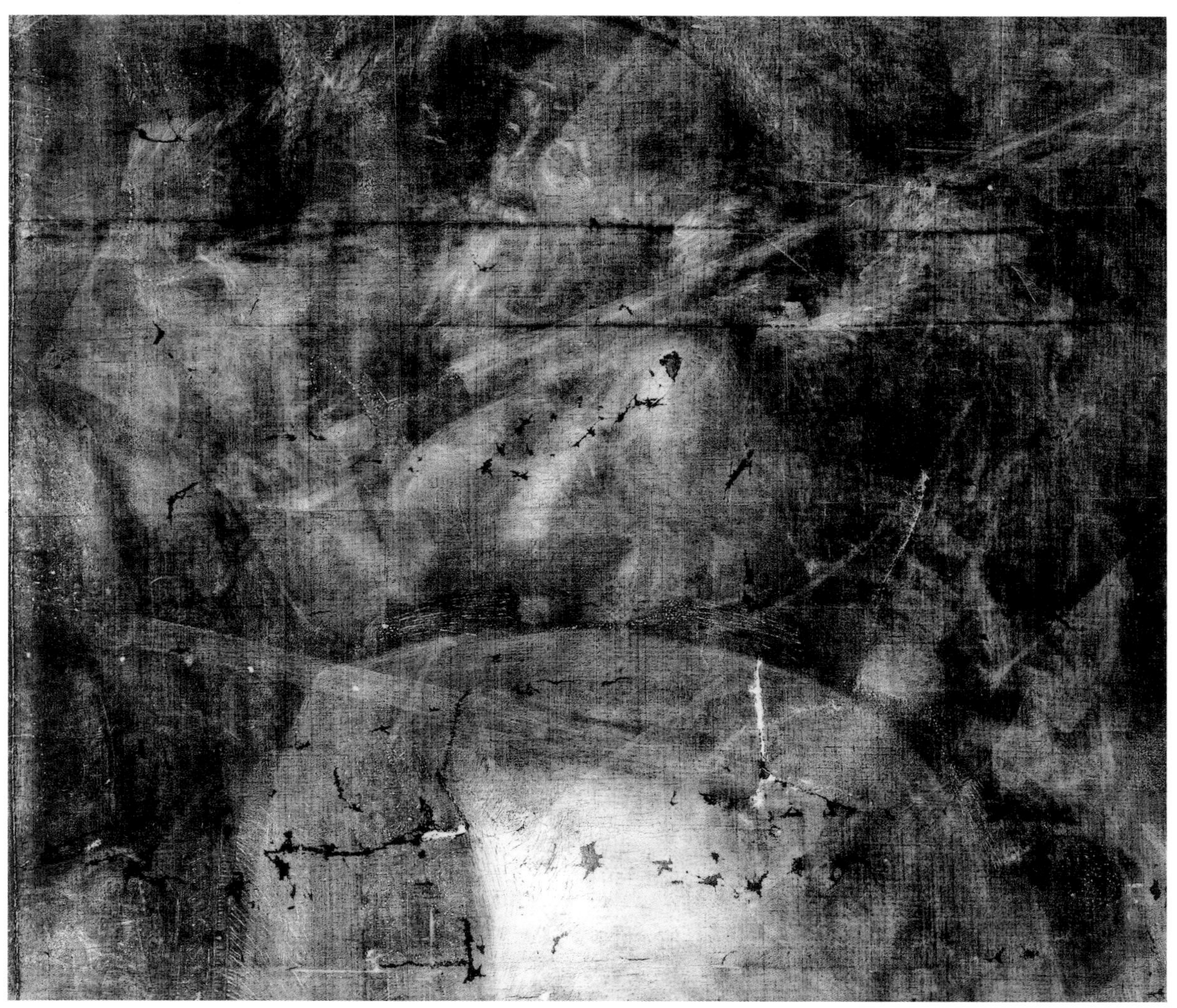

Fig. 9 X-radiograph assembly of area behind Prince

underlying image appeared quite intact, with no signs of severe abrasion.

The Prince's armour and face, which had not been overpainted apart from local retouchings and strengthened highlights, were in good condition. This encouraged our assumption that the reason for overpainting the background had to do with the iconography of the painting, rather than with its state of preservation.

Cross-sections showed that the thick layer of brown varnish underneath the landscape had penetrated into cracks of the original paint-layer, indicating that the overpainting had been carried out a considerable time after the painting's completion (plate 9, p. 39). We were confident that it would be possible to remove the landscape without risk to the original composition.

There remained the problem of evaluating the possible gains of uncovering the original, against the loss of the landscape, an important part of the painting's history. The landscape would be lost, in which the use of indigo suggested that it had been painted before 1724 and which for stylistic reasons could be dated to the late seventeenth century.

The quality of the landscape was poor, the impastoed leaves woodenly repeated and the recession into the distance, even with the varnish removed, very uncertain. The removal of the landscape would, it was hoped, reveal intact a major royal commission.

The treatment of the painting

The relining canvas of 1902 was very weak at the tacking edges. The adhesion between all the relinings and the original was still very good. It was decided therefore to strengthen only the edges, by means of a strip-lining. The adhesive used was BEVA 371, a mixture of synthetic resins and waxes. Once it had been established that the original painting was in good condition, the decision was made together with the owner to remove the landscape to regain the original painting by Robert Peake. The addition along the top was left in place, but the oily paint-layer of the fourth restoration was removed. With the aid of remaining traces of blue, green and yellow along the top of the wall and the few leaves still visible, a new area of foliage and sky was reconstructed. The missing part of the plumes on the Prince's hat were dealt with on the same principle. Comparison with contemporary portraits helped with the reconstructions.

The retouchings were done using powder pigments, with egg tempera as a medium. The varnish is MS2A, a synthetic resin based on polycyclohexanol dissolved in white spirit. The same varnish was used as a medium to apply glazes to the tempera retouchings.

Notes

1. For an account of the Prince's brief life see: Gervase Jackson-Stops, *The Treasure Houses of Britain*, exhibition catalogue, Washington, National Gallery of Art, 1985, Catalogue No 56, p. 132, entry by Roy Strong; Roy Strong, *Prince Henry and England's Lost Renaissance*, London 1986.
2. For a description of the Golden Section see: H. E. Huntley, *The Divine Proportion, a Study in Mathematical Beauty*, New York 1970, pp. 24 and 27.
3. For the significance of geometric proportion and numbers in late renaissance art theory see: R. Wittkower, *Architectural Principles in the Age of Humanism*, 4th ed., London 1972, Appendix II p. 161. As Wittkower points out, it is a major achievement of late renaissance art theory to incorporate geometric proportions into the numeric system. Fig. 3 shows how geometric figures closely relate to the numeric grid of 16 × 16 in this composition.
4. Giovanni Paolo Lomazzo, *Trattato dell'arte della pittura, scoltura, ed architettura*, Milan 1584, translated by: Richard Haydocke, as *A Tracte containing the Artes of Curious Paintinge, Caruinge and Buildinge*, Oxford 1598; Henry Peacham, *The Gentlemans Exercise*, London, 1612; Henry Peacham, *The Compleat Gentleman*, London, 1634. A good bibliography of 17th century English treatises can be found in R. K. R. Thornton and T. G. S. Cain, *A Treatise Concerning the Arte of Limning by Nicholas Hilliard*, Mid Northumberland Arts Group, 1981, pp. 137–9.
5. Theodore Turquet de Mayerne, 'Pictoria, sculptoria et quae subalternarum artium', manuscript, 1620, British Museum, Sloane 2052; Ernst Berger, *Quellen für Maltechnik während der Renaissance und deren Folgezeit*, München 1901, reprinted Walluf/Nendeln 1973; Johannes Alexander van de Graaf, 'Het De Mayerne manuscript als bron voor de schildertechniek van de Barok', dissertation Univ. Utrecht, Mijdrecht, 1958; Camille Versini et Marcel Faidutti; 'Le Manuscrit de Turquet de Mayerne', Lyon n.d. (post 1967).
6. Sally Thirkettle, 'The Cleaning and Examination of "Henry Prince of Wales on Horseback" and other works by Robert Peake', unpublished report, Hamilton Kerr Institute, University of Cambridge, 1986.
7. Pigment analysis was carried out by Karin Groen.
8. See Peacham, *The Compleat Gentleman*, p. 111, 'To begin a picture'.
9. Peacham, *The Compleat Gentleman*, p. 116.
10. Prussian blue was discovered accidentally c. 1705 by Diesbach in Berlin. The method of production was published by Woodward in *Philosophical Transactions* 1724. Prussian blue has been identified in a work by Hogarth dated to the early 1730s (*Music Party*, Fitzwilliam Museum). See: R. D. Harley, *Artists Pigments c. 1600–1835*, London 1970, pp. 65–68; H. Kühn, *Reclams Handbuch der Künstlerischen Techniken*, Stuttgart 1984, p. 38.
11. The inscription is written on the *inside* of the stretcher, i.e. facing the canvas. It reads 'Re-lined by J. & H. Reeve, 1902, London, W'.

The Judgement of Solomon[1]

Keith Laing

Unknown artist
The Judgement of Solomon
Oil on canvas, 208.3 × 315 cm
National Trust, Kingston Lacy

The date of this painting's execution, and the identity of the artist, remains a subject of much debate; no contemporary records appear to have survived. The first known reference to the work is by Ridolfi,[2] writing in 1648, who attributed it to Giorgione. More recently, however this attribution has been rejected in favour of his pupil, Sebastiano del Piombo.[3] It is generally considered to have been painted at the turn of the sixteenth century.

The Judgement of Solomon (fig. 1) is exhibited after the removal of extensive overpaint,[4] dating possibly from a period shortly after Bankes's acquisition in 1820. In 1869, when the painting was exhibited at Burlington House, it was noted that it had 'undergone scaling and repainting by which several bits and some heads have been injured' and 'the semi-dome of the niche daubed with yellow'.[5]

In his description of the painting, Ridolfi acknowledged that it is unfinished.[6] The most obvious confirmation of this fact is the absence of the two babies, essential to the scene. However, the full extent to which it was left incomplete can only be properly appreciated after the recent removal of thick, discoloured layers of varnish and several layers of overpaint (plate 11, p. 40). Traces of the white gesso in the interstices of the unprotected canvas are visible in many unfinished areas, most notably the right arm of the true mother. The wavy lines on the shirt front of the figure next to the executioner (fig. 2) are merely scored into the still wet paint as an indication to guide later detailing. His feet are unfinished and the blue stockings freely sketched in. There is some confusion in the modelling of the old man's red drapery around his hands, which are themselves incomplete. Much of the architectural detailing is only loosely indicated, or absent altogether.

Fig. 1 Whole, after cleaning and restoration

2

Fig. 2 Detail, figure to the left of the executioner, showing the lines scored into the wet paint on his shirt

Fig. 3 Reconstruction of the earliest architectural scheme from the existing evidence. Solomon is included as he was present from the very beginning; each composition is painted around him.

Fig. 4 Reconstruction of the second architectural scheme

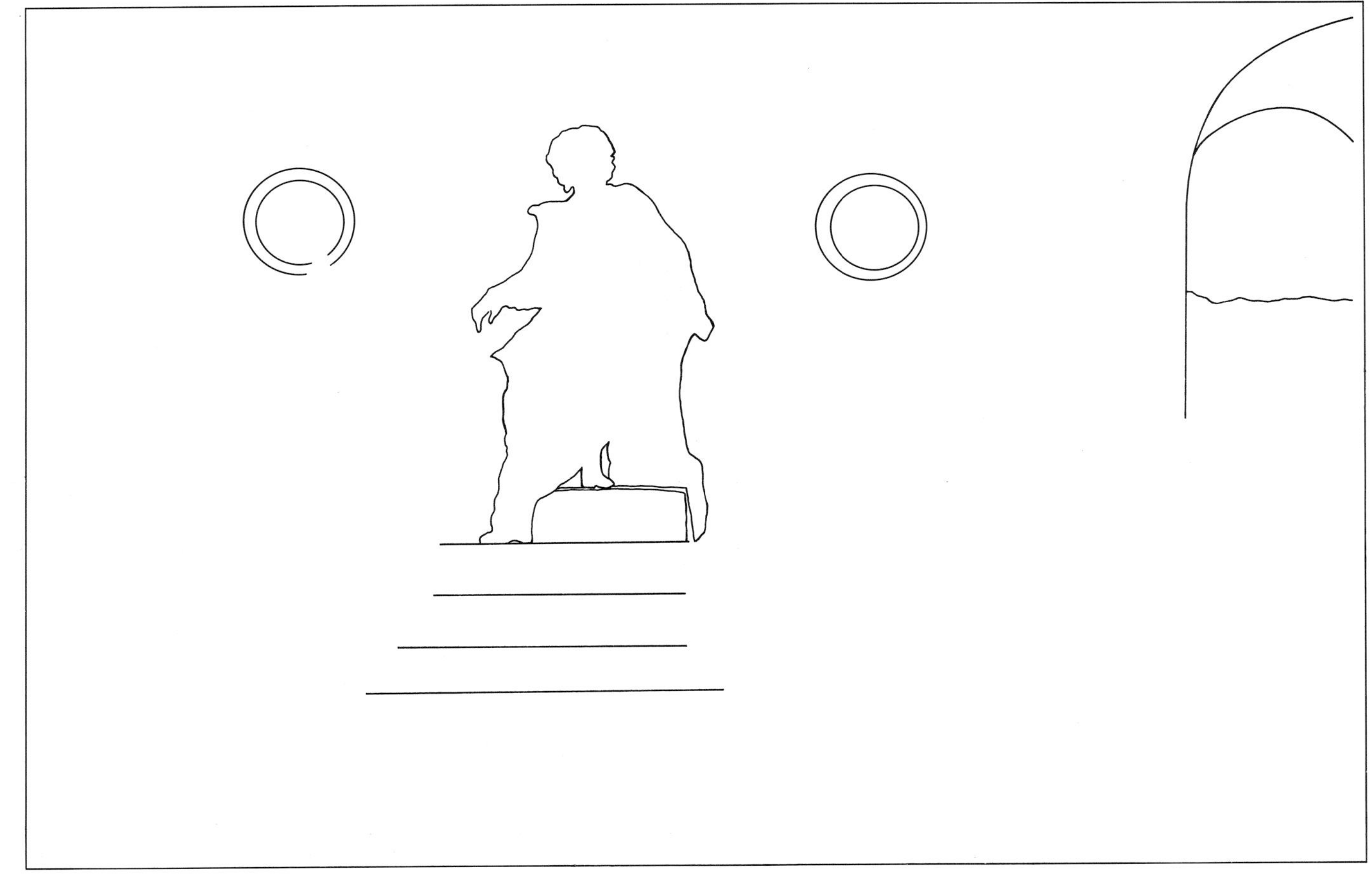

3

Conversely, there are passages in the painting which show a high degree of completion. The brooch at the waist of the false mother is carefully articulated as are several of the Corinthian capitals, and the green drapery of the true mother displays an almost pedantic attention to detail.

Cleaning revealed numerous *pentimenti* and traces of underdrawing and architectural features unrelated to the present composition. It became clear that major changes had taken place in the painting's evolution, and that at least two different interpretations of the same subject lie below the incomplete top layers of paint. The extensive overpaint was an attempt to cover up the more ambiguous passages and present the spectator with a more completed image.

The orange/yellow paint of the apse behind Solomon's head appeared both stylistically and technically incongruous. An X-radiograph revealed losses and damages below, while a study of paint cross-sections from this area identified a thin layer of damaged gold-leaf below (plate 12, p. 40). The removal of this thick overpaint uncovered a pink cloth of honour and a white arch with gilded spandrels which belong to an earlier composition, not yet reworked by the artist, in the upper region. He had, however, proceeded with his change of plan far enough to lay in a thin layer of grey paint applied over the lower part of the cloth as a first stage in the articulation of a projected apse. Plate 13 (p. 40) illustrates how part of Solomon's left shoulder and thick curls were covered by this overpaint.

Paint samples were taken from selected areas of the painting for microscopic and microchemical analyses.[7] The results, together with a series of X-radiographs and infra-red reflectograms,[8] provided fascinating and valuable information in establishing the painting's evolution.

Three different architectural schemes could be deciphered. The earliest (fig. 3) revealed remnants of a painted arch on the right hand side, open to a blue sky and indications of a landscape. Traces of blue paint in a corresponding area on the left hand side suggest a complementary arch. Roundels flanking Solomon's throne were perhaps intended to display a coat-of-arms, or are possible openings in a wall. In the second scheme (fig. 4), Solomon is flanked by large columns placed before a receding arch. Tall lateral tabernacles and a pavement comprising red and white square tiles complete this now interior setting. The floor design is revised in the present composition: the simple square tiles are abandoned in favour of an elaborate pavement. A basilican interior with Corinthian columns replaces the previous more two-dimensional design.

The extensive underdrawing, revealed by infra-red (fig. 5), illustrates how the figures underwent similar major revisions. Below the present composition lie smaller-scale figures, some of which are completely painted, while others have been merely sketched in. Fig. 6 is a reconstruction

4

5

of this earlier arrangement.[9] A delicate drawing of a dead child was discovered in the centre foreground (fig. 7), and a very fine drawing of a horse and rider is seen on the right hand side (fig. 8). The executioner is fully painted and is shown holding a baby upside down.

Many of these figures are adapted to comply with the larger-scale group forming the present composition. The old man acquires a hat and a voluminous red cloak, providing extra height and bulk respectively. Previously positioned behind Solomon's throne, he is now brought forward and placed on the first step to increase his height further. The true mother's legs are lengthened and the green drapery added in an attempt to conceal the figure's now awkward elongation. Her head is now inclined and enlarged by including part of the first head, disguised as extra hair. The guard on the left hand side is enlarged by means of his armour and a hat. The difference in scale between the two designs can still be appreciated with the naked eye: the head and shoulders of the first executioner are visible through the back of the present executioner (fig. 9). There are even alterations in the evolution of this final composition: *pentimenti* of the head and right arm of the false mother (fig. 10) and the legs of the executioner are visible.

The technique employed in the execution of this painting is highly informative. Major compositional changes and the juxtaposition of complete and incomplete passages acknowledge an *ad hoc* approach which is quite contrary to our understanding of painting techniques at this juncture. The numerous alterations imply that the artist had no fixed, predetermined image but rather achieved his end result through a gradual evolution of ideas and representations. The complex perspective of the pavement was, however, more carefully planned: small holes can be seen at the intersection of each tile (fig. 11), suggesting that this design was transferred from a cartoon. Furthermore, the perspective is worked out with the use of the incised line scored into the paint while still wet.[10]

The relining of the painting provided an opportunity to examine the original canvas.[11] It is made up of three sections, with the seams running horizontally. The widths of the three strips measure 76.5 cm (top), 76 cm (middle), and 64.5 cm (bottom). It is possible that the bottom has been reduced slightly; the first floor design continues around the turn-over edge. As the selvage edge is visible along the top edge and along the oversewn edge of the seam, a width of approximately 78 cm might well reflect the size of the loom. The canvas is of a closely woven plain weave, with a thread count averaging 17 (warp) by 18 (weft) per cm^2. The original turn-over edge is missing on the left hand side, which could suggest that the painting has been reduced on this side. The fact that the present composition, and indeed the two earlier ones, are not symmetrically placed strengthens such an argument. There is, however,

6

Fig. 5 Whole, infrared

Fig. 6 Reconstruction of the earlier figure group. The dotted line indicates figures which have been drawn only. The broken lines correspond to an overlapping of figures where each belong to a separate stage.

Fig. 7 Infrared detail, showing the drawing of the dead child in the centre foreground

Fig. 8 Infrared detail, the right hand side, showing the drawing of a horse and rider

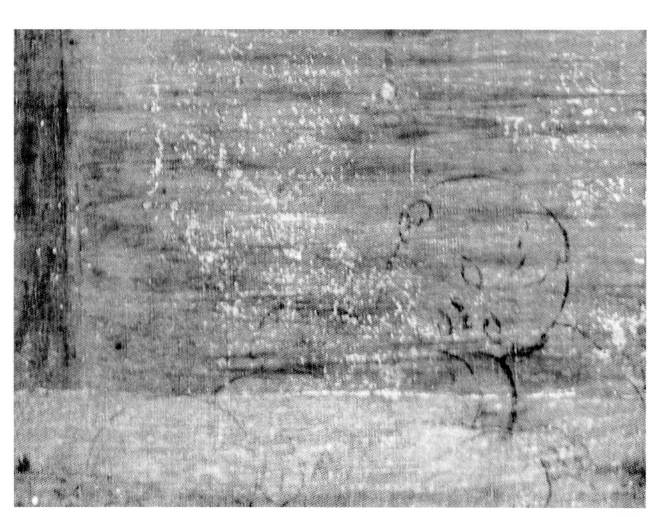

7

8

9

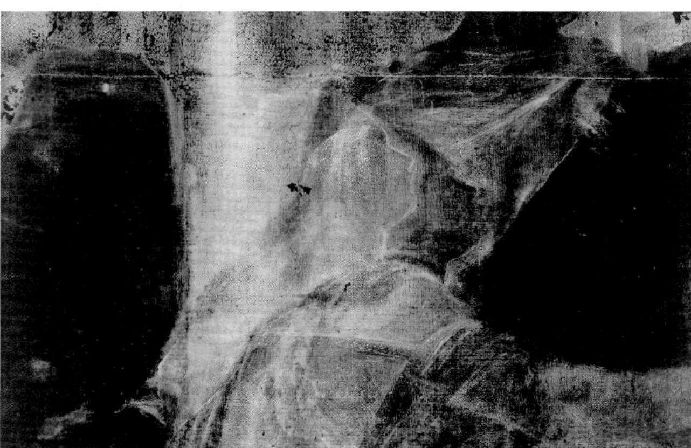

10

little evidence to support this. The left hand edge shows a strong cusping, quite as pronounced as that along the other three edges. This is, of course, not sufficient proof that the present dimensions are original: if the painting was cut soon after it was abandoned, and then restretched, evidence of cusping now would not be unexpected.

The gesso ground was found to be wholly calcium sulphate dihydrate (Ca SO 2H O),[12] a composition particular to the grounds of Venetian paintings of this period.[13] It was noted above that the thin gesso is visible in many unfinished areas. It is darkened by the absorption of adhesives, now discoloured, from previous lining.

The extensive charcoal underdrawing was executed directly above the gesso. The style of this drawing varies considerably. The soft, delicate line of the dead child (fig. 7) and many of the earlier figures contrasts with the heavier, bolder handling in the drawing of the false mother and the later executioner. Different again is the delineation of the old man's bowed head with its short, staccato strokes (fig. 12). It is perhaps unwise to read too much into these differing styles, however, as the quality and strength of the infra-red image is conditioned to a great extent by the thickness and composition of the paint lying above. This can vary considerably in different areas of the painting.

Many paint samples examined in cross-section revealed a layer of black pigment particles suspended in a transparent brown medium lying above the gesso. It is difficult to determine the precise function of this layer. The transparent medium may be an oil layer applied over the gesso to render it non-absorbent, during which process it absorbed any carbon particles from the drawing. It is, however, more likely that this layer is associated with a wash or *abozzo* which loosely established the composition prior to the application of colour.[14]

The pigments identified were typical of the period. Besides the ubiquitous lead-white and earth colours these included red-lake pigments, lead-tin yellow, copper resinate and vermilion.

11

Fig. 9 Detail, the executioner, showing the earlier, smaller-scale executioner below

Fig. 10 X-radiograph detail, showing the alteration to the false mother's head

Fig. 11 Detail, the floor design, showing the holes at the intersection of each tile, which probably acted as a guide in the transferring of this design

Fig. 12 Infrared detail, showing the old man's bowed head

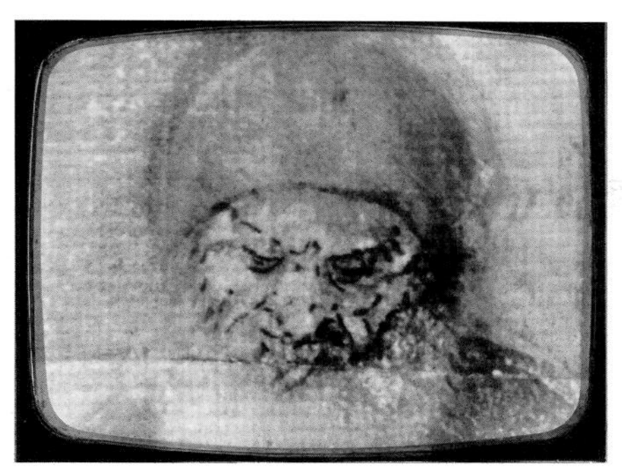

12

Ultramarine was almost exclusively used for the blues, often mixed with lead-white and other pigments, where the less costly azurite would have been expected. No examples of the use of orpiment and/or realgar were found, although these were much favoured by Venetian painters of the period. Traces of gold-leaf were identified below the overpaint in the apse, and this formed part of the decoration in the spandrel of the earlier architecture. The use of gold-leaf is unusual at this date; by the beginning of the sixteenth century artists preferred to imitate gold with pigments,[15] although gold-leaf has been found on Sebastiano del Piombo's 'Crisostomo Altarpiece'.[16] The medium was identified as essentially linseed oil, but there were indications of the use of egg-tempera in the lower layers.[17]

The varying complexities of different areas of the painting are further illustrated in an examination of the cross-sections. The figure of Solomon represents one of the few areas in the painting not subjected to revision. This is reflected in a study of a paint sample from his blue cloak (plate 14, p. 40), which shows a simple layer structure above the thin gesso ground. The majority of the samples, however, reveal a complex mixture of pigments in a multi-layered structure. This is, of course, largely due to the many alterations, but perhaps also reflects a search for a wider range of chromatic nuances. For example, layer 4 in plate 15, (p. 40) corresponds to the green mantle of an earlier figure and comprises copper-resinate, red-ochre, black, lead-white, and lead-tin yellow. This combination of opaque and transparent pigments in one layer is a further departure from traditional painting methods, but is characteristic of the technical innovations noted in the works of Giorgione.[18]

The restoration was confined to losses and damages. No attempt was made to complete the unfinished areas or to resolve the many architectural ambiguities. Such an approach would demonstrate little respect for the painting's original condition when abandoned, and would merely result in a duplication of its previously over-restored state. Any attempt to rationalise the apse behind Solomon's head would involve substantial alterations based on pure conjecture. The painting must be appreciated for what it is: an unfinished masterpiece. In addition, it provides a unique insight into the working methods of a Venetian artist, closely associated with Giorgione, at the turn of the sixteenth century.

Notes

1. The material for this essay is taken from an article by Laing and Hirst, 'The Kingston Lacy Judgement of Solomon', *Burlington Magazine*, cxxviii, 1986, pp. 273–282.
2. C. Ridolfi, *Le Maraviglie dell'Arte*, ed. Von Hadeln, Berlin, 1914–24, I, p. 102.
3. M. Hirst, *Sebastiano del Piombo*, Oxford, 1981, pp. 13–23
4. The cleaning and restoration of the painting was carried out at the London studio of the Hamilton Kerr Institute.
5. Crowe and Cavalcaselle, *A History of Painting in North Italy*, London, 1871, pp. 138 & 139, f. I.
6. C. Ridolfi, *op. cit.* n. 2 above.
7. Micro-analyses of paint samples were undertaken by Karin Groen, Research Chemist at the Hamilton Kerr Institute.
8. As normal infrared photography and reflectography proved unsuitable due to the thin, non-reflecting ground, infrared plates were exposed by transmitting infrared rays through the painting. This work was carried out by Christopher Hurst.
9. All reconstructions were compiled by the author.
10. The vanishing point for this design, and the background architecture, is located about 10 cm below the ram's head.
11. Relining work was carried out by Simon Bobak.
12. Identified by X-ray diffraction powder analysis carried out by Joyce Plesters, Scientific Department, The National Gallery.
13. R. J. Gettens and M. E. Morse, 'Calcium Sulphate Minerals in the Grounds of Italian Paintings', *Studies in Conservation*, I, 1954, pp. 174–88.
14. C. Eastlake *Methods and Materials of Paintings of the Great Schools and Masters*, Dover Publications, 1960, p. 294.
15. J. Plesters, 'The Gold in European Paintings', *The Whiley Monitor*, 1963, p. 12.
16. L. Lazzarini, 'Studi Veneziani', *Bollettino d'Arte*, Supplement no. 5, Rome, 1983, pp. 135–44.
17. Gas-chromatography by Raymond White, Scientific Department, The National Gallery.
18. Lazzarini, *op. cit.*, n. 16 above.

The Hunt in the Forest by Paolo Uccello

Ann Massing and Nicola Christie

Paolo Uccello (1396/7–1475)
The Hunt in the Forest
tempera and oil? on panel, 73.3 × 177 cm
Ashmolean Museum, Oxford

The restoration of Paolo Uccello's *The Hunt in the Forest* (fig. 1) was first considered following the discovery of an area of flaking paint near small splits on the right edge of the panel. Simple treatment of the blistering paint might well have necessitated the application of yet another layer of varnish on top of the existing varnish which had considerably discoloured, and was, in the upper half of the painting, patchy and opaque. The Visitors of the Ashmolean Museum therefore proposed that the panel be cleaned and restored, with treatment beginning in the summer of 1987 for completion in time for the restored painting to be displayed during the exhibition marking the first ten years of the Hamilton Kerr Institute. As this article goes to press, the restoration of the panel itself nears completion (plate 16, p. 41), but the analysis of the information gathered during restoration is, as yet, incomplete. In a subsequent publication it is intended to present a more comprehensive documentation illustrating Uccello's painting technique, discussing more fully some of the findings reported here. Uccello's interest in perspective is well known, but *The Hunt* has been considered to have been painted in a more empirical manner, without any evidence of preparatory drawing or perspective lines. During cleaning, however, indications of a perspective grid were discovered which had hitherto been overlooked.

The artist

Paolo di Dono, called Paolo Uccello, was born in Florence c. 1397, the son of Dono di Paolo, a barber-surgeon. Uccello trained in the workshop of Lorenzo Ghilberti for four or five years and assisted with the work on the doors of the Florentine Baptistry. In 1415 he was admitted to the Physicians' Guild in Florence as a painter. There are few records concerning Uccello's studio, although we know that Antonia, his daughter, was a painter and that Antonio di Papi worked with Uccello in 1459. Uccello was active in Florence, Venice, Padua, and Urbino, painting many panels and frescoes, his best-known works being the three panels depicting *The Rout of San Romano* now in the National Gallery, the Uffizi, and the Louvre.[1]

Few factual details are known about Uccello's life or working methods, although Vasari recounts several anecdotes about him in his *Lives of the Artists*.[2] Vasari tells us that Uccello 'loved painting animals, and in order to do them well he studied them very carefully, even keeping his house full of pictures of birds, cats, dogs, and every kind of strange beast whose likeness he could obtain, since he was too poor to keep the animals themselves. Because he loved birds most of all he was called Paolo Uccello, Paolo of the Birds.'[3]

Uccello lived to an old age, and *The Hunt* is often considered his last work.[4] Vasari tells us that Uccello 'left a daughter, who had some knowledge of drawing and a wife who told people that Paolo used to stay up all night in his study, trying to work out the vanishing points of his perspective, and when she called him to come to bed he would say: "Oh, what a lovely thing this perspective is!"'[5]

Preliminary examination

The Hunt in the Forest, now in the Ashmolean Museum, was in the Fox-Strangways Collection until 1850. In the Museum files it was classed as Early Italian until 1898, when the attribution to Uccello was first made.[6] An old label attached to the reverse of the panel with four blobs of red sealing wax describes it as: 'Una caccia nelli Boschi di Pisa di Benozzo Gozzoli'. Another label reads 'The Hon. ble Wm. Fox Strangways, No. 2', while a third refers to the Ashmolean Museum, 'ASH MUS'.

The wood of the panel is poplar, the most commonly used wood for Italian panel paintings.[7] Two planks, both tangentially cut but close to quarter-sawn, are joined just below the centre of the painting,[8] the grain running horizontally. The joint is stable, and in fact is difficult to see since the panel was retooled after the joint was glued, both on the front and on the back of the panel.[9] On the reverse, tool marks, visible in raking light, continue smoothly over the joint. Several repairs have been made to the irregularities of the panel; thick white paint covers knots and deformations of the wood (fig. 2). These repairs seem original and similar to repairs on the front of the panel visible in the X-ray, where, in addition, small rectangular pieces of canvas cover the knots of the wood (fig. 4).[11] The panel is almost as it was when it left the artist's studio, with the

1

2

3

Fig. 1 Paolo Uccello *The Hunt in the Forest*, before restoration. This photograph includes the painted grey border (covered by the frame) which surrounds the painted composition.

Fig. 2 Reverse of the panel

Fig. 3 Detail of the reverse of the panel in raking light

4

Fig. 4 X-radiograph assembly.
Due to the thickness of the panel, the grain of the wood and the irregularities of the panel show more clearly than the paint layer. In the upper right corner for example the roughness of the original panel is very obvious. Ground, paint or putty fills the hollows of the wood grain and the dips in the wood. Tool marks show in the X-ray as lighter vertical streaks, sloping slightly to the right near the top and bottom of the panel. Knots and irregularities in the panel are covered with paint or putty and show on the X-ray as light patches; the knots are also covered with patches of finely woven canvas. The weave of the canvas is just visible on the original films. There are darker areas either side of the joint in the panel, suggesting the presence of a strip of parchment. Four drops of sealing wax on the corners of a label look similar to the repairs, showing as light areas on the X-ray (probably due to vermilion in the wax). Many small damages, regularly spaced around the edges of the panel, also appear as light areas on the X-ray, presumably because the holes are filled with paint or putty containing lead white. The damages are covered by the painted grey border, and were probably made by nails used either to secure the panel in position while it was painted or afterwards for display. More modern attachments (metal brackets?) were fitted onto the reverse with screws; this is visible on the X-ray and on the photograph of the reverse of the painting. Woodworm exit holes and woodworm channels show as darker areas in the X-ray. Other darker areas include the losses around the edge of the panel; some damages in the paint layer are also noticeable.

5

Fig. 5 Detail of the left side before treatment

6

Fig. 6 Ultraviolet fluorescence photograph of the left side. Examination of the panel in ultraviolet fluorescence before restoration showed strong fluorescence overall, except in three areas. In this detail of the left side, the dark patch indicates an area where the varnish was removed during a previous cleaning; the paint layer is abraded in this area as well.

exception of a few nail and screw holes: an example of a 15th century panel which has not been thinned, flattened, cradled, reinforced, or overpainted.

On the right side of the reverse of the panel several parallel incised lines slanting from the right downwards towards the centre can be seen on the photograph taken in raking light (fig. 3). Woodworm exit-holes are visible on both sides of the panel, but there are no signs of live infestation. There are some small splits on the end grain of the right side, otherwise the panel is in good condition. A thin strip of wood (1 cm thick) has been nailed onto the lower edge.

On the front of the panel, the composition is surrounded by a painted grey border which is slightly narrower on the sides than on top and bottom (fig. 1). It is possible that the sides of the panel were trimmed before this grey border was painted. The grey paint continues just slightly over the side edges. Black repaint covers the older greyish paint of extremely coarsely ground particles which is not consistent with the rest of the paint layers. The border extends slightly over the original paint layer. It is expected that further analysis will confirm that it is of a later date than the rest of the painting.

The small area of flaking paint on the right side just above the joint and above a small split just below it was re-adhered with isinglass (fish glue) before any further treatment or investigation. The discoloured opaque varnish made it difficult to judge the condition of the paint layer although it was obvious that the composition survived everywhere. The features and details of many of the figures and animals are abraded, or, in some instances, missing altogether; small damages are visible in normal light, on the X-ray or with the infrared reflectograph. The opacity of the varnish was especially disturbing in the foliage of the upper half of the painting where the forms of the trees and the impression of recession was almost completely obscured (fig. 1). The thick varnish was uneven and partially reformed; in addition, white paint had been splattered over the painting. The paint splashes were undoubtedly on the panel for a very long time since they were underneath the layer of varnish and both these paint drops and the varnish had taken on a craquelure pattern of their own. In ultraviolet light the varnish fluoresced evenly as one would expect of an old varnish, except for three dark areas. Figs. 5 and 6 illustrate one of the areas which appeared dark in ultraviolet light, the others were in the foliage of the trees near the centre. In all three areas, the paint layer underneath the dark patches appeared to have been disturbed, i.e. abraded by a previous cleaning (this was subsequently verified). In the grass on the left, the upper glazes and some of the detail is missing; in the areas in the trees, the losses are in places down to the ground layer.

Restoration

After removal of a layer of surface dirt with swabs moistened with warm distilled water, the varnish and later repaints (for example plate 23, p. 41) were removed with a solvent mixture of industrial methylated spirit and white spirit 1:5. The older repaints as well as the original paint layers were not affected by this solvent mixture. The removal of the thick varnish revealed an unexpected subtlety of colour and tones, especially in the figures in the foreground. Many small details which had been obscured by the varnish were revealed; the features of the figures for example are painted in brown glazes so similar in colour to the discoloured varnish that small details such as the ears of the figures turning away from the viewer were not visible before varnish removal.

Removal of varnish and repaint uncovered, as expected, areas in the foliage which had been previously overcleaned, sometimes down to the ground. Most areas gained in detail however, the form of the trees became clear and the impression of recession was restored to the undamaged areas. The grass, ferns, and ivy in the foreground are in excellent condition in many areas, although covered with a brownish layer. Where the brownish layer is absent, the greens are often abraded or damaged. In some areas, the discolouration is definitely a glaze applied by the artist himself; elsewhere the brownish layer is of such an uneven application that one suspects the painter would not have been responsible. At this point cleaning was discontinued to investigate more closely Uccello's painting technique. It was necessary to differentiate between possible discoloured original copper resinate glazes and later discoloured resin/oil repaints.

Technical examination and Uccello's painting technique

Examination with the stereo miscroscope provided most of the information concerning Uccello's painting technique. However some small paint samples were taken from areas of damage in order to determine the paint layer build-up and for pigment analysis. The minute paint particles were embedded in polyester resin and ground and polished on one side, so that the layer build-up and pigments could be studied. Remaining portions of the samples were retained for microchemical analysis.

Preparation of the panel

A small sample of the ground layer was taken from an area of damage and analysed microchemically. It was found to be gypsum (calcium sulphate) bound in glue, which is the preparation typically used in Italian panel paintings. Although several layers of gesso were probably applied, it was difficult to identify more

7

8

9

10

Fig. 7 Detail in raking light. The relief is created by the thickness of the paint layers.

Fig. 8 Infrared reflectograph assembly of the three running dogs. Uccello changed the position of the dog's tails, and of the open mouth of the third dog.

Fig. 9 Detail of the three running dogs before cleaning

Fig. 10 Infrared reflectograph detail of the 'hornblower' showing lines of underdrawing, probably in carbon black

Fig. 11 *The Hunt* with the incision lines visible on the painting marked in bold black lines. The broken lines illustrate most of the perspective lines of the underdrawing visible with infrared reflectography.

Fig. 12 *The Hunt* with perspective lines marked on fig. 11 continued

11

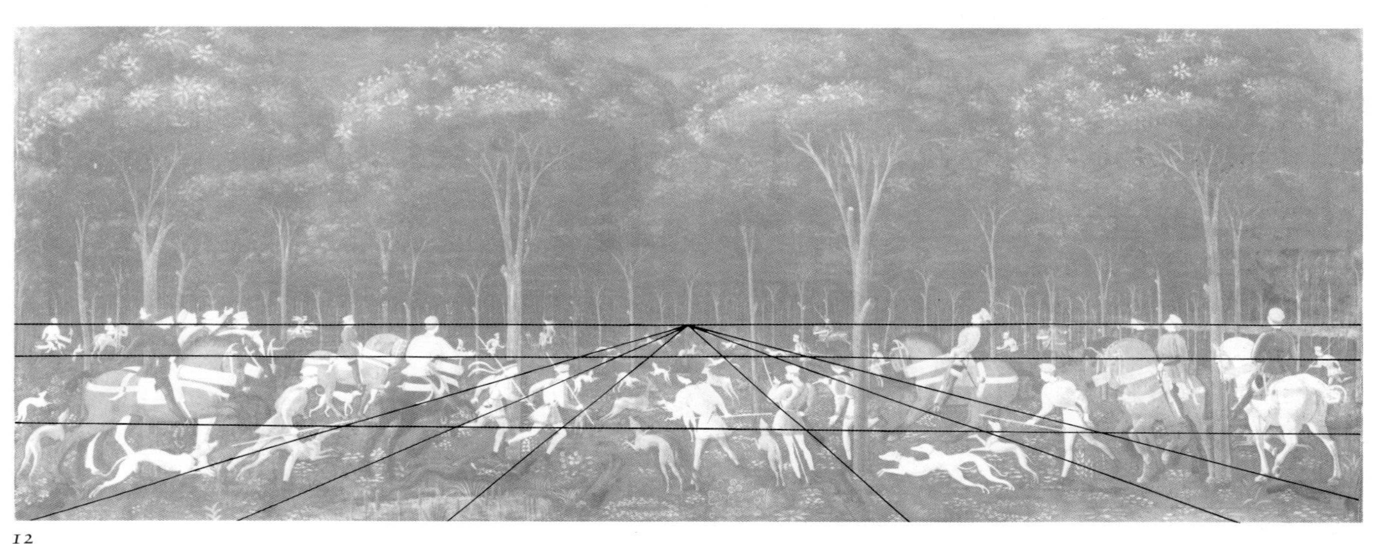

12

than one layer in the samples examined. In one of the samples the upper part of the ground layer next to the paint layer was darker, probably indicating a sizing layer of animal glue which was partially absorbed. The gesso ground does not extend underneath the painted grey border, but forms a ridge or *malrand* around the edges.

The underdrawing

Due to the application of dark underlayers containing a high proportion of black (carbon?) pigment over virtually the whole surface of the painting (see discussion of the paint layer which follows), the underdrawing is visible with the infrared vidicon in only a few areas. Nonetheless it does provide much information on the way in which the artist worked out his perspective scheme.

A detail of the 'hornblower' viewed with the infrared vidicon shows faint parallel lines running diagonally through the figure (fig. 10). Similar lines can be see in the dog and the running huntsman on the left.

Close examination of the surface of the painting in raking light revealed a number of incision lines following the diagonals of the fallen logs in the foreground. Other incised lines were used by the artist as a form of underdrawing; the trunks and branches of some of the trees in the middle distance are incised, also a number of flat oval shapes roughly corresponding to the areas of shadow in the trees (fig. 11).

If the lines of the underdrawing seen with infrared reflectography and the incised lines following the diagonals of the fallen logs in the foreground are continued across the picture plane, they clearly form the orthogonals of a perspective grid, extending from the logs lying in the foreground to a vanishing point situated on the horizon line (plate 25, p. 42). The position of these converging orthogonals is illustrated in fig. 12.

The incision lines which are now visible in raking light as slight indentations were used by the artist to work out areas of the design and were later obscured by layers of paint. Perhaps more of the composition was incised into the ground, but as successive paint layers have filled up the incisions, this is difficult to detect. The contours of the figures were not incised. In many places the contour of the figures and of the underlayer of the green foreground does not meet exactly, leaving the gesso ground visible, here no incision lines are visible. Some deeper, sharper incisions, along the lances of the huntsmen, appear to have been made into the paint rather than the gesso ground (plate 26, p. 42). Microscopic examination shows sharp, defined edges of the incising tool cutting through thick paint layers and interrupting the brushstrokes of the blades of grass. Parts of the horizon line also appear to have been incised through the upper paint layers at a later stage in the painting sequence.

The paint layers

THE GREENS

The dark underlayer The green foliage and the green foreground were painted onto a dark underlayer. The purpose of this dark underlayer is to affect the final tone of the green pigment, and this technique seems to be characteristic of Uccello's painting technique. In the paintings depicting *The Rout of San Romano* in the National Gallery and in the Louvre, Uccello also used a dark underlayer beneath the greens.

This dark underlayer also provides areas of relief by contouring the figures and animals (plate 20, p. 41), thus forming a three-dimensional frame emphasizing their decorative qualities (fig. 7, also plates 17 and 18, p. 41). When viewed in raking light, the relatively high relief of the dark underlayer can be seen to conform to the original position of the figures as seen in infrared light (as for example the three running dogs, figs. 8 & 9).

A cross-section from an area of foliage shows the underlayer to be very thin. In samples taken from the foreground, the underlayer is also thin but slightly varying in thickness. A sample taken from the 'ridge' forming the outline of the treetops against the sky was found to contain a proportion of blue particles as well as of black. Viewed in transmitted light, these particles appear very similar to the ultramarine identified in samples of the sky. When viewed under higher magnification, white crystalline particles are visible in cross-section; this has yet to be confirmed by further analysis, but is probably calcite, added as a 'bulking agent' to form areas of impasto.

The foreground As described above, a black underlayer of varying thickness is found beneath all the foreground greens. On top of this is a layer, also of varying thickness, consisting of malachite in a discoloured medium. Details of grass and plants were then applied, often in thick, raised paint, in a mixture of malachite, white and a yellow, as yet unidentified, in varying proportions. Cracking has developed in some of the top layers due to the slower drying rate of the thicker, underlying leaves.

The rounded regular shape of the particles of

continued on p. 45

Fig. 13 Detail of grass showing the build up of paint layers

Fig. 14 Detail of foliage showing the build up of paint layers

Plate 1 Studio of Joos van Cleve *Adoration of the Kings*, Fitzwilliam Museum

Plate 2 Copy of *Adoration of the Kings* by Mary Allden

Plate 3 Peake *Henry, Prince of Wales* (Mrs P. A. Tritton), before restoration

Plate 4 After restoration

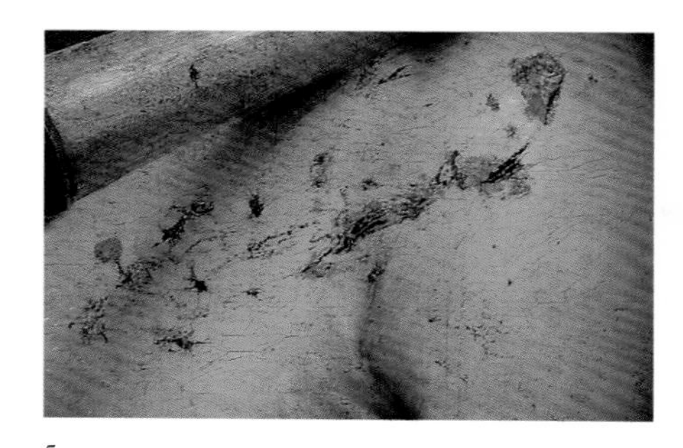

5

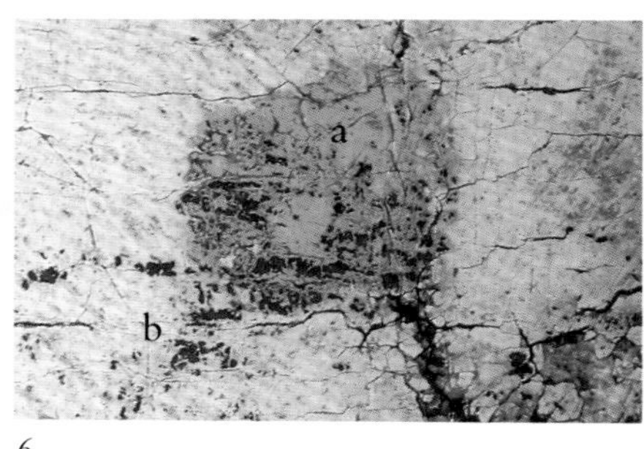

6

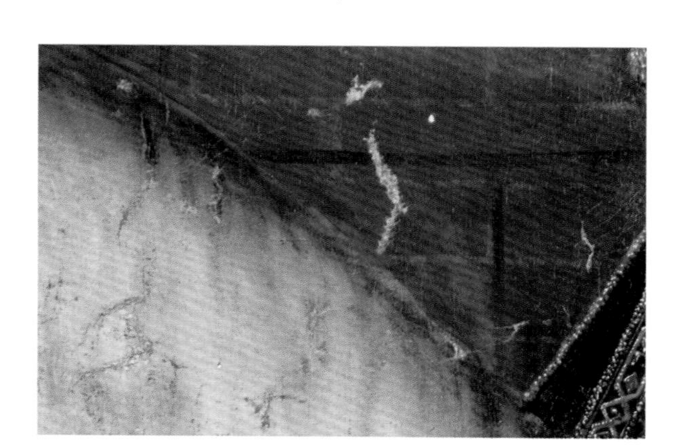

7

8

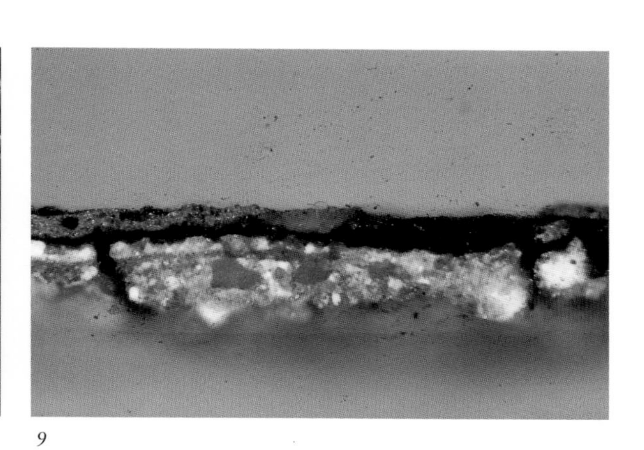

9

Plate 5 Retouched damages on Father Time's chest and shoulder; the first restoration

Plate 6 Detail of plate 5. (a) darkened retouches to flesh paint, (b) blue sky of landscape

Plate 7 Detail of damage caused by creasing in horse's neck and background

Plate 8 Detail to left of horse's bit

Plate 9 Cross section from top edge of plate 8

Plate 10 Initial test to establish condition of original paint layer

10

Plate 11 *The Judgement of Solomon* (National Trust, Kingston Lacy), detail, showing the removal of the discoloured varnish and overpaint in the lower half. The upper right area is uncleaned, while the top left area shows the later overpaint after varnish removal.

Plate 12 Paint cross-section from the apse showing the thin layer of damaged gold-leaf (a) lying between an orange/red bole layer (b) and a thick layer of overpaint (c)

Plate 13 Detail, to the right of Solomon's head during the removal of the orange/yellow overpaint

Plate 14 Paint cross-section from Solomon's blue robe

Plate 15 Paint cross-section from columns, right, with green drapery of a female figure, overlapped by two separate architectural schemes

11

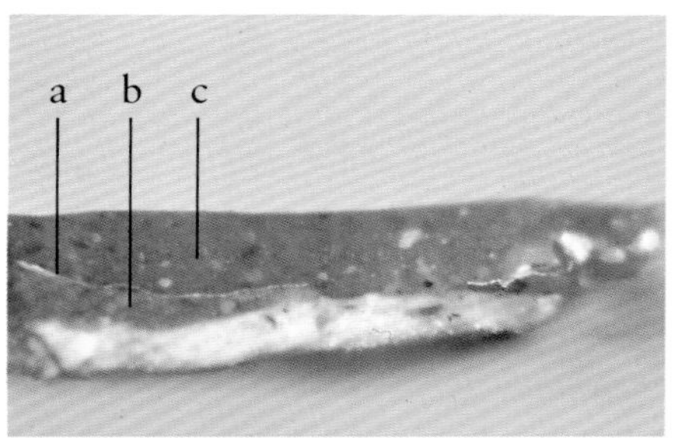

12

13

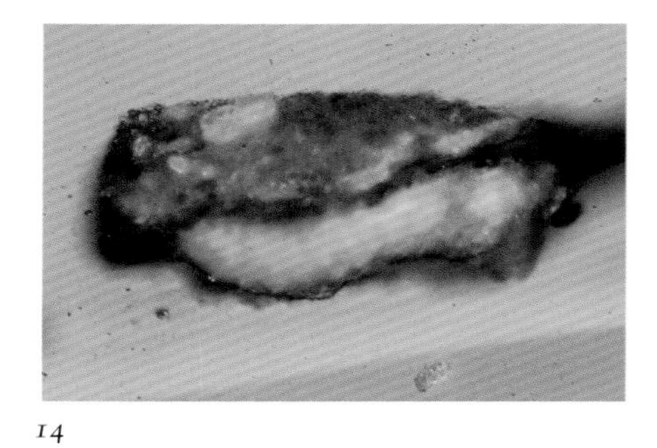

14

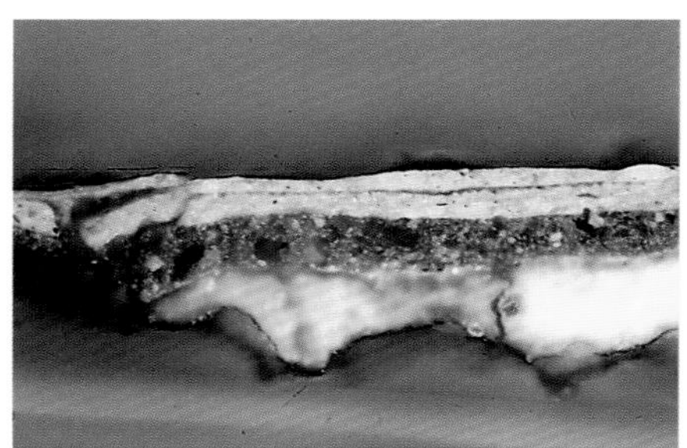

15

16

Plate 16 Paolo Uccello, *The Hunt in the Forest*, The Ashmolean Museum, Oxford. After restoration.

Plate 17 Detail in raking light. Considerable relief is created by the thick underlayers of paint.

Plate 18 Detail in raking light illustrating the raised black underlayer outlining the shape of the horse. The light ground is visible in worn areas of the thinly painted black legs.

Plate 19 Detail of the rump of the 'braking' horse. The outline was changed by the artist to a more rounded shape.

Plate 20 The light shape of the dog is outlined by the black underlayer, over which the tree trunk was painted. The altered refractive index of the paint medium has increased the transparency of this top paint layer revealing the layers beneath.

Plate 21 Area of foliage showing the build up of paint layers in the leaves and the 'scraped-out' shapes at the centre of each cluster

17

18

19

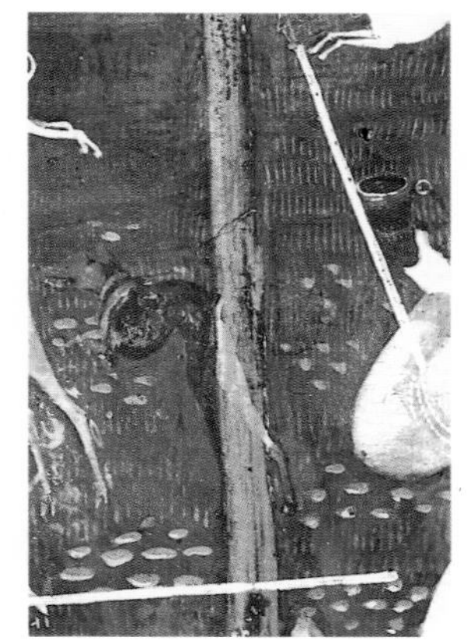

20

21

Plate 22 Oak leaves painted in a semi-transparent olive green glaze in the forest just above the river

Plate 23 Detail of overpaint in the foliage

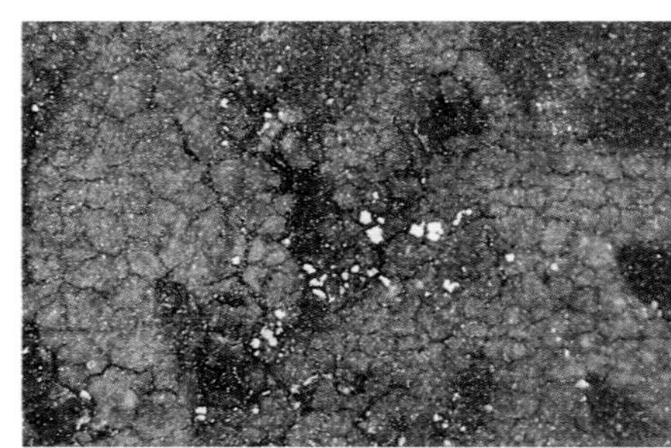

Plate 24 Macrophotograph of a fragmentary leaf painted in gold in the foliage, top left

Plate 25 Detail of the incised perspective lines converging toward a central vanishing point

Plate 26 Incision lines of the lance and dog lead of the hunter with the three dogs

Plate 27 Detail of the sky showing the grey underlayer beneath a thin layer of ultramarine

Plate 28 A scraping of paint from the sky photographed in transmitted light shows particles of ultramarine

Plate 29 Coarse particles of malachite are clearly visible on the surface of the painting. This detail is from the foreground just above the three running dogs.

Plate 30 The foliage, top left. Large rounded particles characteristic of artificial malachite.

a. stained gesso
b. very thin layer of black
c. malachite mixed with black in a discoloured medium
d. large rounded particles of malachite in a discoloured medium
e. malachite mixed with a little lead white

There is a little ochre in the three green layers.

Plate 31 The rump of the white horse is painted on a blue underlayer which is visible in a worn area of the horse's crupper

Plate 32 The white horse's crupper.

a. gesso
b. thick layer of yellow and red ochre mixed with lead white and a little black in a discoloured medium (light brown shadow of the white horse)
c. translucent greyish layer with blue particles (thin layer, indistinct from d.)
d. lead white with coarsely ground blue particles found mainly at the surface
e. finely ground vermilion with a little organic red (red crupper)

Plate 33 Detail of the rider on the white horse. The saddlecloth is glazed in red lake; the orange highlight on the garter resembles red lead.

Plate 34 Sword of the rider on the white horse.

a. discoloured gesso
b. lead white with coarsely ground blue particles found mainly at the surface (underlayer); there is possibly another layer, similar in composition to layer c, plate 17
c. large particles of organic red mixed with a small proportion of lead white (saddlecloth)
d. finely ground vermilion with very little organic red and black

25

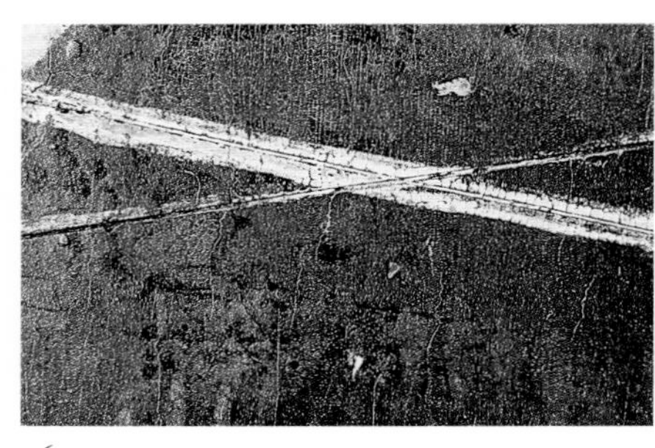

26

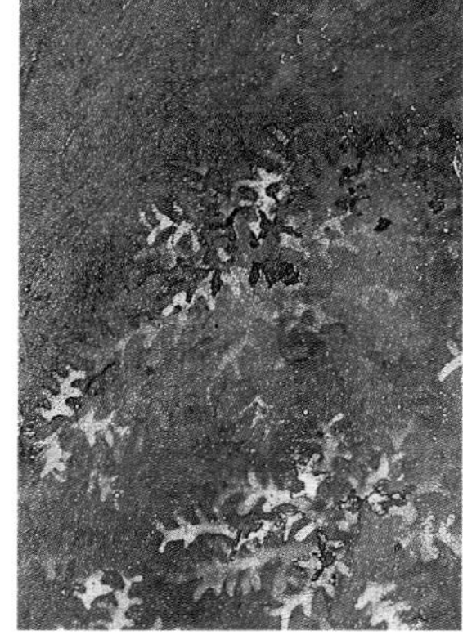

27

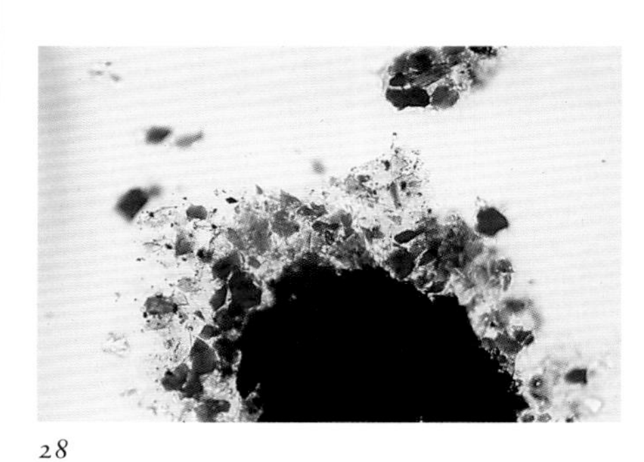

28

29

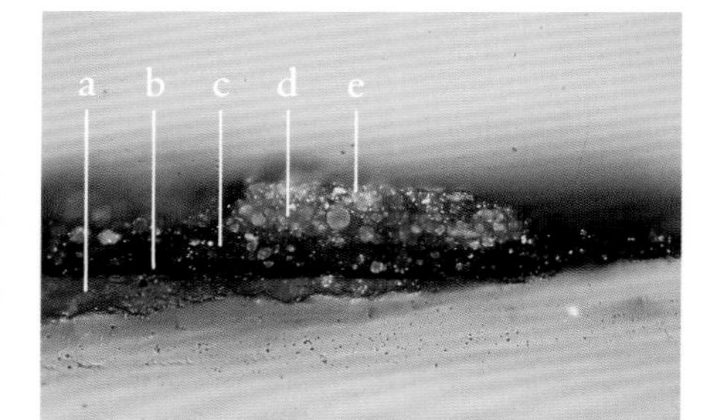

30

31

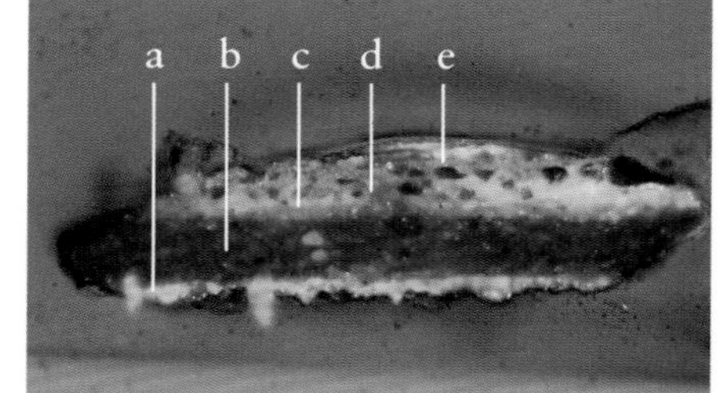

32

33

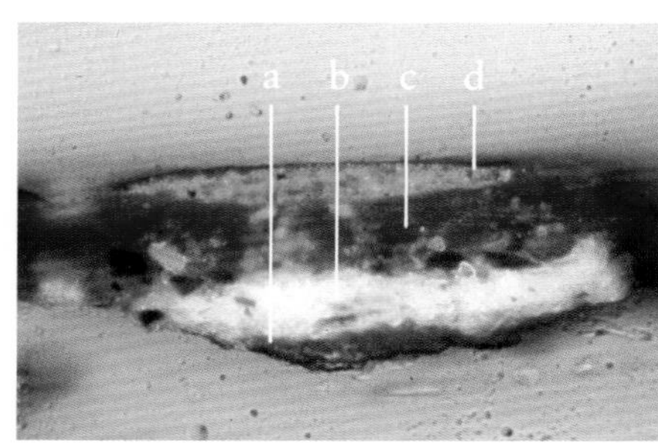

34

Plate 35 Claude Lorraine *Crossing the Ford* (National Trust, Anglesey Abbey). The paint layer in this painting does not show blanching

Plate 36 Gaspard Dughet, *View of Tivoli* (Ashmolean Museum), detail, blanching in the foreground

Plate 37 Gaspard Dughet, *Classical Landscape* (National Trust, Stourhead), the surface of a sample from a badly blanched tree, ×200

Plate 38 The same painting as in plate 37, cross-section of a paint sample from badly blanched green bushes, ×200

Plate 39 The same painting as in plate 37, thin-section of a sample in a blanched area in light green leaves, polarized light, showing mainly chalk and quartz in the ground, ×400

Plate 40 Claude Lorraine, *Father of Psyche sacrificing to Apollo*, (National Trust, Anglesey Abbey), cross-section through tree and sky, × 200

Plate 41 Claude Lorraine, *Crossing the Ford* (National Trust, Anglesey Abbey), dark paint of an underlying first tree can be seen where the blue sky is worn, c. ×2

Plate 42 Claude Lorraine, *Ascanius shooting the stag of Sylvia* (Ashmolean Museum), numerous superimposed, thin paint layers were sometimes found in the trees, ×200

35

36

37

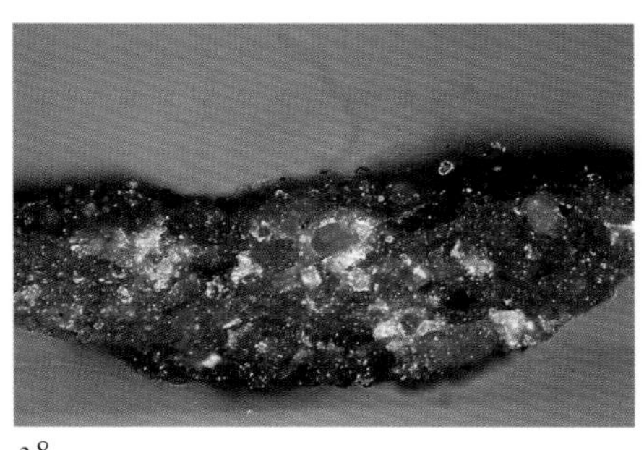

38

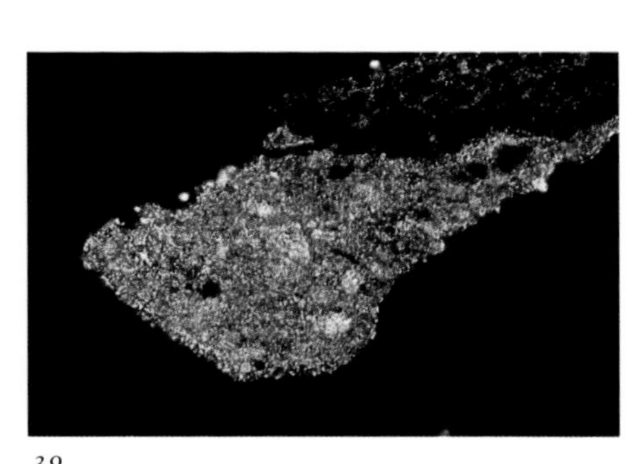

39

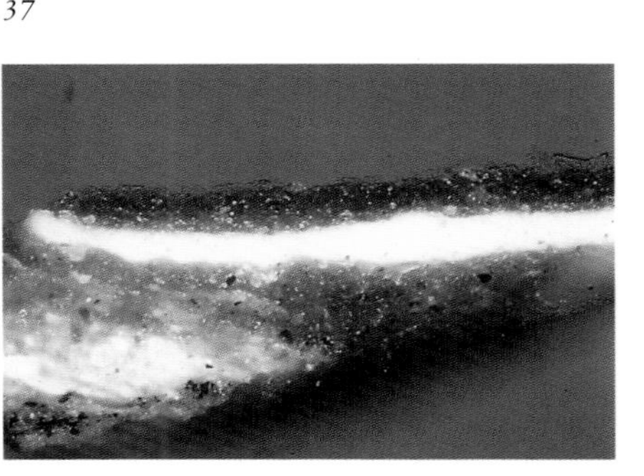

40

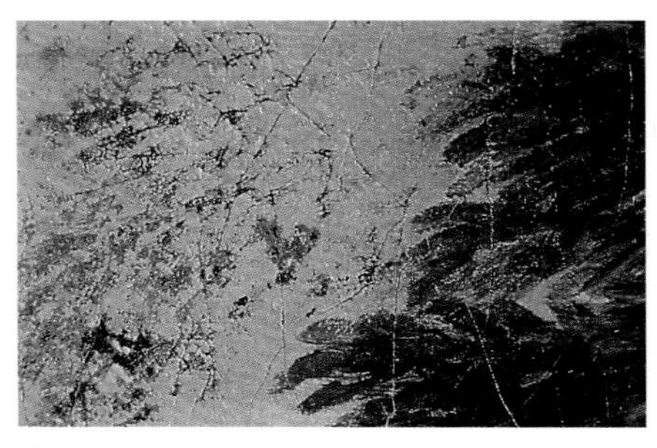

41

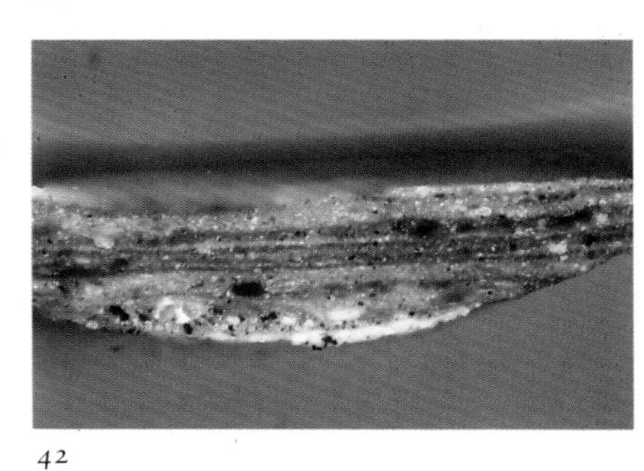

42

Plate 43 Claude Lorraine, *Laban and his Daughters* (National Trust, Petworth), green earth was found mixed with ultramarine, smalt, ochre, chalk and quartz, all very finely ground, magn. × 400

Plate 44 As plate 43, polarized light

Plate 45 Chalk with a little ochre and black in an egg/oil emulsion, painted out on glass. The escaping solvent left holes and a thin skin of paint where it got trapped under the surface, ×110

Plate 46 The same as in plate 45, but with the 'typical Claude mixture'

Plate 47 Gaspard Dughet, *Landscape near Rome* (Fitzwilliam Museum), the top half before, the bottom half after treatment with dimethylformamide vapour, c. ×10

Plate 48 The same painting as in plate 47, surface of a paint sample, ×110

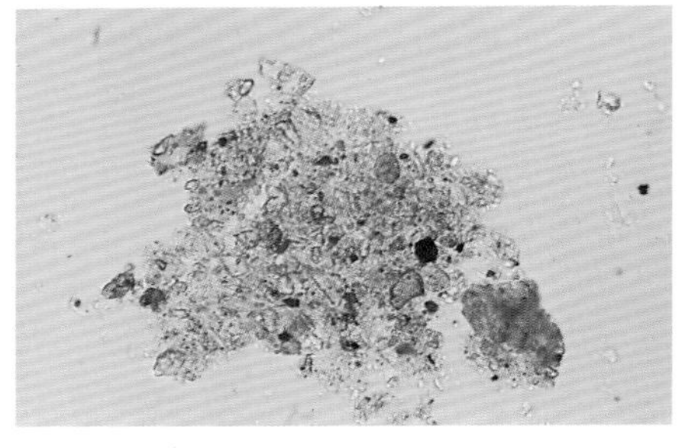

43

44

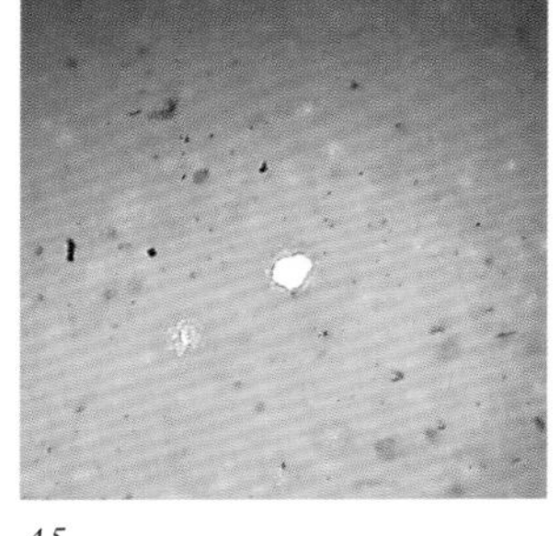

45

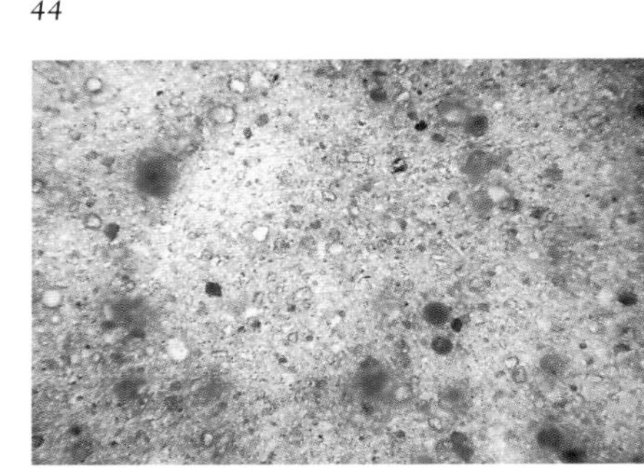

46

47

48

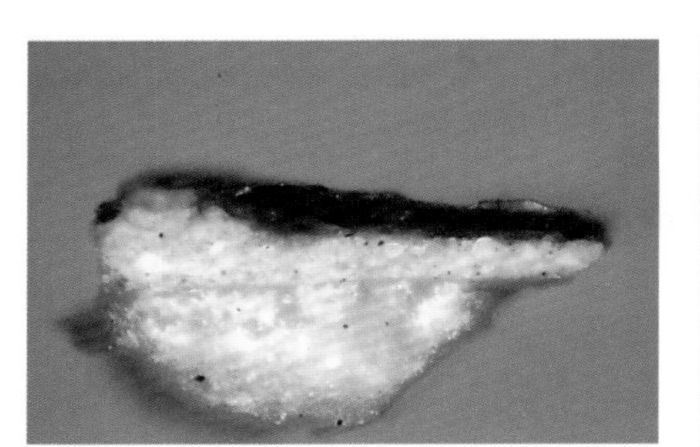

Plate 49 Paint cross-section from black cloak, near the bottom edge. The chalk-glue ground is covered by a light brown *imprimatura* and smooth brown-black overpaint.

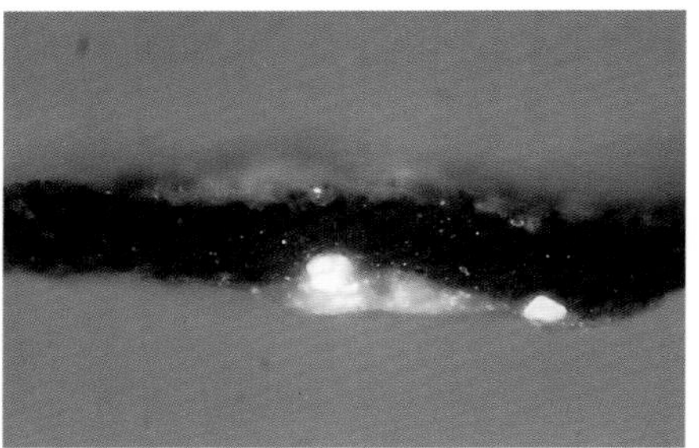

Plate 50 Cross-section from a sample slightly higher up in the cloak, showing a mixture of chalk, lead white and a little ochre underneath the dark paint

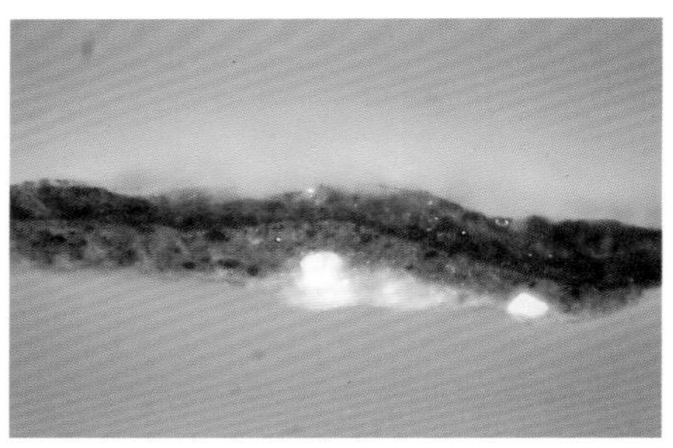

Plate 51 The same sample as in plate 50, viewed in ultraviolet light. The dark paint layer consists of two layers, the top one very smooth.

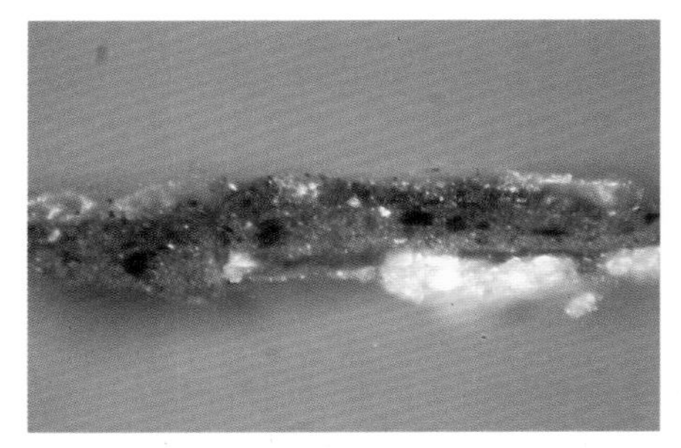

Plate 52 Cross-section from the background on the right hand side, showing an abraded light-coloured underlayer, covered by a thin layer of varnish and brown paint

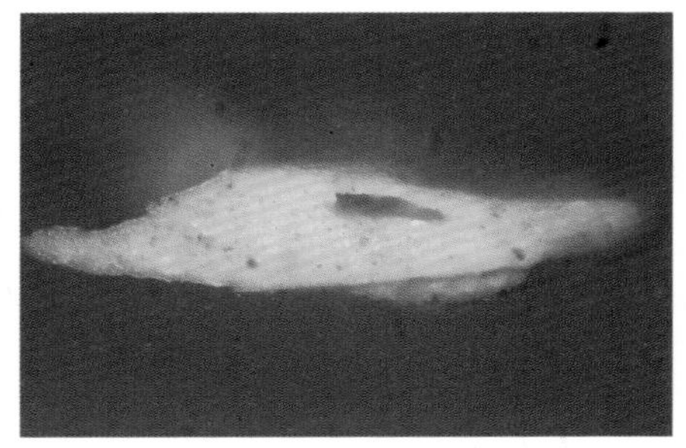

Plate 53 Cross-section of flesh paint from the right cheek, showing thin white and pink paint, wet-in-wet, on top of thin ground layers

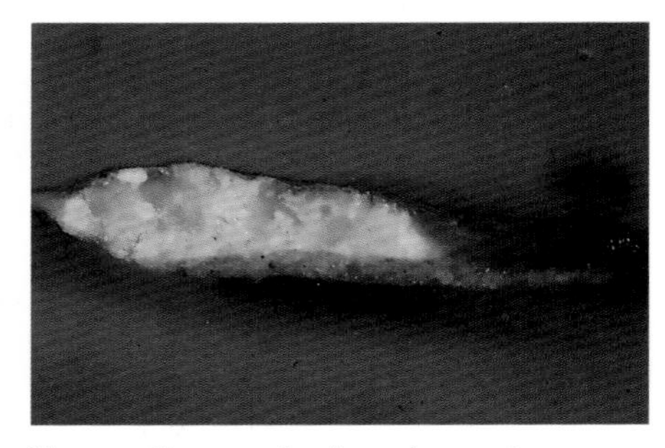

Plate 54 Cross-section from the ear-ring, which is painted in thick lead-tin yellow. The sample shows the red paint of the shadow in his ear underneath. The shadow contains lead white, red ochre and a little red lake.

continued from p. 36

malachite in all the cross-sections suggest that this is an artificially produced copper carbonate green (plates 29 and 30, p. 42), although this has still to be confirmed by X-ray diffraction.[13]

In some areas of the foreground, a thin brown semi-transparent layer is present, often outlining the contours of the figures, but entirely absent in other areas. This had the appearance of a discoloured or tinted varnish, still only partially removed. However the layer did not fluoresce in ultraviolet light, unlike remains of old resin varnishes in the trees which were of a similar appearance. Also, closer inspection revealed that in places the brown layer continued underneath original paint layers. Grass-like forms on the near bank of the river on the right of the panel are painted in a brownish glaze. A positive test for copper indicates that this layer is a discoloured copper resinate glaze which originally would have been green. If elsewhere in the foreground the now brownish glaze were green, the effect would be less uneven.

Microscopic examination of the foreground reveals that in those areas where the brown layer is absent, the paint surface appears rough and worn. Additionally, these bright green areas have lost much of the detail of grass and plants (painted in thinner, lighter layers). It is thus concluded that the upper paint layers in the foreground were much abraded by a previous restorer and the resulting damage partially concealed by overpaint and partially by the thick layer of discoloured varnish.

The foliage The black underlayer continues beneath the trees, but it is generally much thinner than underneath the greens of the foreground. One sample shows a second dark layer with more green pigment, less black and a few yellow particles. Painted wet-in-wet with the black underlayer this dark olive green was used to paint leaves, and, unlike the majority of the foliage, is not painted in impasto (plate 22, p. 41). Brighter green leaves in thicker, raised paint consisting of the same copper carbonate green in a discoloured medium as in the foreground greens, form the larger part of the foliage. Lighter green leaves of varying proportions of malachite, white and yellow are superimposed onto these in several layers, as with the foreground greens. The thinner layers of the highlights have formed cracks due to drying rates which differed from those of the thicker layers beneath. Flat oval shapes of a semi-transparent brown glaze are found in the lower regions of the trees, corresponding in some places to the raised leaves, but overlapping them arbitrarily in others. This glaze has not been analysed but is similar in appearance to the brown glaze found in the foreground which proved to be copper resinate.

The scattered clusters of leaf shapes in the trees revealing the light ground have given rise to several interesting theories concerning their presence. Close examination reveals that the brushstrokes of the light green leaves are interrupted by these shapes indicating that the paint was removed from these areas after the foliage had been completed. The edges of the hollows are not consistent, some are smooth whilst others are rough and jagged, often with patches of the dark underlayer remaining in the hollows. It has been suggested that these are accidental 'losses' caused by the flaking off of paint or mordant due to poor adhesion or contractive forces exerted by an upper layer. However, the perfectly-formed shapes of some of these hollows (plate 21, p. 41) have an appearance of deliberation not usually associated with areas of paint loss.

Small specks of gold found in the foliage were initially believed to be losses from the gilded frame. However, their concentration in this area of the painting led to closer inspection. Plate 24 (p. 41) shows a macrophotograph of a fragmentary gold leaf found in the second tree from the left. Small particles of gold were also found in some of the hollowed-out leaf shapes. A number of recipes for applying gold in various forms to paintings exist. In his *Il Libro dell' Arte*, Cennino Cennini explains how to grind gold leaf with egg white and to use it as a pigment if, amongst other things, 'you want to make a tree to look like one of the trees of Paradise'. He continues further on, recommending the artist to 'mix with this gold a little finely ground green for the dark leaves', or with other colours depending upon the desired effect.[14] However, as yet, no evidence has been found to confirm that Uccello applied his gold in this manner.

Uccello painted his gold leaf shapes directly onto the green of the foliage. It is possible that in order to create even brighter gold leaves, he scraped the paint from certain areas, applying the gold directly onto the gesso ground, either, as Cennini describes, ground up and tempered with egg, or on a mordant which was a more common practice. Gold applied onto a white ground appears much more luminous and sparkling than painted on a dark underlayer, and would have created a most striking and decorative effect.[15]

THE REDS

Two small paint samples were taken from the huntsman on the far right of the painting, the first from a damage in the red crupper of his horse (plates 31 and 32, p. 42), the second from a damage in his sword (plates 33 and 34, p. 42). These reds are painted in finely ground vermilion with a very small proportion of black particles added. The saddlecloth over which the sword is painted is composed of large particles of organic red with a small proportion of lead white, giving a deep pink hue. In the cross-section made from the sample taken from the crupper the red is composed of vermilion mixed with a little organic red. Although further samples were not taken, it is expected that other areas of the 'flat' scarlet are similar in composition.

Beneath the red layer in both cross-sections, and indeed beneath all of this horse's red tackle, is a blue layer composed of coarsely ground lead white and ultramarine particles. This underlayer may be intended to lend a bluish tone to the upper layer of red; however, given the high density and covering power of vermilion, this would seem unlikely. It is more probable that the artist originally intended the tackle to be blue, changing his mind and the colour at a later stage in the painting. A similar layer of coarsely ground blue and white particles is also visible beneath the red bridle of the foremost horse of the pair to the right hand side, but this is the only other area in which it has been observed beneath vermilion. A blue and white layer does, however, occur beneath the saddlecloth of the 'braking' horse. There it is used for deliberate effect beneath a very thin translucent layer of pink (probably organic red lake and lead white mixed) to produce crimson. The decorative motifs are then applied in a pure lake glaze. In a similar fashion, the tunic of the 'portly' rider to the left of the painting is composed of a main colour of ultramarine, white and a small amount of organic red, with a larger proportion of white added in the lights. Over this, the shadows are applied in a red lake glaze, producing a subtle range of hues from deep crimson to violet.[16]

Another paint sample was taken from the shoulder of the foremost huntsman of the pair to the right side of the painting. There a thick vermilion underlayer can be seen, over which is applied a red glaze with a few small black particles added. The modelling of the tunic is achieved in this upper layer, which varies from a cool pink (organic red, white and a very small amount of blue) in the lights, to deep crimson (red lake and black) in the shadows.

THE BROWNS

A sample taken from the brown horse of the 'portly' rider shows a very finely ground and dense layer of yellow and red ochre, black, white and a small amount of vermilion. The light brown shadows of the white horse (plates 31 and 32, p. 42) show a thick layer of yellow and red ochre mixed with lead white and a small amount of black.

THE FLESH

Only one small sample was taken from a damage in the face of the running figure to the left of centre. The flesh is painted in a thin layer of white mixed with either vermilion or red ochre. Small particles of black observed between the ground and paint layer may be underdrawing. Microscopic examination of the paint surface shows that the modelling was glazed over this layer but has been almost completely lost. Small touches of a deep pink are found on the cheeks and around the noses, whilst the lips are probably coloured with vermilion. Modelling of the features is executed in a semi-transparent brown glaze in which particles of black are visible at × 40 magnification.

THE BLUES

A cross-section taken from the sky in the top left corner shows a thick, dark layer of blue over a grey underlayer composed of black and white particles (plate 27, p. 42). This grey layer is visible in the top left corner of the painting where the blue upper layer is particularly thin. The coarsely ground particles looked very much like azurite, however when viewed in transmitted light, their colour was of a more violet-blue (plate 28, p. 42) and, unlike azurite, they were isotropic, i.e. they possess a single refractive index. A separate sample was treated with hydrochloric acid which caused loss of colour, a reaction occurring in lapis lazuli or ultramarine.

Paint samples were not taken from the blue tunics or stockings of the huntsmen. However microscopic examination suggested that these areas were also composed of ultramarine and perhaps a very small amount of azurite mixed with lead white.

Conclusion

Uccello's painting technique is consistent with the methods and procedures of the period. After preparation of a poplar panel with pieces of canvas covering the joint and knots and deformations of the wood, a gesso ground was applied, probably in several layers, then sized with a coat of animal glue. Underdrawing and incision lines, before and after the first layers of paint, defined the composition.

The subject of the painting dictated that much of the painted surface would be green. Uccello's technique was to cover a dark underlayer with layers of green, superimposing detail upon detail: ivy leaves on top of ferns, on top of grass (fig. 13). In the trees, the foliage is also built up with a succession of paint layers (fig. 14); clusters of leaves are painted one on top of the other in increasingly lighter tones, culminating with sparkling gold leaves. The figures were painted in bright colours, the contours changing slightly as the artist adjusted his composition (plate 19, p. 41). The result is that the horses, the huntsmen and the dogs are painted on a reflective white ground in bright colours, which stand out all the more against the dark greens of a background made darker by the underlayer. The figures thus form a bright parade of arching contours against the 'backdrop' of the forest.

The diminution of these bright shapes towards a central vanishing point provides a smooth transition from the decorative surface to accurate perspectival recession. Subtle variations of hue in the lower branches and tree trunks provide rhythmic alternations of light and shadow, leading the eye into the depths of the forest. With great care in the planning of the composition and a methodical build up of the paint layers, Uccello succeeded in uniting two seemingly contradictory elements: a predilection for the decorative possibilities of shape and colour with a 'Renaissance' interest in the accurate representation of figures and objects in space.

Acknowledgement

We would like to thank Karin Groen who supervised the analytical work and is still processing some of the information gathered during restoration.

We are also grateful to the staff of the National Gallery, London and of the Louvre, Paris who gave us the opportunity to study and discuss the documentations concerning *The Rout of San Romano*.

Notes and references

1. For a summary of Uccello's life and a catalogue of his work, the standard volume on Uccello is still: J. Pope-Hennessy, *Paolo Uccello*, London, 1950.
2. G. Vasari, *Lives of the Artists*, translated by George Bull, Penguin Books, 1965, pp. 95–104.
3. Vasari *op. cit.* p. 98.
4. P. Hennessy, *ibid*, p. 24.
5. G. Vasari, *ibid*, p. 104.
6. C. Loeser, 'Paolo Uccello' *Repertorium für Kunstwissenschaft*, xxi, 1898, pp. 87–88.
7. The confirmation of the wood as poplar has not yet been made microscopically.
8. The measurements of the panel are slightly irregular. The panel is 73.2 cm high on the right side, 73.4 cm on the left side. The length is 177 cm at the top, 176.7 cm at the bottom. The thickness varies between 2.5 and 2.9 cm. The joint in the panel is 37 cm from the top, 36.2 cm from the bottom.
9. The joint is a simple butt-joint with no additional reinforcement. The X-ray shows no dowels or cleats.
10. The painted border is 1.5 – 2 cm wide on the sides, but 3 cm wide top and bottom (not including the strip of wood along the bottom edge).
11. The presence of canvas was confirmed during cleaning. The removal of putty from one of the damages in the foliage exposed a small area of canvas, stained brown due to the glue with which it had been soaked during its application to the panel. The filling of knots or defects in a panel with sawdust bound with glue is described by Cennino Cennini in his *Il Libro dell' Arte*, Dover Publications, Inc., New York, 1933, p. 69. Cennino also recommends that canvas strips be adhered to the entire surface of the panel prior to the application of the ground layer. (This seems to be the case for *The Rout of San Romano* in the Louvre; canvas is clearly visible over most of the X-ray.) The method of covering only the joints and flaws of the wood with canvas was common practice, however, and is also found in the panel of *The Rout of San Romano* in the National Gallery.
12. The panel has been considered to be a cassone panel (J. Pope-Hennessy, *ibid.* pp. 23–24, *et al.*). These holes may be related to this function.
13. Microchemical tests were carried out on a small paint sample from the foliage and positively identified both copper and carbonate ions.
14. Cennino Cennini, *Il Libro dell'Arte*, translated by D. Thompson, Yale University Press, 1933, p. 102. The earliest surviving manuscript of *Il Libro dell' Arte* is dated 1437; the *Libro* may have been written, however, at the end of the 14th century.
15. W. Boeck 'Uccello-Studien', in *Ztschr. f. Kunstgesch.*, II, 1933, p. 268. In 1933 Wilhelm Boeck wrote that Uccello painted *The Hunt* onto a gold ground. It is interesting to speculate if Boeck noticed bits of gold, or whether he interpreted the white ground covered with yellowed varnish (which Uccello left uncovered in several places) as gold: 'Uccello [hat] die 'Jagd' gar eine offenbar durchgehende Golduntermalung gegeben, auf die die Lokalfarben so transparent aufgetragen sind, dass das durchscheinende Gold ihnen zu eigenem Leuchten verhilft.'
16. It was not possible to carry out analysis of the lake glazes due to the size of the sample required and the relatively few and small areas of damage. However, a similar red lake from the National Gallery *Rout of San Romano* was analysed by thin layer chromatography and found to have properties matching those of madder.

Scanning electron-microscopy as an aid in the study of blanching

Karin Groen

Some paintings by Claude Lorraine (1600–1682) and Gaspard Dughet (1615–1675) have been examined, paying special attention to blanching which so often occurs in works by these artists.[1] The term *blanching*, literally, 'to make white by withdrawing colour', is used to describe the whitish appearance in a painting due to a defect in the paint film. The following entries in Hess's *Paint Film Defects*[2] seem worth consideration: cissing, pinholing, cratering, hazing, blooming, whitening by immersion in water, blushing and milkiness. Most of these terms, or the definitions given for them, indicate that microvoids and moisture play a part.

When restorers in England were asked about their experience with blanching, it seemed clear that water is the main contributor to the problem, whether used in cleaning, blister laying or relining. Ammonia and heat were occasionally mentioned. Frequently the paintings already showed blanching when they were received for restoration. When painters were named, those from the seventeenth century working in Italy and especially Rome were often cited as examples.

It seemed worthwhile, therefore, to look for holes or pits in the paint layers and to examine the technique and materials used by painters working in Rome in the seventeenth century. It seemed likely that they would have materials and techniques in common, maybe a legacy from such sixteenth century sources as Caravaggio and the Caravaggesque.

Paintings by Claude and Dughet were chosen with this purpose in mind; however when other paintings, by Salvator Rosa (1615–1673), Gerard Honthorst (1590–1656) and others, were restored, particular attention was paid to any areas of blanching.

It was hoped that examination of the painting technique would also shed some light on problems that seemed to be associated with individual artists, for example poor adhesion between undermodelling and main body paint layers in Claude, and perished greens in Claude and Dughet.

Methods used

The investigation involved examination of the paintings using a stereo-microscope, the study of paint cross-sections, polarized light microscopy, micro-chemical and electron microprobe analysis with X-ray diffraction in a few instances, micro-chemical and staining tests and gas-liquid chromatography for analysis of the medium, and a scanning electron microscope for study of the surface.[3]

In the paintings by Claude and Dughet the blanching seemed more or less restricted to dark areas, especially greens and browns (plates 36 and 37, p. 43). In the paintings by Salvator Rosa and Honthorst the blues were affected as well. Early in the investigation there was evidence to assume that the blanching was not solely due to a peculiarity of the paint used for these areas, but that the composition of the ground layers had to be taken into account. Observations that led to this conclusion were:

1. In some of the Claude paintings the edge of a blanched tree did not show blanching. From studying Claude's working method it is clear that the edges of trees overlap the sky, which consists mainly of dense lead white. The edges seemed to be protected from something trying to penetrate from underneath.
2. Blanching was more pronounced in thin paint layers than in the thick impasto of the same brushstroke.
3. A characteristic of blanched paintings seemed to be that the embedded samples from them were not easily made into useful cross-sections. It seemed as if the cross-sections themselves were obscured by blanching. Obtaining a clear image depended on the liquid used for grinding the sample, whether it was viewed dry or wet and even on the length of time between grinding and examination under the microscope. This annoying problem arose especially when ground and/or paint layers contained a high proportion of medium. Apart from an overall dull image, material which was whitish because of the scattering of light could be seen around larger particles and holes in the paint layers and in the ground. This phenomenon was most pronounced in Dughet[4] (plate 38, p. 43).

Although the study of the build-up and composition of the layers provided useful information, evidence such as voids was hard to come by in this way. The embedded samples even seemed to obscure any evidence that might possibly be present. Also, the process of grinding the samples could alter the texture, when moisture was used on samples from paintings susceptible to moisture. Besides the difficulty in interpreting the cross-sections, there existed the possibility that there were holes too small to be visible with the light microscope, i.e. smaller than 0.3 μm. Use was then made of a scanning electron microscope. Hardly any material is available on the interpretation of electron micrographs from paint surfaces for comparison.[5] Therefore, non-blanched areas in the same paintings were studied with the same methods, as well as a few samples from a painting that had proved not to be prone to blanching. Further comparative material was provided by prepared teststrips, for which green earth was chosen. Green earth was used in all the greens in the paintings by Claude and Dughet. A wide range of media was chosen for the preparation of the test strips, because the medium could very well be responsible for the phenomenon.[6] The test strips were exposed outdoors for two years before examination under the electron microscope (SEM).

Results of microscopic examination and analyses

The results obtained from fifteen paintings are listed in the table on pp. 50–53. The table shows rather a simplification of the actual build-up of the paint layers, which, especially in Claude, is more complex. Some of the boxes in the table are blank. The reason for this is that access to the paintings was spread over a period of ten years and those features that now are seen as relevant were not perceived to be so at the time. Also, it was not always possible to carry out an extensive examination, and analytical methods such as gas chromatography were not available at the beginning of the project. The amount of sample material needed for gas chromatography (GLC) was another restricting factor.

Results show that the same range of pigments was found in the greens of the landscapes and in the blue skies in Dughet and that similarities exist among the paintings by Claude. A surprising find was the large quantity of chalk in the grounds of the Dughet and in some of the Claude paintings. Grounds which at first sight appeared ochreous, judged from the colour, on thin-sectioning and analysis turned out to be composed mainly of calcium carbonate, with a little ochre added for colour (plate 39, p. 43). Hess holds the presence of chalk in oil paint responsible for the formation of blisters.[7] Silicious material was found in many of these grounds. The main constituent of the greens in all the Dughets is green earth. Admixtures of other pigments, such as lead white, ochre, bone black, lead-tin yellow, charcoal black, umber and smalt, were found and in the most perished greens there was usually a large proportion of chalk. The presence of green earth (glauconite or celadonite) and quartz was confirmed by X-ray diffraction.[8]

The layer structure in the Dughet paintings is in general quite simple: often there is only one paint layer sometimes there are two. In the latter case dark underpaint was used, often medium-rich and translucent, containing bone black, ochres and umber besides chalk and green earth. Highlights were often set directly on this medium-rich underpaint. The second ground layer of the usually double ground was found to be applied very unevenly and as a result missing in places. The blanching seemed most pronounced where the paint layer was rich in medium, chalk and quartz, and where it was sitting directly on the ground; alternatively where the paint layer was very thin and overlaying a translucent underpaint. Even when there was an addition of lead white, paint layers often appeared greyish, as if a medium other than oil had been used. Staining and heating tests seemed to confirm the presence of proteins. The sequence of painting could be demonstrated in many of the paintings by Dughet, as well as in Claude: first came a grey underlayer for the sky, then the dark underlayer for the trees, then the blue sky and finally the finishing layer for the trees (plates 40 and 41, p. 43).

The grounds in Claude's paintings are more opaque, due to the presence of lead white, except in paintings examined dating from before c. 1660. The way in which the materials were used in Claude's early pictures resembles Dughet's painting technique much more than the method Claude used later. A striking thing in many of Claude's paintings is his use of intermediate layers of medium (varnish or glue?) and the large number of superimposed paint layers. The lack of adhesion between paint layers is clearly due to these intermediate layers. The reason for them could be excessive 'oiling-out'; for example in *Crossing the Ford* and *The Rape of Europa* areas already painted were covered up and repainted. Painting each painting twice seems to be inherent in Claude's working method: underlying trees can often be seen shimmering through the final sky and in *Ascanius Shooting the Stag of Sylvia*, one of his late pictures, one unexpectedly finds thirteen thin superimposed paint layers in the seemingly freely painted bushes (plate 42, p. 43). Dark areas often consist of piled-up medium-rich paint, the total thickness exceeding a quarter of a millimetre (*Jupiter and Europa*). For painting the highlights, thin opaque paint was applied on top of the thick translucent paint.

A similar dark translucent underpaint was used for the trees and the water in some of the paintings, the paint layers on top showing a variety in thicknesses and opacity in both the light and dark areas. In dark areas one can find the translucent brown-greens covered up by thick, dense layers of ochreous paint. Claude used his pigments very finely ground, mixing green earth, ultramarine, smalt, ochres, blacks and whites into what could almost be called the 'typical Claude mixture' (plates 43 and 44, p. 44). In Dughet as

Comparative analysis of fifteen paintings by Dughet and Claude

Painting	First ground layer: colour	Average thickness	Electron microprobe analysis[1]	Composition[2]
1 Gaspard Dughet *Classical Landscape* National Trust, Stourhead, canvas, 157×226.6 cm	brown	c. 200–300 μm	(Mg), Al, Si, (Pb), K, Ca, Fe	chalk, quartz, a little brow ochre
2 Gaspard Dughet *Landscape near Rome* Fitzwilliam Museum, no. M73, canvas, 73.7×110.5 cm	reddish-brown	minimal c. 80 μm	(Mg), Al, Si, (Pb), K, Ca, Fe	chalk, red and brown och a little black
3 Gaspard Dughet *Classical Landscape* Birmingham City Museum and Art Gallery, canvas, 124.9×141cm	reddish		(Mg), Al, Si, (Pb), K, Ca, (Ti), Fe	chalk, large particles of quartz, a little red and brown ochre
4 Gaspard Dughet and Jan Miel *Landscape with River* Fitzwilliam Museum, canvas, 126.4×174.6 cm	yellowish-brown		Mg, Al, Si, (Pb), K, Ca, Fe	chalk, quartz, a little lead white, very little red, brow and yellow ochre
5 Gaspard Dughet *Hilly Landscape with Classical Figures* Museum of Wales, canvas, 36.8×48 cm				
6 Gaspard Dughet *View of Tivoli with Rome in the Distance* Ashmolean Museum, canvas, 76×126 cm	reddish-brown	up to c. 110 μm	(Mg), Al, Si, (Pb), K, Ca, Fe	chalk, a little red ochre, quartz
7 Claude Lorraine *Tivoli with trees at Sunset* 1637/8, private collection, canvas, 96×131 cm	reddish-ochre	up to c. 110 μm	Al, Si, Pb, K, Ca, Fe	chalk, quartz and/or glass little red ochre, very little black
8 Claude Lorraine *Coast View with the Rape of Europa* 1647, Rijksdienst Beeldende Kunst, The Hague, canvas, 93×118 cm	brown	c. 150 μm	Al, Si, (P), Pb, K, Ca, Fe	lead white, chalk, a little ochre, silicates, a little bla
9 Claude Lorraine *Laban and his Daughters* 1654, National Trust, Petworth, canvas, 143.5×251.5 cm	reddish-brown		(Mg), (Al), Si, Pb, K, Ca, Fe	quartz, lead white, chalk, ochre
10 Claude Lorraine *Italian Landscape* 1660, Wallace Collection, canvas, 74×109 cm	orange-red	minimal 80 μm	(Al), (Si), Pb, (Ca), (Fe)	lead white, a little red ochre, red lead (?)
11 Claude Lorraine *Father of Psyche Sacrificing to Apollo* 1662(3), National Trust, Anglesey Abbey, canvas, 174×220 cm	orange-red			red ochre, silicates, lead white, chalk
12 Claude Lorraine *The Rape of Europa* 1667, Her Majesty the Queen, canvas, 102×134.7 cm	red		Al, Si, Pb, K, Ca, Fe	red ochre, lead white
13 Claude Lorraine *Crossing the Ford* 1670s, National Trust, Anglesey Abbey, canvas, 67.8×95.5 cm	orange-red	> 40 μm	Al, Si, Pb, (K), (Ca), Fe	lead white, fine red ochre, charcoal black
14 Claude Lorraine *The Discovery of Coral* 1674, Holkham Hall, canvas, 100×127 cm				
15 Claude Lorraine *Ascanius shooting the Stag of Sylvia* 1682, Ashmolean Museum, no. A376, canvas, 120×150 cm	orange-red	> 55 μm	Pb, (Ca), (Fe)	lead white, red ochre, charcoal black

1. ( ) = trace; __, ═, = large amount present
2. Identifications are through microscopical and analytical techniques
3. Analysis done by Raymond White, National Gallery

ɔnd ground layer					
our	Average thickness	Electron microprobe analysis	Composition	GLC ground layers	
lish-brown	c. 130 μm	(Al), Si, (K), Ca, (Fe)	chalk, quartz, a little red ochre	linseed oil	1
m grey	c. 30–110 μm	(Al), Si, Pb, K, Ca, (Fe),	chalk, lead white, a little red and brown ochre, charcoal black, a little silicious material		2
	uneven thickness, absent in the green sample		lead white, charcoal black		3
					4
lish-brown			lumps of lead white, very little red ochre, a little black		5
					6
	c. 10–80 μm	(Al), (Si), (P), Pb, Ca	lead white, bone black, very little brown and red ochre		7
brown	c. 100 μm	(Al), Si, Pb, (K), Ca, Fe	lead white, a little chalk, a little ochre and black, silicates		8
					9
brown	c. 5–50 μm		black pigment in matrix of fine brown ochre		10
brown	c. 30 μm		charcoal black in brown matrix		11
oon	0 – c. 100 μm	(Al), Si, Pb, (K), Ca, Ti, Fe	charcoal black, red ochre, lead white	egg and oil lipids (maroon layer)[3]	12
grey, towards maroon ur	c. 34 μm	Al, Si, Pb, (Ca), (Fe)	bone(?) black, lumps of lead white, red ochre, a little quartz		13
oon			bright red ochre, charcoal black, chalk, lead white		14
		Si, Pb, (K), Ca, (Fe)	lead white, charcoal black		15

Comparative analysis of fifteen paintings by Dughet and Claude (*continued*)

	Sky			*(Blanched) green in trees*	
	First paint layer	*Second paint layer*	*GLC sky*	*Electron microprobe analysis*[1]	*Composition*
1	lead white, smalt, ultramarine	lead white, ultramarine	egg	(Mg), (Al), Si, (Pb), K, Ca, Fe	green earth (glauconite c celadonite), quartz, calc
2	lead white, chalk, fine pale smalt	lead white, ultramarine		Mg, Si, K, Ca, Fe Mg, (Al), Si, P, Pb, K, Ca, Ti, Fe	green earth, chalk green earth, ochre, bone black, a little lead white (dark area)
3		lead white, ultramarine	egg, a little oil	Al, Si, (Pb), K, Ca, Fe	green earth, ochre, carb black, chalk, quartz
4				Mg, Al, Si, P, Pb, K, Ca, Ti, Fe	green earth, ochre, bone black, chalk
5				(Mg), (Al), Si, (Pb), K, (Ca), Fe	green earth, ochre, a litt lead white and chalk
6	lead white, fine pale smalt	lead white, ultramarine		Al, Si, Pb, K, Sn, Ca, Fe	green earth, lead-tin yel chalk, (lead white in pla
7	lead white, smalt, a little charcoal black and ochre	lead white, ultramarine, a little brown and yellow ochre, very little black			green earth(?), ochres, charcoal black, chalk
8	lead white, fine smalt	lead white, fine ultramarine	walnut oil	(Mg), (Al), Si, (P), Pb, (K), Ca, Fe, Cu	green earth, a green cop pigment (malachite?), ultramarine, yellow and brown ochre, bone blac
9	ultramarine, pale green earth, isotropic green, blue and colourless material (glass?)			Mg, Al, Si, Pb, K, Ca, (Ti), Fe	green earth, ultramarine ochre, quartz, a little lea white and chalk, a little smalt
10	lead white, smalt	lead white, fine smalt and ultramarine		Mg, Al, Si, S/Pb, K, Sb, Ca, Fe	dark green: green earth, gypsum(?), a little yellov and red ochre and a blac pigment, Naples yellow. Grass: ultramarine adde
11	lead white, chalk, fine smalt	lead white, ultramarine		Mg, Al, Si, Pb, K, Ca, Fe	green earth, lead white, chalk, quartz
12	lead white, smalt (plus fine ultramarine in places)	lead white, ultramarine (plus fine smalt in places)	walnut oil	Mg, Al, Si, P, Pb, K, Ca, (Mn), Fe, Co	green earth, bone black, umber, chalk, a little lea white, smalt
13	lead white, coarse and fine smalt, a little fine red added in places	lead white, fine ultramarine and smalt		Mg, Al, Si, Pb, K, Ca, Fe, Co	green earth, lead white, chalk, ochre, a little carb black. Green was found mixed with ultramarine, smalt, and yellow and re ochre as well. All pigme very finely ground
14	lead white, smalt				green earth, chalk, a littl smalt, red ochre and bla
15	lead white, fine ultramarine and smalt	lead white, fine ultramarine, a little fine smalt		(Mg), Al, Si, Pb, K, Ca, Fe, (Cu)	green earth, ultramarine yellow ochre, chalk, (massicot?), a little of a green copper pigment

1. ( ) = trace; __, ═, = large amount present
2. Identification by X-ray diffraction

LC 'anched) trees	*Other pigments present in the landscape*	*Average thickness of the paint layers*	*Remarks*	
: sample: egg d sample: hydrocarbons ɔ oil or egg)	bone black, lead-tin yellow	c. 20 µm	Starch was identified in the relining paste and in the ground layer. The starch must have penetrated the ground. The second sample for GLC analysis of the blanched green trees had been treated with water and a few drops of ammonia in order to remove a discolouring, later applied, surface layer. Staining tests for proteins in the green were positive. Before restoration, the craquelure was raised and there was incipient flaking in many areas.	1
	bone black, yellow ochre	c. 30 µm	There are dark underlayers, with bone black and ochres mixed through green earth in the dark areas of the trees and the landscape. Highlights in the trees are set on top of medium-rich, translucent paint layers. The blanching is most pronounced where there is a large amount of calcium carbonate in the more translucent greens. The pigments seem dispersed in a greyish medium. On treatment with 4N NaOH only part of the medium is drawn out.	2
			Only three paint samples were available. The second ground layer is not present in the sample of perished green. Perhaps the grey is not an overall ground layer but a local underpaint for the sky. On treatment with 4N NaOH, a flaky, brown organic material appeared.	3
;?	umber		Only one sample, purposely taken from a blanched green, was available. Therefore it is not possible to decide whether there is a double ground.	4
nched top layer: egg k underlayer: egg, a little a conifer resin	ultramarine, smalt (both ground finely), charcoal black, a light yellow pigment (massicot? Sn absent)		Starch was identified in the relining paste. A resin seemed to be present as well. The paint samples were very small, therefore the ground layers were incomplete (not measured). There is a greater variety of pigment mixtures in the greens of this painting than in the other Dughets. The blanching was not very pronounced. Test for proteins was positive.	5
			Badly blanched greens. Too few paint samples to decide whether there is a double ground, although a grey layer was found under the paint layers of the sky. The trees and bushes were first sketched in using a translucent brown-green, thicknesses 15–85 µm. Highlights and middle tones were set on top. In the most obvious perished greens this top layer is very thin, 10 µm on average, which does not seem to have been caused by abrasion.	6
		c. 18 µm	No obvious blanching. There are thin layers of medium in between paint layers. Parts of the sky have an additional, dark underlayer.	7
nut oil	umber	ranges from c. 5 to c. 85 µm. Paint layers wet-in-wet with a total thickness of c. 240 µm	No blanching, only a few turbid patches in dark areas. Wrinkled paint in dark areas. Bad cupping of the paint and flaking. Wide craquelures in places.	8
			Blanched greens. Wide drying cracks. The pigments can hardly be distinguished in the cross-sections because of the darkened medium and the low refractive index of the pigments. Separate layers are also not clearly visible.	9
	Zn is present together with Cu. Green crystals are similar to those in Claude's *Father of Psyche*	c. 27 µm	There are thin layers of medium in between paint layers in the sky. No blanching.	10
, plus oil	Naples yellow. Zn is present together with Cu. The green crystals are similar to those in Claude's *Italian Landscape*	variations in thickness from 15–c. 110 µm	The final paint layer in the leaves is a c. 110 µm thick ochreous mixture. There are layers of medium in between paint layers. No obvious blanching.	11
	red, yellow and brown ochre	c. 5–80 µm	Thick intermediate layers of glue(?), up to c. 40 µm, are present between the paint layers and the ground, resulting in flaking paint. Bad blanching in restricted areas.	12
	Naples yellow?	c. 20 µm, the underlayer in the sky is up to c. 120 µm thick	There is an additional dark underlayer under part of the sky and the water, very similar in composition to the second ground. The sky is further locally underpainted in a greyish-blue, locally in a pink hue. In some of the perished greens no green pigment could be found in the thin top layer. Although the top layers contain lead white they look greyish, as if too much medium or a medium other than oil was used. There are thin layers of medium (varnish?) in between the paint layers.	13
		c. 20 µm. The underlayer in the sky up to c. 120 µm thick	Only three paint samples were available. Either a first ground is missing in the samples, or there is only one ground layer.	14
	a light yellow pigment (massicot? Sn and Sb absent)	c. 17 µm. Sometimes many overlying much thinner paint layers	Numerous superimposed, thin, green and bluish-green paint layers in the landscape. Some of the thin top layers contain only a white and a blue pigment.	15

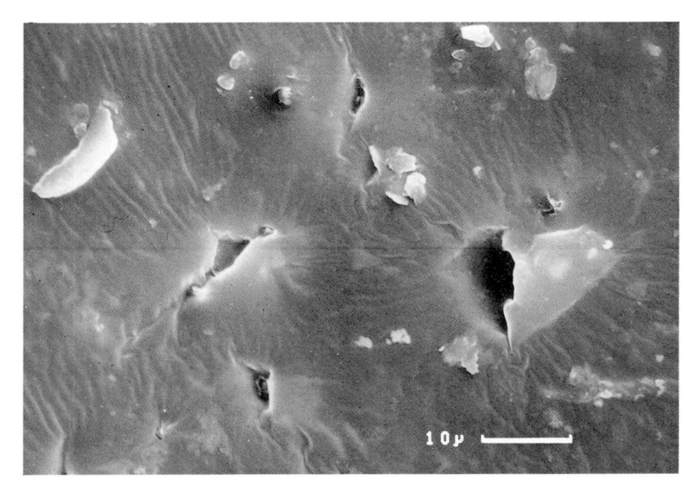

Fig. 1 Test strip, green earth/drying oil, thinned with turpentine

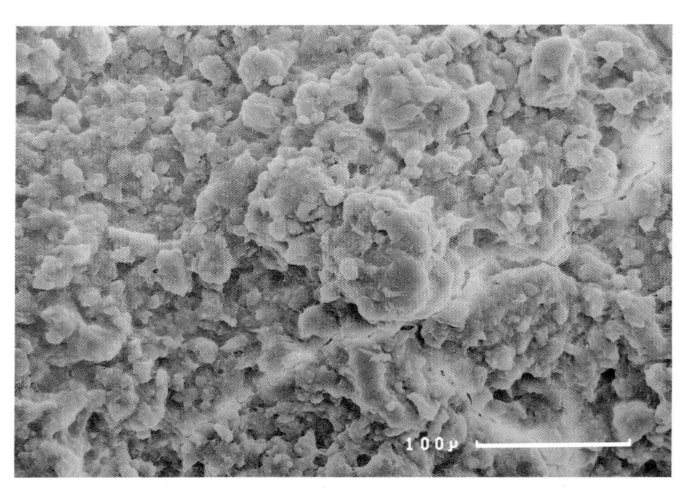

Fig. 2 Test strip, green earth/rabbit skin glue (7 gr. glue in 100 ml water)

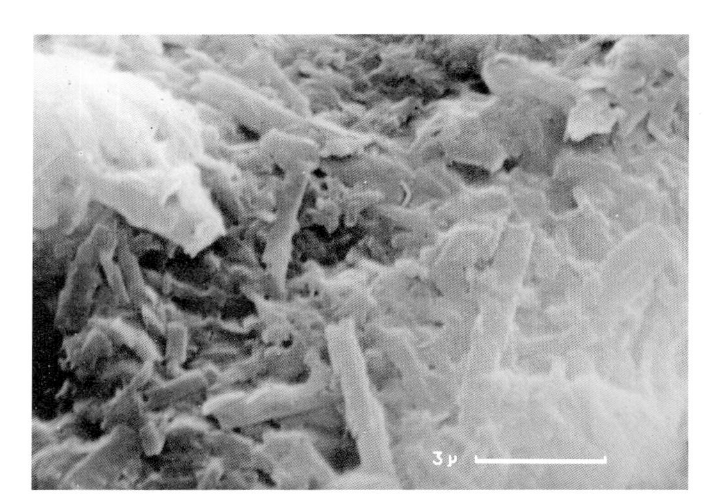

Fig. 3 Same test strip as in fig. 2

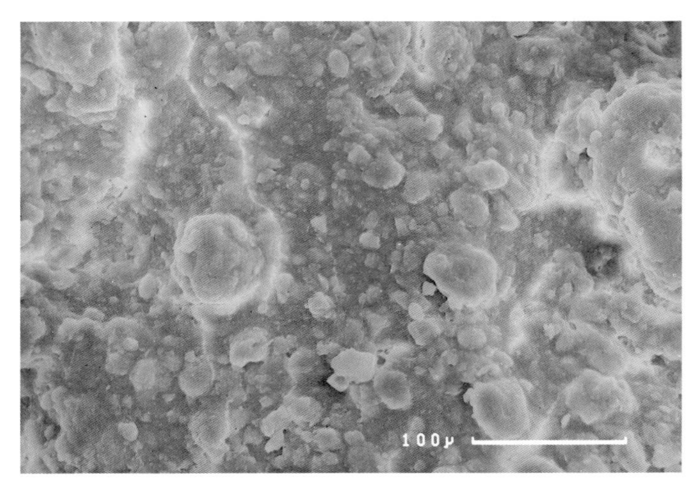

Fig. 4 Test strip, green earth/whole egg (whole egg/water, 1:1 by volume)

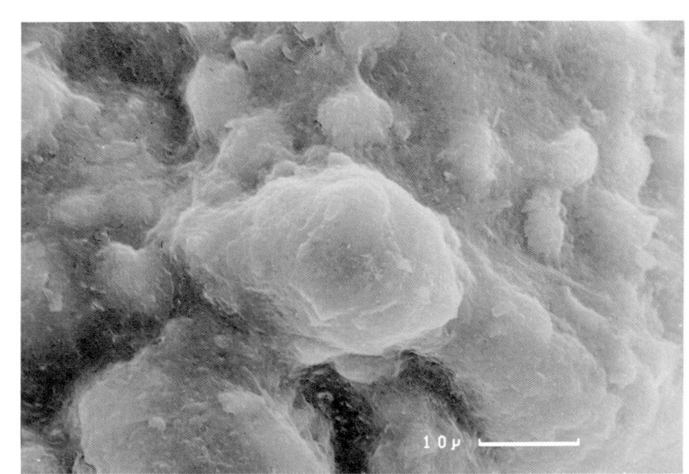

Fig. 5 Same test strip as in fig. 4

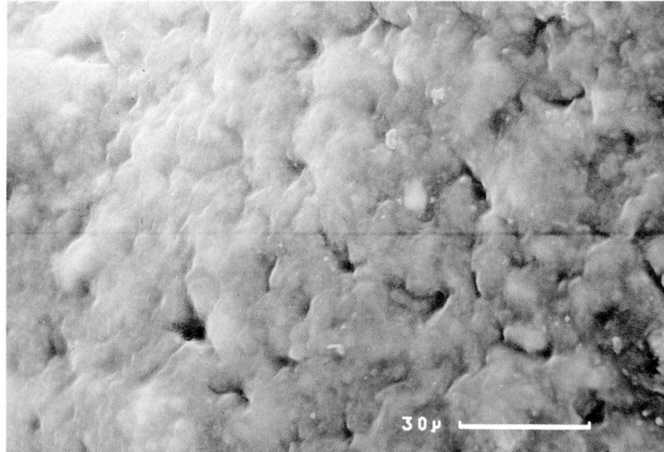

Fig. 6 Test strip, green earth/whole egg/linseed oil (whole egg/linseed oil, 1:1 by weight)

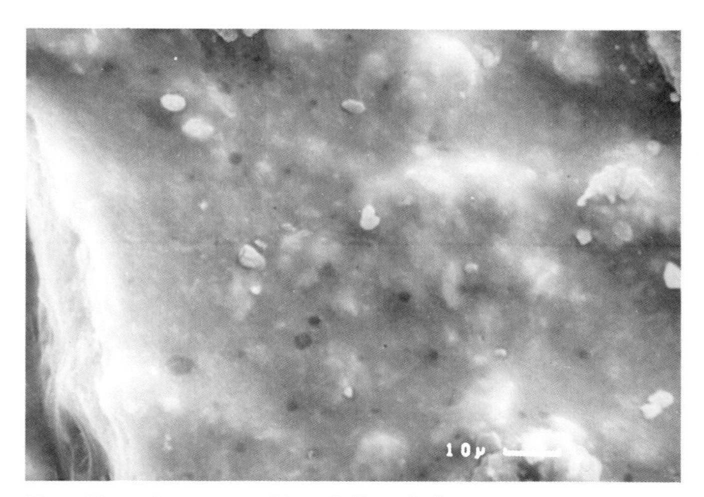

Fig. 7 Test strip, green earth/mastic/linseed oil (mastic/linseed oil, 1:1 by weight at 150°C, thinned with a little turpentine)

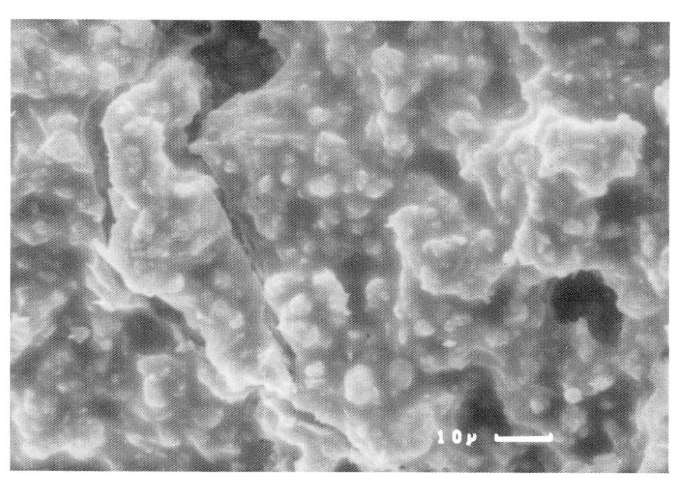

Fig. 8 Test strip, green earth/dammar/linseed oil/glue (dammar/linseed oil/glue 1:1:1 by weight)

well as in Claude, holes can be seen in the cross-sections, with a whitish material gathered around the holes and around the larger pigment particles.

Electron micrographs of test strips

The electron micrograph in fig. 1 shows green earth in a drying oil, thinned down with turpentine oil. Although the pigment volume concentration was such that the paint had the right consistency, there is a nearly continuous film and dispersed pigment particles can hardly be distinguished. Ripples, their 'wavelength' in the order of the diameter of the average pigment particle, are especially pronounced in the left-hand side of the photograph.[9] The surface of the film has cracked, both parallel and perpendicular to the ripples, illustrating that oxidation of the surface took place too rapidly, causing an increase in surface area.

Fig. 2 shows the same pigment painted out in rabbit skin glue. Individual and clusters of pigment particles are coated with glue. Fine drying cracks run through the sample. Occasionally there are fine fibrous structures, which, when magnified and measured, suggest the remains of collagen fibres (aggregates of collagen fibrils, see fig. 3).

A green earth/whole egg mixture (fig. 4) shows again an irregular surface texture and fine drying cracks. Higher magnification exposes aggregates of platelets, green earth being a mica, coated by the medium (fig. 5). In an emulsion of whole egg and oil (fig. 6) individual pigment particles are not easily distinguished; the pigment particles seem to have clustered together leaving gaps from which solvent (or water) might have escaped during drying. In fig. 7, mastic/linseed oil 1:1, thinned with turpentine oil, shows a rather smooth surface with some dark spots which appear to be craters rather than deposition of carbon caused by the instrument, and some particles on top of the surface. (The dark horizontal line running through the middle of the photograph indicates that the beam has had some impact on the paint film). The addition of glue to this oil/resin mixture (fig. 8) makes the paint set before the solvent has time to escape. The paint was too viscous for its 'second flow' and a homogeneous film surface could not be produced. 'Premature cracks' and holes formed instead.[10]

Electron micrographs of samples from paintings

Moving from the especially prepared test strips to actual paintings, figs. 9 and 10 show the topography of a painting by Lambert Sustris, *Diana and Acteon*, (Christ Church Picture Gallery, Oxford) where the medium is linseed oil and the paint layers are not susceptible to blanching. The surface is quite smooth with pits which are nearly all associated with tiny cracks, obviously drying cracks. The sample was taken from the trees in this landscape painting, since many of the samples examined in the blanched paintings derived from such areas.

When the first samples of blanched areas in Dughet's *Classical Landscape* (Stourhead) were examined by SEM one feature was immediately apparent; part of the surface was covered by tiny holes, c. 0.5 μm in diameter, many smaller (fig. 11). The presence of these pits was not restricted to the surface layer; in the micrograph (fig. 12) they are also sitting underneath. Some seem to be peeping out from under the top layer which itself consists of thin, overlapping sheets of paint, although the cross- section suggested only one homogeneous layer. The hills in the sheets could be clusters of pigment, unless they have to be explained as caused by the vacuum to which the samples are being exposed. There are also lumps of a very fine material which can be seen spread out in places (fig. 12). Fig. 13 shows quite clearly the consistency of the paint. Fig. 14, a different sample from the same area, shows minuscule pits below the surface in addition to the more obvious ones. From the latter tiny cracks radiate out.

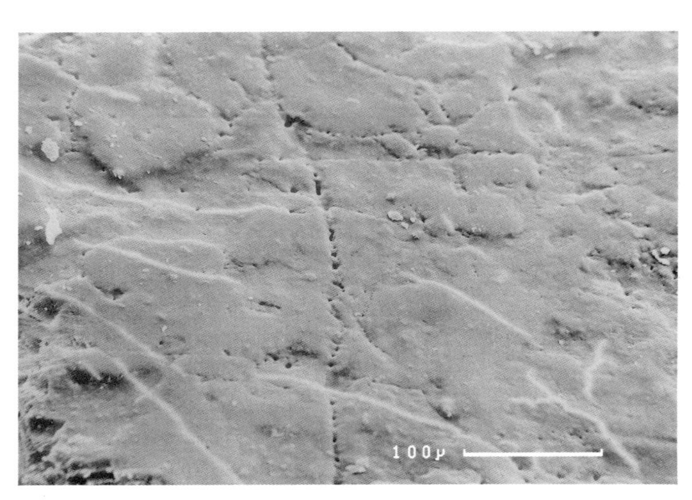

Fig. 9 Sample from a painting not prone to blanching (Lambert Sustris, *Diana and Acteon*, Christ Church Picture Gallery, Oxford)

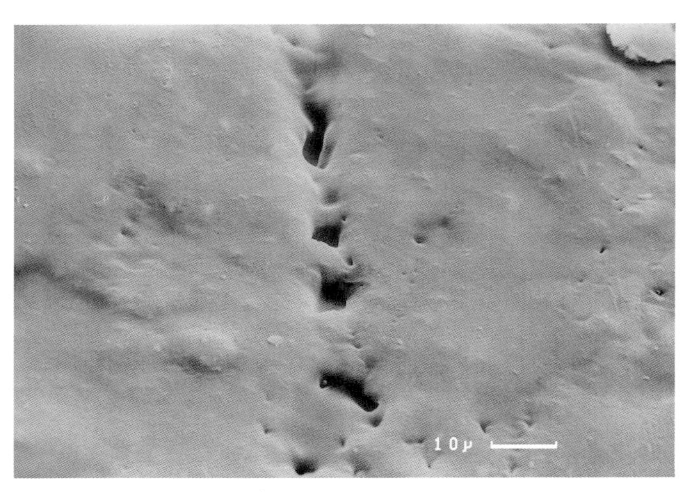

Fig. 10 Same sample as in fig. 9

Clusters of globular shapes can be seen especially in the top part of the photograph.

The sky in this painting did not show obvious blanching. The micrograph in fig. 15, taken from the sky, shows a topography not entirely consistent with a drying oil, confirming the GLC analysis (egg). Of course the pigment volume concentration in the dense paint from the sky is higher than in the green earth test strips, and the Claude samples are older, but even so, by now familiar aspects of a quick-setting paint can be distinguished. These are: overlapping sheets of paint, a porous film, cracks and an irregular surface with particles that seem only loosely bound. Under higher magnification the globular texture of the paint and the hexagonal shape of some of the holes can be seen (fig. 16).

Two samples were examined from Dughet's *Landscape near Rome*. Fig. 17 is from a blanched area in the trees where the paint has been used in a glazing way; fig. 18 from a (blanched) more opaque light green which is sitting on top of a dark grey underpaint. Fig. 17 shows areas which are quite smooth and others where there are sheets of paint and holes in and below the surface: an indication of the setting of the paint before the solvent was completely evaporated. In the centre top two round shapes resemble lids on hinges, suggesting a cavity underneath from which solvent escaped without producing a pit; the paint must still have had enough elasticity to hold the 'lid' in place. Fig. 18 shows a nearly side view, exposing the porous dark grey underlayer.

Fig. 19 shows a blanched area of blue-green paint in Claude's *Laban and his Daughters*. Unfortunately no results of medium analyses are available. Under the optical microscope a lot of glass-like material could be observed. Fig. 20 shows one of the craters magnified. Fig. 21, a sample of badly blanched green in the same painting, again seems to show a quick-setting paint, although effects of former restorations can not be excluded. Former restoration seems to be the only explanation when examining fig. 22, which was made from the same sample; a ring of precipitate left after evaporation of a drop. A few electron micrographs of Salvator Rosa's *Mr Altham as a Hermit* (National Trust) are included here, since the picture showed the same type of blanching. Fig. 23, made in a greyish highlight in the drapery and in which the optical microscope revealed pale blue smalt and colourless glassy material, shows a porous underlayer for the discoloured smalt. Figs. 24 and 25, from a greyish-appearing green leaf, show all the aspects of a quick-setting paint.

In Claude's *The Rape of Europa* a green area was recently recovered from under an old putty. The non-blanched recovered surface is shown in figs. 26 and 27. The surface is quite smooth, though covered by remnants of the putty. This suggests that the cleaning of paintings could be responsible for their blanching. A blanched green in the same painting, fig. 28, shows again a porous paint, resulting in overlapping sheets of paint. A cross-section through the fractured (not embedded and polished) sample can be seen in fig. 29, with its back-scattered image in fig. 30. The back-scattered image shows that most of the material in both the paint layers and the ground consists of compounds with atoms of low atomic number. The scattered white dots (high atomic number) are probably lead white. The fine material in the left hand bottom corner is the silverdag coating, which is visible in both the lower corners in the back-scattered image. From the middle of the micrograph towards the top right the sample is under a slight slope, so the rather smooth appearing top layer is the top surface. The cross-section shows the porous paint layer and a coarser textured ground.

Discussion

Most of the pigments used by the painters under investigation are hygroscopic, namely chalk, green

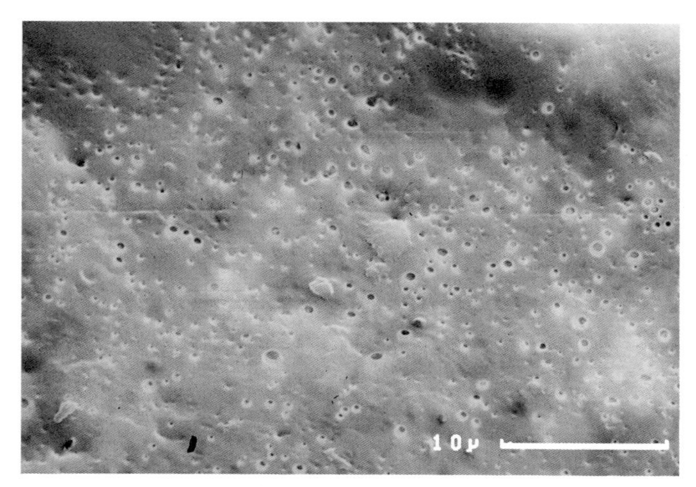

Fig. 11 Paint sample, Dughet, *Classical Landscape* (National Trust, Stourhead), blanched area in the green bushes

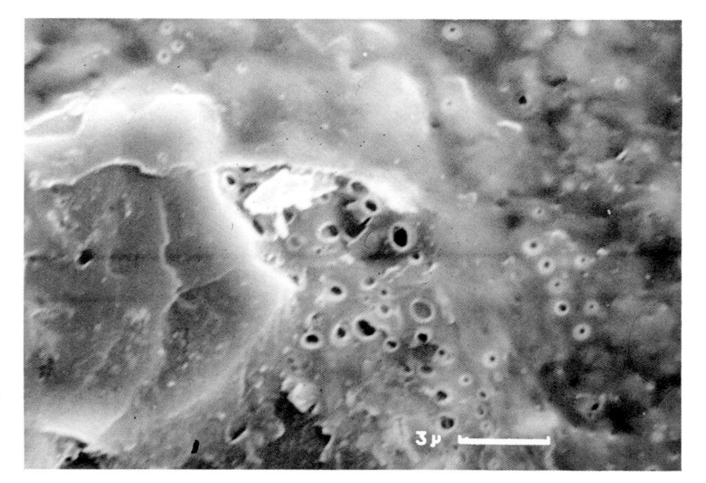

Fig. 12 Same sample as in fig. 11, slightly different area

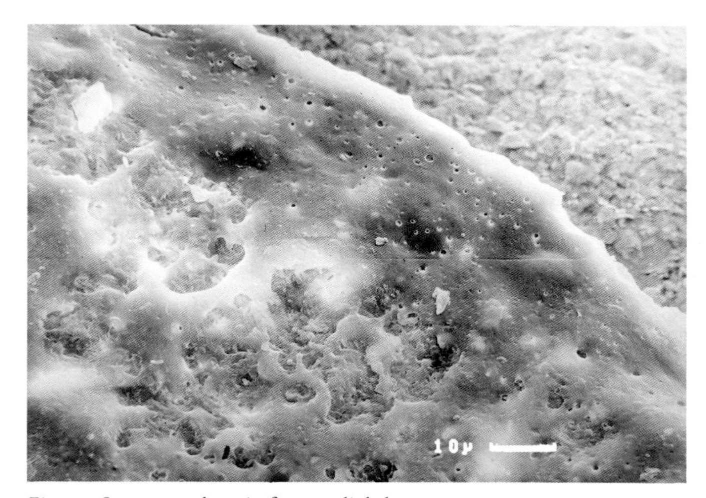

Fig. 13 Same sample as in fig. 11, slightly different area

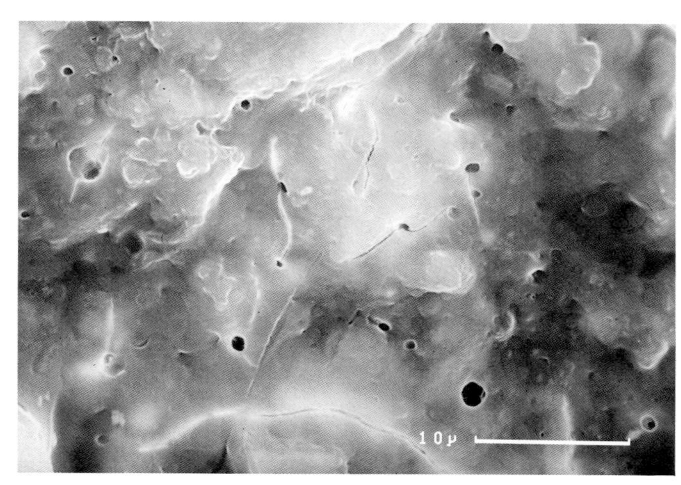

Fig. 14 Same painting as in fig. 11, different sample. An area in the green in the landscape showing bad blanching

Fig. 15 Same painting as in fig. 11. Blue sky, where there was no obvious blanching in the painting

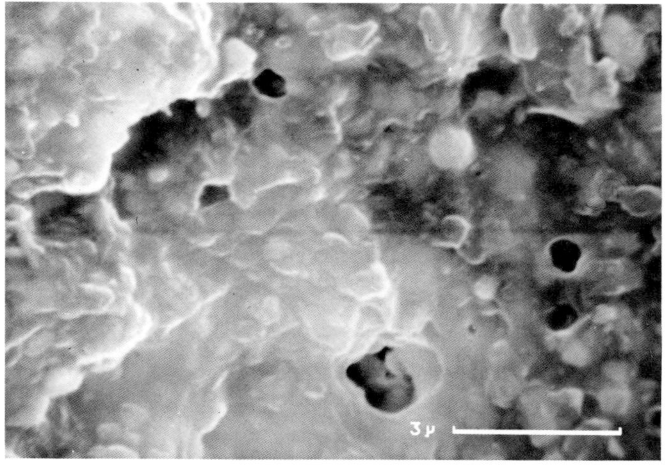

Fig. 16 Same sample as in fig. 15

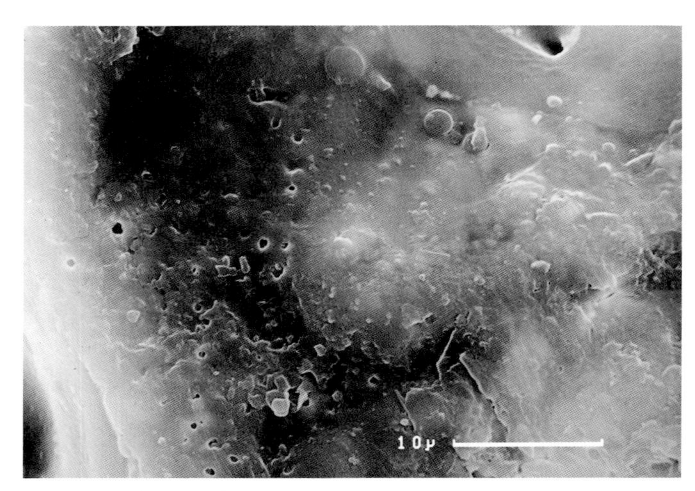

Fig. 17 Dughet, *Landscape near Rome*, Fitzwilliam Museum, blanched green in the trees

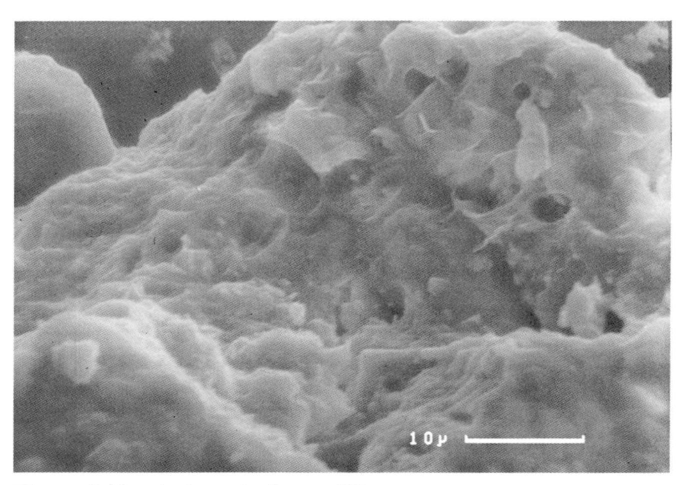

Fig. 18 Same painting as in fig. 17, different sample. Blanched light green in the trees, overlying a dark green

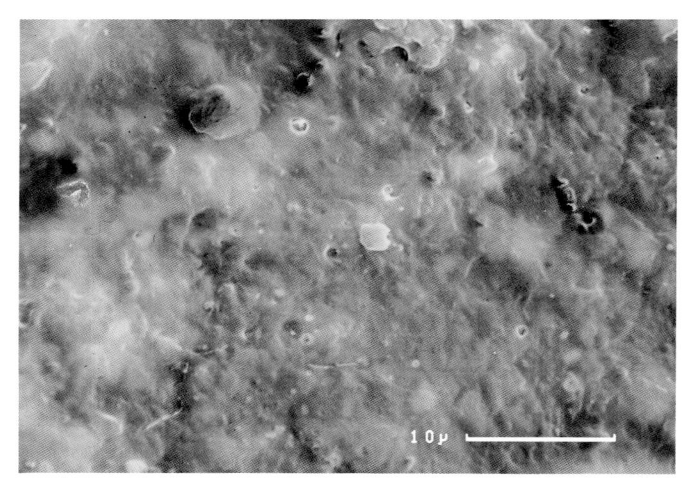

Fig. 19 Claude Lorraine, *Laban and his Daughters* (National Trust, Petworth), blanched blue-green in distant trees

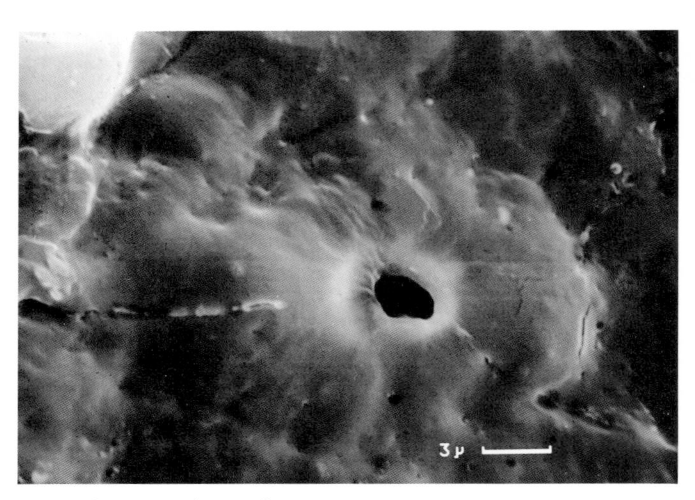

Fig. 20 Same sample as in fig. 19

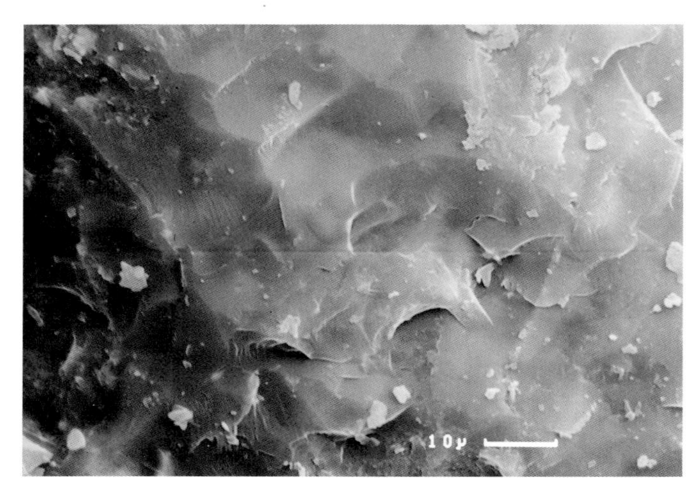

Fig. 21 Same painting, different sample. Blanched area in bushes

Fig. 22 Same sample as in fig. 21

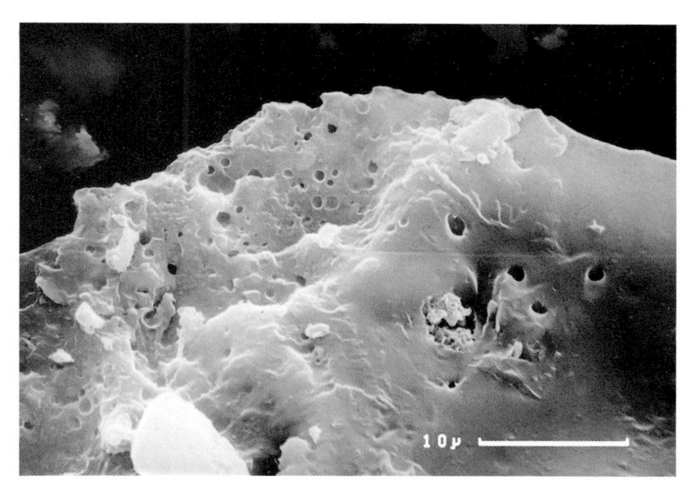

Fig. 23 Salvator Rosa, *Mr Altham as a Hermit* (National Trust, Kingston Lacy), blanched area in greyish clothing

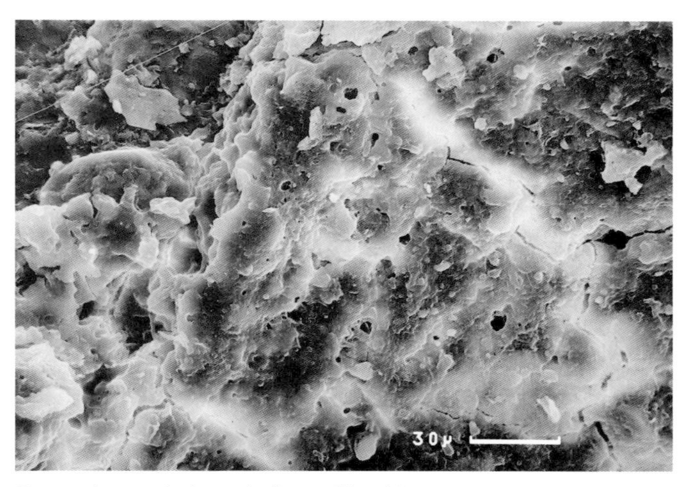

Fig. 24 Same painting as in fig. 23, blanching in a greyish-green leaf

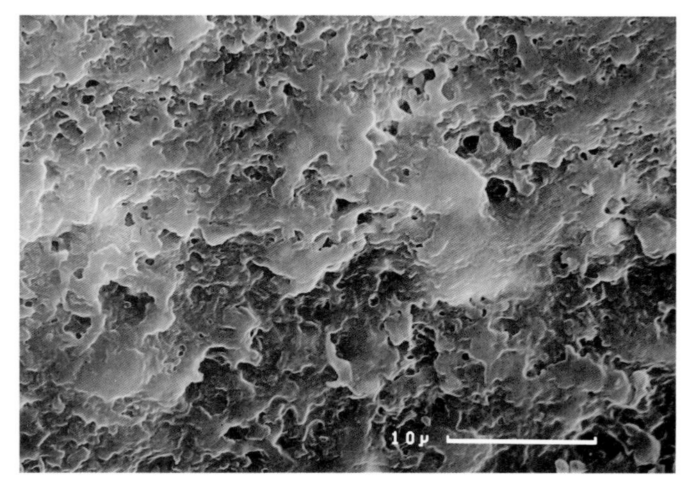

Fig. 25 Same painting as in fig. 23, blanching in a greyish-green leaf (same sample as in fig. 24)

earth, natural ochres, ultramarine and smalt. As a consequence these pigments are not easily wetted by organic media (wetting meaning the replacement of air on the particle surface by oil). Nowadays, in the industrial manufacture of paints, this problem is overcome by adding surface active agents, which, by adsorption onto the surface of the particles, give them hydrophobic properties. An example of this is the deposition of stearic acid on whiting or on precipitated calcium carbonate. Free fatty acids, present in oil media, would have the same effect.

It was surprising to find that in some of the paintings, especially in Dughet, the bulk of the pigment in the ground was not lead white with ochre, but chalk, although we initially seemed to be dealing with oil-grounds. Richard Symonds, in his Italian Notebooks, says that 'To make imprimatura wch shall stand abroad in ye ayre, tis best to use olio Cotto. Also tis good dare una mano di gesso prima & poi oglio suopra'.[11] In another recipe, which also describes ground layers applied to canvas by the painter Canini, the latter complains that primers sometimes left out the lead white from the ingredients red ochre, lead white, chalk (or a white clay) and charcoal black.[12] Although insufficient results of GLC analyses of the media used for the grounds have yet been gathered, other evidence, such as the electron micrographs, seem to indicate that the medium is often not oil alone. On the basis of the evidence, and the fact that hygroscopic pigments work better when a hydrophilic phase is added, the conclusion seems obvious; these painters used a mixed medium. This medium could be a purposely made emulsion or an oil medium in which hydrophilic substances, used for grinding the pigments, got trapped.

The same applies for the paint layers, where a few more GLC results are available. Noteworthy here are the large proportions of chalk found together with the green earth. The identification of egg in the GLC analyses is based on the low and sometimes absent azelate peak.[13] With the limited number of GLC results gathered so far, it is difficult to say whether this medium was used only in restricted areas. By trying out different formulations of egg/oil emulsions, mixed with chalk, green earth and the 'typical Claude mixture', a paint, which was very easy to handle and which showed a similar porosity, was obtained. This emulsion was made with 10 ml egg yolk, 10 ml drying oil and 20 ml of distilled water. It could easily be diluted with turpentine, suggesting a fatty or water-in-oil emulsion.[14] However, when using it with chalk, diluting with water was possible as well; this was not so when using other pigments. Green earth for instance became crumbly and it was not possible to make it into a paste. The handling of the paint and the smell were like good oil paints, but it had more impasto quality.[15] Besides the working qualities,

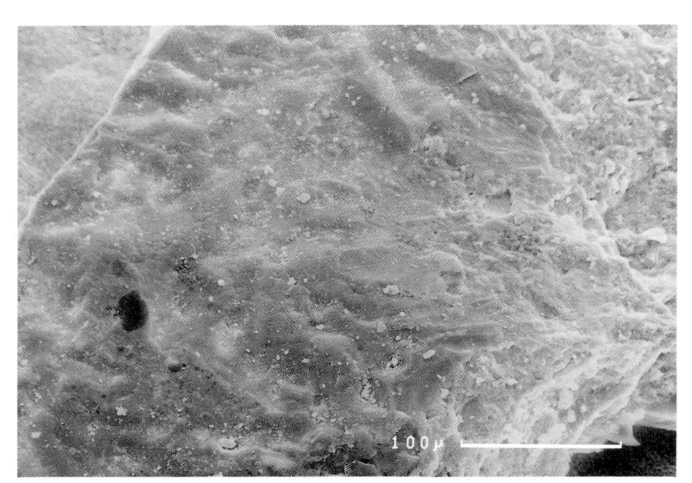

Fig. 26 Claude Lorraine, *The Rape of Europa* (Her Majesty the Queen), green in the foreground that was recently recovered from under a putty

Fig. 29 Same sample as in fig. 28, now seen in cross-section

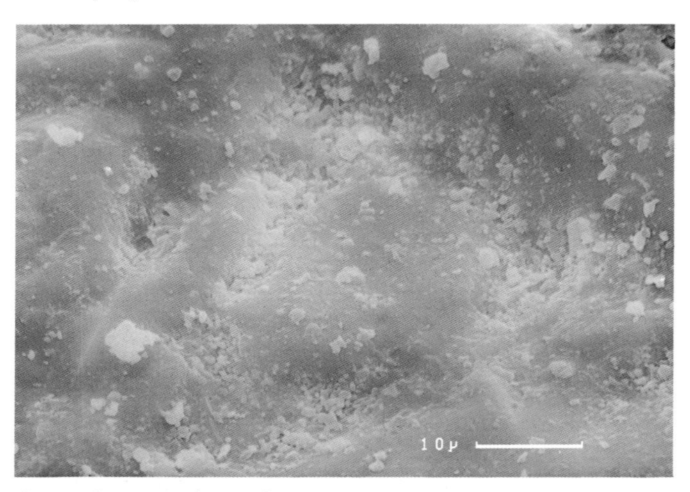

Fig. 27 Same sample as in fig. 26

Fig. 30 Back-scattered image of fig. 29

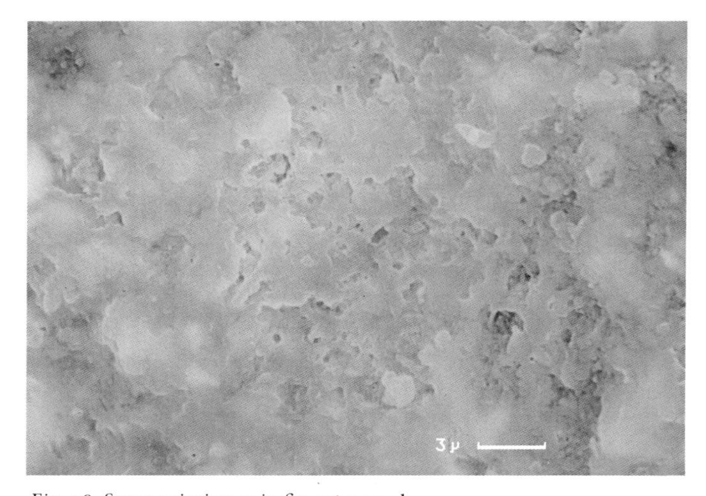

Fig. 28 Same painting as in fig. 26, very dry, blanched paint in the tree in the middle

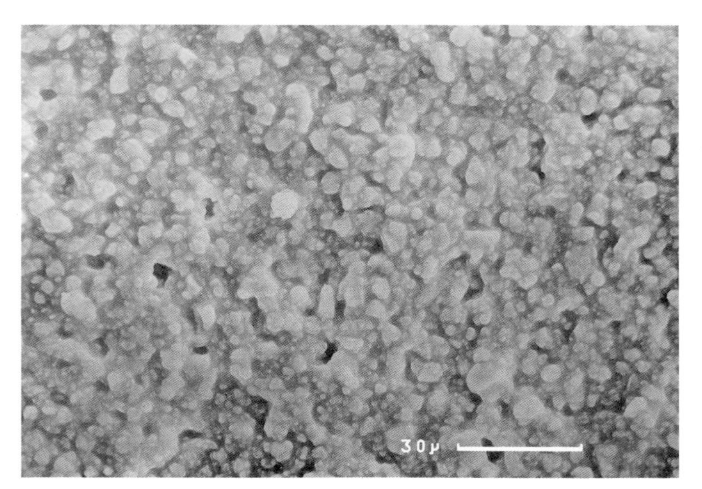

Fig. 31 Test strip, chalk in an emulsion of egg and oil, diluted with turpentine

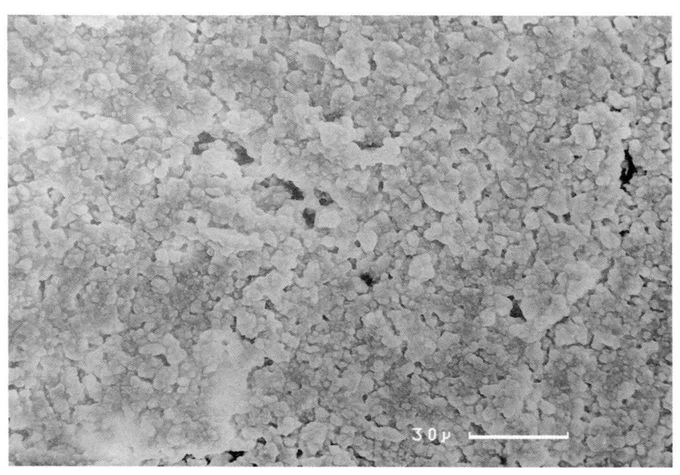

Fig. 32 The same test strip as in fig. 31, after three rolls with a cleaning swab with white spirit, then three rolls with 2½% ammonia, then three rolls with ethanol (industrial methylated spirit)/white spirit, 1:5

the emulsion thinned with turpentine had characteristics similar to those in Claude and Dughet when samples were examined under the microscope. One could observe the formation of the porous structure by the bubbles of turpentine escaping or trying to escape, a phenomenon absent when the tests were done with oil as the medium or water as the diluent. These observations combined with the results of analyses, seem to justify the conclusion that these painters used a water-in-oil type emulsion, or, in painters' terms, oil-tempera, thinned with an organic solvent such as turpentine or lavender oil.

Egg yolk is itself an emulsion of finely divided oil globules in water. This oil-in-water type emulsion is stabilized by lecithin, which is present in the yolk, lecithin acting as an emulsifier or surface active agent. It is a phospholipid and its action, like that of all surfactants, stems from the fact that it has both polar ends and long non-polar chains. However, cholesterol, present also, favours the water-in-oil type of emulsion, which may be thinned with turpentine. When oil is added, varying proportions of egg and oil give either the oil-in-water or the water-in-oil type of emulsion. According to Ralph Mayer, over one-third of egg or egg-solution gives the oil-in-water type.[16]

The electron micrograph in fig. 31 shows the topography of chalk painted out in the prepared emulsion (see also plates 45 and 46, p. 44). What seems to be the case is that an apparently water-in-oil type of emulsion (since it can be diluted with turpentine) separates out on application, leaving a porous film. On the use of egg/oil emulsions not much is to be found in early manuscripts, and where an obscure term is interpreted as possibly such an emulsion, this interpretation is dismissed by later writers.[17] However, Vasari mentions mixtures of egg and oil on at least two occasions and in recent years such mixtures have been identified by other investigators.[18] The passage in the Marciana Manuscript is of interest because green earth is mentioned as one of the pigments 'which have no body', continuing: 'The tempera of these colours, prepared "a putrido", is water and the yolk of an egg . . .'.[19] The Dutch painter and writer Samuel van Hoogstraeten recommends glue and egg paints for paintings that are to be hung opposite the light or a window, avoiding the gloss of oil paint.[20] Assuming that the paintings did not look blanched when they were first made, although the paint film was porous from the beginning, then porosity alone is not enough to explain blanching. So-called Benard cells in the paint film have been reported, photographed using X-ray micrography, on which occasion blanching was not mentioned.[21] Although pits do make the paint film look more opaque or whitish, due to the increased scattering of light, there must be an additional factor. Pits or microvoids are, for reasons of economy, introduced on purpose in the paint industry for making white paint without the use of a white pigment. The conclusion of researches in these areas is that when both voids and a pigment of high refractive index are present, the scattering is optimal.[22] The reason for this is that the difference in refractive indices is optimal: the high refractive index of the pigment, often titanium white, against that of the air-filled voids with r.i. 1, or 1.33 when they are filled with water.

In the paintings under discussion both voids and pigment particles are present. However, the r.i. of most of the pigments used is relatively low and the voids are probably filled with moisture for periods, bearing in mind the hygroscopic nature of the pigments and of the intermediate glue layers, resulting in a small difference in r.i. between particles and voids. When the chalk and green earth (and other) emulsions were painted out, the formation of holes and bubbles of solvent trapped

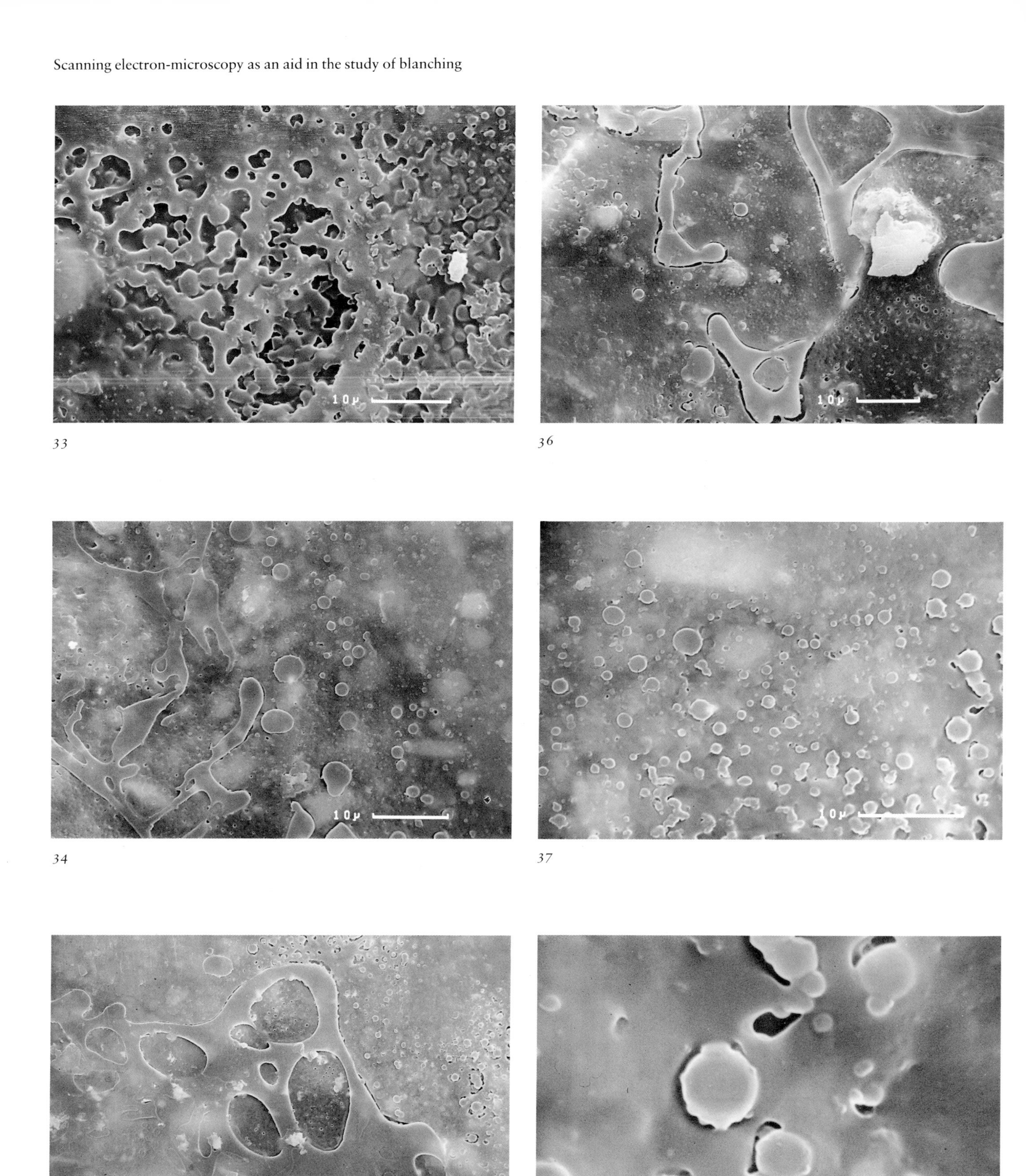

Figs. 33–38 Dughet, *Landscape near Rome* (Fitzwilliam Museum), paint surface after reforming treatment with dimethylformamide vapour.

underneath an often very thin skin of paint were observed, and it could be seen that the pigments (and possibly the emulsion) was separating out; the solvent drew compatible particles along with it. These particles included chalk and the fine silicious material present in green earth. The coarser particles of glauconite were left behind. The compatible materials were concentrated together and deposited around the holes or underneath the thin skin of paint where the lid had just been closed above the bubble. It is not difficult to imagine that the surface is easily broken, releasing the solvent and precipitating the material it carries with it. An increase in humidity, whether caused by the environment or due to restoration, will result in moisture being drawn up in the capillaries and the moisture subsequently being released on a decrease in humidity. Attracted, loosely bound, fine material will be deposited again. During cleaning part of this material is probably being leached out as well, with subsequent deposition of a new supply around the holes. (It is not surprising that 'cleaning-swabs' do not show that any paint has been removed: the fine silicates and chalk, and the aqueous medium, are colourless when the swab is wet and even when dry one could not distinguish them with the naked eye.)

From this study on blanching it appears that in these particular paintings there was a paint film defect from the start and that the process responsible for the defect is continuously being repeated whenever there is a change in moisture. Cleaning makes the situation worse, and the blanching goes on until no more material can be removed from the paint layer, leaving behind a completely porous film. Since 'like dissolves like' the effect is made more pronounced by the use of a more polar solvent. Cleaning tests done on the test strips showed that micro-fissures and additional micro-voids appeared after only three rolls with a swab with 2½% of ammonia in water and on treatment with methylated spirit/white spirit, 1:3 (fig. 32). In at least some of the cases, the blanching must be due to a relining treatment, done in the past. Nearly all of the paintings had been relined with a water-based starch paste. The formulations for these pastes differed widely and one can expect to find all sorts of additives on analysis, which could either prevent or promote blanching. Unfortunately, not many relining mixtures have as yet been analysed, although starch has been identified in several of the relined paintings in this project, indicating that the mixture was water-based. In the one case where the paste has been more fully investigated, a mixture of oil, wax, resin, animal glue and dextrin was found.[23] One wonders what solvent was used here. However, the picture relined with this mixture does not show blanching.

Some of the observations mentioned in the beginning also apply to relining being involved.

The peculiarity of blanching is that it is not dispelled by varnishing. The varnish seems to be too viscous to fill the pores and of course it does not remove the loosely bound material; at most it redistributes it. Reports of treatment of blanched paintings include impregnation of the paint layers with a methacrylate-pine oil mixture[24] and reforming the medium using dimethylformamide vapour.[25] Ten years and more after both treatments, blanching had not re-occurred. The second method seems preferable, since no substances that are completely foreign to the painting are introduced into it. For the improved appearance of the surface of Dughet's *Landscape near Rome* see plates 47 and 48, p. 44. The electron micrographs of a sample of the same painting are difficult to interpret with regard to the improved surface of the painting (figs. 33–38). What they do clearly illustrate, however, is that the medium was liquefied during the treatment with dimethylformamide and that two different substances in the medium have separated out: an emulsion separating out.

Notes

1. M. Wyld, J. Mills and J. Plesters, 'Some Observations on Blanching (with Special Reference to the Paintings of Claude)', *National Gallery Technical Bulletin*, Volume 4, 1980, pp. 49–63.
2. M. Hess, *Paint Film Defects*, second and revised ed., 1965.
3. A short description of methods used recently appeared in: M. Jaffé and K. Groen, 'Titian's 'Tarquin and Lucretia' in the Fitzwilliam', *The Burlington Magazine*, vol. CXXIX, 1987, note p. 165.

   Debye-Scherrer X-ray powder diffraction patterns were made, using a Philips diffractometer at the Department of Earth Sciences. Electron microscopy was done at the Department of Material Science and Metallurgy, using a Camscan S4. The samples were glued onto aluminium stubs with silverdag and coated with gold. The sample was positioned at 45°. Using a voltage of 20 kV the secondary electron image was produced. The image was photographed on Kodak FP4 film. In a few instances the backscattered electron image was produced as well.

   Gas chromatography was done using a Perkin Elmer PE 881 with packed column after saponifation and methylation of the sample. Some of the GLC analyses were done in the Scientific Department of the National Gallery on the Perkin-Elmer PE F70 with capillaries.
4. S. Bergeon, G. Mondorf, S. Delbourgo and J-P. Rioux, 'Le Blanchiment, Un Cas Precis d'etude', *ICOM Committee for Conservation*, 6th Triennial Meeting, Ottawa, 1981, 81/20/3. The same phenomenon was observed on brown paint in a painting by Romanelli.

5. Examples of more or less applicable articles are the following: R. L. Eissler and F. L. Baker, 'Critical Pigment Volume Concentration in Linseed Oil Films', *Applied Polymer Symposium*, no. 16, pp. 171–182; L. C. Princen, 'Vehicle Compatibility in Emulsion Coatings', *Applied Polymer Symposium*, no. 16, pp. 209–220; M. Dauchot-Dehon, 'Les Effects des Solvants sur les Couches Picturales', *Bulletin Institut Royal de Patrimoine Artistique*, XIV, 1973/4, pp. 89–104; H. G. Birkett and J. Rooney, 'Study of paint films by electron microscopy', *Pigment & Resin Technology*, 6, no. 8, 1977, pp. 14–18; G. Kampf, W. Papenroth, H. G. Volz and G. Weber, 'Time-lapse observation of chalking under the electron microscope', *16th FATIPEC Congress*, Liege, *Proceedings*, Vol. 3, 1982, pp. 167–174; L. E. Plahter and U. S. Plahter, 'The Young Christ among the Doctors by Theodoer van Baburen' *ACTA* (Institutum Romanum Norwegiae), Series altera in 8°, 3, 1983, pp. 183–229.
6. J. Mills, 'Blanching of the paint film involving possible changes in the medium', *National Gallery Technical Bulletin*, vol. 4, 1980, p. 60.
7. Hess, *op. cit.* n. 2, 83, 14a 'On account of the hygroscopic properties of chalk, oil paint containing it must not come in contact with moisture, in order to prevent the formation of blisters'.
8. X-ray diffraction data found:

	d(Å)	I
glauconite or celadonite	10.2	100
	4.52	80
	3.65	40
	3.33	60
	3.05	40
	2.57	100
	2.39	60
	1.71	10
	1.50	60
quartz	4.25	35
	3.34	100
	1.82	17

From the X-ray diffraction data it is difficult to say whether the d-value of 3.05 can be assigned to calcite as well. The presence of chalk was confirmed in several of the samples by micro-chemical tests.

Glauconite occurs almost exclusively in marine sediments, but has been reported to occur in alluvial deposits (transported by a river) and the nearly identical mineral celadonite seems to occur usually in vesicular cavities in vulcanic rocks (W. A. Deer, R. A. Howie and J. Zussman, *Rock forming minerals*, London, 1982, p. 35; R. L. Feller ed., *Artist's Pigments*, Cambridge, 1986, pp. 148–150).

Calcite and quartz, present in the Dughet samples of green earth, could be either accessory minerals or purposely added fillers. Since in the most perished greens the proportion of calcite was often found to be extremely high, one has to assume either that batches of pigment of different purity were used or that chalk was added. The reason for the latter could be that it would give the pigment 'more body'; de Mayerne has remarked: 'Pour vert un bol vert venant d'Italie qui a fort peu de corps et sert a glacer' (Th. T. de Mayerne, *Pictoria, Sculptoria, Tinctoria*, 1620, Edition Audin Imprimeurs Lyon, p. 131).
9. Princen, *op. cit.* n. 5. Examples are given of micro ripples, superimposed on buckles (ripples on macro scale). Experiments carried out by Princen showed that buckling is caused by metal driers and that without these, rippling remains but buckling is eliminated.
10. Pinholing as a result of Vortex-ring action is described very realistically by M. Hess in 'Pinholing and Cissing of Coatings', (*The Oil and Colour Trades Journal*, 1943, pp. 664–668), where he refers to F. E. Bartell and M. van Loo and their theory of the phenomenon, published in 1925 (*Ind. and Eng. Chemistry*, 1925, p. 925 and p. 1051). See also S. Keck, 'Mechanical Alteration of the Paint Film', *Studies in Conservation* 14, 1969, pp. 9–30.
11. M. Beal, *A Study of Richard Symonds*, London, 1984, p. 218. Beal transcribes olio Cotto as linseed oil boiled with litharge to make a quick-drying medium.
12. Beal, *op cit.* n. 11. 'Terra Rossa, biacca da Corpo a little & Creta un tantino negre Carbone. He complyned the ordinary imprimers putt in no biacca. Creta is usually sifted & grind in oyle.'

In f28 (Beal p. 228) he gives a recipe for a white made of egg shells, which, when powdered, may be mixed with oil.
13. J. Mills and R. White, 'The Gas Chromatographic Examination of Paint Media', Part I. Fatty Acid Composition and Identification of Dried Oil Films', *Studies in Conservation*, Vol. 11, no. 2, 1966, pp. 92–107. J. Mills and R. White, *The Organic Chemistry of Museum Objects*, London, 1987, p. 142.

No sample material was left over to look for the presence of cholesterol by means of mass spectrometry. Traces of phosphorus detected by electron microprobe analysis could not with certainty be assigned to phospholipids and phosphoproteins present in egg and casein.
14. L. Masschelein-Kleiner, *Ancient Binding Media, Varnishes and Adhesives*, Rome, 1985, p. 2.
15. I appreciate the efforts of Renate Woudhuysen and Ann Massing in preparing and trying out many different paint formulations. In their opinion green earth did have more body when used in egg than in oil, although the pigment volume concentration was found to be much higher in oil. This they found not only in egg (whole egg and yolk) but also in glue, whole egg/linseed oil, egg yolk/drying oil, mastic/linseed oil and mastic/linseed oil with the addition of glue. When resin was present the mixture had to be diluted with turpentine, or the paint would not come off the brush. Although with the oil/resin mixtures the impasto stayed, the paint was much easier to handle after the aqueous medium was added. With oil alone, the paint just flattened out, even when as much pigment as possible was added.
16. R. Mayer, *The Artist's Handbook*, London, 1973, p. 242.
17. H. Kühn, H. Roosen-Runge, R. E. Straub and M. Koller, *Reclams Handbuch der künstlerischen Techniken*, Band I, Stuttgart, 1984, p. 203.

18. Kühn, *op. cit.* n. 17. An egg-walnut oil emulsion was found in the green in a painting by Carlo Crivelli, c. 1490, and a similar emulsion in the blue drapery by Lorenzo Costa, c. 1505. (both analysed in the National Gallery). Other examples include: paintings by Bernt Notke, 1482/83, and a triptique in Turnhout, painted between 1535 and 1540 (C. Waregne-Reyes, H. Coenen, L. Kockaert and J. Vynckier, 'Le triptyque des Saintes Agethe et Apolline de Turnhout', *Bulletin Institut Royal de Patrimoine Artistique*, 20, 1984/85, pp. 43–69).
19. M. P. Merrifield, *Original treatises in the Arts of Painting*, Vol. II, no. 309, p. 610.
20. S. van Hoogstraeten, *Inleyding tot de Hooge School der Schilderkonst*, Rotterdam, 1678, facs. 1969, p. 337. 'The glue- and egg-paints are surely not to be relegated altogether, firstly, because of their spry brightness, and then, because of their handling ability in skillful painting; and especially because they are capable of many uses where oil paint fails. The clarity of the size and egg paint is very efficient for showing something in candlelight or from a distance, as in prospects (vistas) or in intimate theatre stages. Also, when a piece is to hang right opposite the light or a window, glue or egg paint is better than oil paint, since it does not glitter. And since it flows easily from the brush it is more suitable for extensive works such as screens, wall hangings or painted tapestries, for which purpose it has generally been used for more than two hundred years; because one can fold and crease them without harm as was done with the *konterfeitsel* that Dürer sent to Raphael and like Mabuse's beheading of Saint Jacob. Beccafumi, a painter from Sienna, was of the opinion that egg paint was more durable than oil paint since, he said, the works of Brother Joan, Brother Philips Benozzo, made with egg paint and very old, were less perished than the works of Lukas van Kortona or Pollaiuolo, done more recently. But our Netherlandish air would perhaps make the reverse come true.'
21. W. W. Percival Prescott, The Examination of Paintings using High Resolution Contact Micro Radiography, *ICOM Committee for Conservation*, 5th Triennial Meeting, Zagreb, 1978.
22. J. A. Seiner, 'Microvoid Coatings; material and energy savers?', *J. Oil Col. Chem. Assoc.*, 60, 1977, pp. 325–346
23. Analytical results from the Central Laboratory for Research of Art Objects in Amsterdam.
24. P. B. Boissonnas, 'A treatment for blanching in paintings', *Studies in Conservation*, vol. 22, no. 1, 1977 p. 43.
25. H. Lank and V. Pemberton Pigott, 'The use of dimethylformamide vapor in reforming blanched oil paintings', *Conserv. Restor. Pict. Art*, 1976, pp. 103–109.

The examination of the *Portrait of Rembrandt in a Flat Cap*

Karin Groen

Imitator of Rembrandt
Portrait of Rembrandt in a Flat Cap
Panel, 70.5 × 57.8 cm
Her Majesty the Queen

The painting came to the Institute in January 1980 for conservation. During varnish removal with a mild solvent mixture consisting of one part of methylated spirit and six parts of white spirit it was noted that the black part of the cap was soluble in this solvent mixture. The ensuing examination revealed that the hat and cloak were both equally susceptible to solvent action. This is rarely found to be the case in 17th-century Dutch painting and never in paintings by Rembrandt. This curious behaviour initiated further investigation, involving photographic techniques, microscopic examinations and an attempt at dating the panel using dendrochronology.

Comments on the painting made before the examination at the Institute, and those resulting from the examination, are reported by Christopher White in *The Dutch Pictures in the Collection of Her Majesty the Queen.*[1]

Support

The oak panel consists of a single, wide board, cut across the tree.

An attempt was made by J. Fletcher at dating the panel by dendrochronology. However, the ring-width sequence he obtained could not be matched with existing curves. An effort was made by J. Bauch of the Ordinariat für Holzbiologie, University of Hamburg, to match the curve of the painting under examination with those of seven others with a single board cut across the tree, but a similarity in ring-width sequence could not be found. However, out of these seven only four or five could be securely matched and dated.

X-radiograph

The X-radiograph clearly reveals the large pentiment in the hat, which was earlier commented on by Friedrich Winkler, when he says

Fig. 1 Imitator of Rembrandt, *Portrait of Rembrandt in a Flat Cap*

Fig. 2 X-radiograph, revealing the large pentiment in the hat and the way the figure was first blocked in with lead white

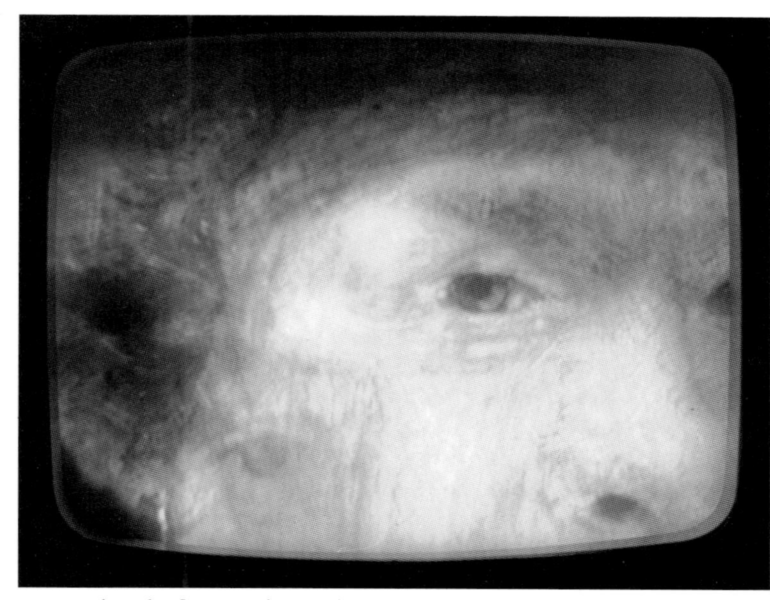

Fig. 3 Infrared reflectograph, revealing a 'third' eye

Fig. 4 Detail in raking light, showing the brushwork

that the painting is a totally overpainted original with a large pentiment by Rembrandt in the beret (fig. 2).[2] Such *pentimenti* are usually clearly visible in X-radiographs of Rembrandt paintings, because of his method of blocking in the figure in dense lead white. For the same reason it can be seen that the space left for the figure was originally planned to be narrower along the right hand side contour, indicating a different position of the sitter. A shape, not visible in the painting, was planned in the lower half, on the right. Although lack of modelling is shown in the sitter's right cheek and nose, there does not seem to be a marked difference from X-radiographs produced by genuine Rembrandt paintings of the 1632–1644 period.

Infrared reflectograph

The infrared reflectograph reveals a 'third' eye situated lower down near the contour of the left cheek, indicating that the head was originally in a different position (fig. 3). The mouth and nose of an earlier version can be recognized as well.

Paint samples

Seven small paint samples were made into cross-sections and examined. Only in samples taken along the edge of the painting could a chalk ground, bound in a glue medium, be found (the other samples possibly being incomplete). The sample taken from the bottom edge shows a thick light brown *imprimatura* on top of the chalk, consisting of lead white mixed with brown ochre (plate 49, p. 44). The excessive thickness of the *imprimatura* in this sample is confusing, since it emanates from the edge. The build-up and composition of these preparatory layers are consistent with panel paintings by Rembrandt and his contemporaries. However, the imprimatura shows abrasion at its top surface with smooth brown-black paint overlaying the unconformity.

Slightly higher up in the cloak there is a mixture of chalk, lead white and a little ochre underneath the dark paint. Examination using long wave ultraviolet light shows that the dark paint consists of two layers, the top one very smooth, the bottom one coarser (plates 50 and 51, p. 44).

A sample from the background on the right hand side shows a damaged light coloured underlay, covered by a thin layer of varnish and then brown paint. The brown paint contains coarse particles of a reddish brown pigment as well as bright red ochre and a red lake. The coarsely ground red lake is situated mainly towards the top of the brown paint (plate 52, p. 44). The flesh paint from his right cheek shows a fairly thick mixture of lead white and with an admixture of red lake, painted wet-in-wet with only lead white (plate 53, p. 44). The bright yellow pigment used in the ear-ring and in the chain is lead-tin yellow (electron microprobe analysis). The yellow paint contains coarse, colourless grains, typical of lead-tin yellow. In the sample from the ear-ring, the thick yellow impasto is sitting on top of the red paint used for the shadow in the ear. The red shadow contains lead white, red ochre and a little red lake. The cross-section shows that the yellow paint is worn; layers of varnish are situated directly on top of the red paint in places (plate 54, p. 44).

Discussion

It is difficult to arrive at a definite conclusion on the basis of evidence from the technical examination and the painting's behaviour towards solvents alone. It was in the end close visual examination that forced one to conclude that the painting could not possibly be by Rembrandt. Both Herbert Lank and members of the Rembrandt Research Project based their conclusion on such an examination, the Rembrandt Research Group stating (in a letter) that the painting is not only not by Rembrandt but also not from his studio. Herbert Lank (in an internal report) noted that the flesh paint revealed the greatest disparity between the modelling in this picture and in other Rembrandt paintings of the period. To cite some of his observations:

- The area around the sitter's right eye is painted with thin radiating streaks which extend into the upper lid and eyebrows. The orange and yellow lines below the eye are crude and formless.
- The reflected light in the eye sockets lacks the transparency usually found (see e.g. the *Selfportrait* of 1640 in the National Gallery) but are a dense and streaky mass.
- Once seen, the hesitant and streaky brushwork becomes apparent all over the face; for instance in the mouth and moustache and in the uncertain way that the sitter's left cheek merges into the background (fig. 4).
- The background is generally pasty and has a crispy uncharacteristic brown/ochre glaze on the top right area.

Herbert Lank concludes that the *Portrait of Rembrandt in a flat cap* is the work of a skilled imitator, that is, someone who composed the picture in the style of Rembrandt. He makes a tentative speculation that the imitator worked in the latter half of the 18th century. Signature and date, *Rembrandt ft./1642*, are part of the pastiche.

This verdict being acceptable as far as stylistic criteria are concerned, some of the technical information obtained seems to indicate that, at least in the first stages of the 'manufacture' of the object, the maker was well aware of the working methods of Rembrandt and his studio. This can be deduced from the way the figure was blocked in, the changes in the hat and the common practice of using a chalk ground with a slightly coloured isolating *imprimatura*. Also, several of the paint samples showed a layer that was already worn when the surface layers were applied. This implies that the imitator used a pre-existing, unfinished or damaged painting. Paintings in their 'dead-coloured' state are mentioned in inventories, when painters' estates came up for sale.[3] The use of such a panel would explain why the X-radiograph is not markedly different from those produced by Rembrandt's studio and from followers of Rembrandt.

Most of the pigments found are those which were used over long periods of time, with the exception of lead-tin yellow. The ear-ring as well as the chain seems to be part of the pastiche, that is the paint layers visible at the surface of the painting. Lead-tin yellow is the pigment one would expect in highlights of such ornaments in 17th-century Dutch paintings, in fact it was most frequently used in the 15th, 16th and 17th centuries.[4] It has been identified in paintings up to c. 1750, occurring less frequently in the first half of the 18th century and seemingly disappearing in the second half. This could indicate that the imitation was done a little earlier than the second half of the eighteenth century.

Notes

1. C. White, *The Pictures in the Collection of Her Majesty the Queen, The Dutch Pictures*, Cambridge 1982, pp. 111–112.
2. F. Winkler, 'Echt, falsch, verfalscht', *Kunstchronik*, 10, 1957.
3. J. Bruyn, B. Haak, S. H. Levie, P. J. J. van Thiel, E. van de Wetering, *A Corpus of Rembrandt Paintings*, I, The Hague, 1982, p. 23.
4. H. Kühn, 'Lead-tin yellow', *Studies in Conservation*, 13, 1968, pp. 7–31.

Cosimo Tura *The Crucifixion with the Virgin and St John*

David Scrase

Cosimo Tura (c. 1431–1495)
The Crucifixion with the Virgin and St John
Tempera ? on panel, 48.9 × 29.5 cm
Fitzwilliam Museum

The panel is generally recognised as by Tura and dated in the 1470s[1] (fig. 1). Miklos Boskovits considers the mourning Virgin and St John in the Fitzwilliam Museum to be very close in style to the figures of the organ shutters of 1469 in the Museo del Duomo, Ferrara, and comments that as the city view in the background recalls Mantegna's Padua he is inclined to date it in the 1460s.[2]

Hardly any drawings known can be securely attributed to Tura. Of the group reproduced in Ruhmer's *Cosimo Tura* (1958), only the drawing in pen and ink of the *Madonna with Saints Sebastian, Francis, Dominic and Agatha* in the British Museum[3] shows the characteristics of penmanship in the underdrawing revealed by infrared reflectography in the *Crucifixion* (fig. 2). Comparison with underdrawing in Tura's *St George and the Princess* on the organ shutters in Ferrara[4] shows a markedly similar handling. The wiry hatching and accentuation of knees is characteristic to both, although the Ferrarese organ shutters are drawn in a looser manner. The tight delineation of form evident in the *Crucifixion* is requisite for a painting on so small a scale and appears to be identical with what can be seen with the naked eye in other small-scale works by Tura, notably the tondi which Longhi considered to be from the predella of the Roverella altarpiece, now in the Isabella Stuart Gardner Museum, Boston, the Fogg Art Museum, Cambridge, Mass. and the Metropolitan Museum, New York.[5] The underdrawing of the main section of the Roverella altarpiece, now in the National Gallery, London, is on the same scale as that in the Ferrara organ shutters and is similar in its rather broader outline to the other paintings by Tura in the National Gallery, most notably to the early *Allegorical Figure* which has recently been cleaned.[6]

The underdrawing revealed by infrared reflectography in the Fitzwilliam painting not only confirms the painting to be by Tura, if anyone still doubted it, but also, in juxtaposition with the underdrawing of the Ferrarese organ shutters and that shown in the National Gallery's pictures, gives confirmation to the attribution of the British Museum sheet to Tura's hand, and will, with luck, enable further attributions of anonymous or wrongly attributed drawings to this most idiosyncratic and important Ferrarese artist.

Notes

1. J. W. Goodison and G. H. Robertson, Fitzwilliam Museum, Cambridge, 'Catalogue of Paintings', vol. II, 1967, p. 177f.
2. M. Boskovits, '*Ferrarese Painting about 1450: Some new Arguments*, Burlington Magazine, vol. CXX, June 1978, p. 378 note 29.
3. British Museum 1855-5-9-1613.
4. Reproduced in the exhibition catalogue *San Giorgio e la Principessa di Cosme Tura*, edited by Jadranka Bentini, 1985, p. 19.
5. R. Longhi, *Officina Ferrarese*, Rome, 1934, p. 36f.
6. For a description of the examination and conservation see Jill Dunkerton, Ashok Roy and Alastair Smith, *The Unmasking of Tura's Allegorical Figure*, National Gallery Technical Bulletin, vol. XI, 1987. I should particularly like to thank Jill Dunkerton and Alastair Smith for giving me access to the files on the National Gallery paintings in their care and for discussing the cleaning of Tura's *Allegorical Figure*.

Fig. 1 Cosimo Tura *Crucifixion*

Fig. 2 Infrared reflectograph assembly

Gert van Lon's *Madonna in the Rosary*

Jean Michel Massing

Gert van Lon (c.1465–c.1530)
Madonna in the Rosary
Oil on panel: c.160.2 × 100.0 cm
King's College Chapel, Cambridge

The *Madonna in the Rosary* (fig. 1) was first attributed to Gert van Lon in 1974; subsequent studies,[1] and the technical investigations done at the Institute have confirmed this attribution.

Gert van Lon was probably born in Geseke (between Paderborn and Lippstadt) around 1465. A Westphalian artist, he seems to have learned his craft in Soest in the workshop of the Master of Liesborn. In 1493 he is recorded as a Master. The first dated document referring to his activities is the commission, dated 5 October 1505, of an altarpiece for the Benedictine monastery of Willebadessen, today in the Westfälisches Landesmuseum in Münster. Later (25 April 1512) he was asked to paint an altarpiece for the Marienkirche in Lemgo. The last document referring to him dates from 1529. He must have died a few months later, as his son Johannes van Lon was in possession of his father's property by 1531.[2]

A relatively large number of paintings have been given to Gert van Lon. The Cambridge panel is said to have come from a women's convent in Soest.[3] It is an autograph work and can be linked in iconography and style to one of the wings of the *Altar of the Holy Kinship* (*Sippenaltar*), now in Münster, which is clearly by the master (fig. 2).

The painting from King's College represents the Virgin and Child within a rosary.[4] The Virgin is crowned as *Regina coeli*, while her Immaculate Conception is symbolised by the crescent moon at her feet and the rays of light all around recalling, literally, the description of the woman of the apocalypse (Revelation xii, 1): *Mulier amicta sole et luna sub pedibus eius* (A woman clothed in the sun and with the moon at her feet). She is presenting a basket of cherries to the infant Christ who has already taken some. This is only too appropriate as the fruit stands for the heavenly reward for piety;[5] in its colour, it also alludes to the passion. Mother and child are surrounded by a rosary formed of a garland with five groups of ten white roses separated by the five wounds of Christ – indicating a rosary in which every ten 'Hail Marys' were followed not only by an 'Our Father' but also by a meditation on one of Christ's wounds. This kind of iconographic 'contamination' (between the imagery of the rosary and that of the wounds of Christ) in fact only occurs around 1500.[6]

Gert van Lon's *Madonna in the Rosary* had a devotional function; like Veit Stoss's *Engelgruss* in the Lorenzkirche in Nuremberg, it was painted as a visual aid to meditation on the rosary, a form of prayer which became popular in the last quarter of the fifteenth century with the institution of Confraternities of the Rosary. The rosary was especially popular among Carthusians and Dominicans.[7]

The painting from King's College was cleaned by Max De Liss in 1971.When the panel was examined by the Hamilton Kerr Institute in June 1984 as part of an inspection of paintings in King's College Chapel, it was noted that separation of the paint layers had previously occurred along the three joints which had been puttied. Fresh splits had also opened, notably along the middle joint, producing raised cleavages of the paint layer along the edges of the split. Small flaking losses had taken place at the bottom of the two left-hand splits where the apex of the warp had been constricted by the frame.[8] The panel had been so tightly fitted into its frame that it could not move in response to changes in relative humidity.

The support consists of four planks joined vertically. The panel was presumably painted on both sides but has at some time been divided by being sawn down the middle. This has caused the two sides to respond differently to fluctuating levels of relative humidity, producing a marked convex warp. As part of an earlier treatment the panel was evidently planed down, somewhat unevenly, and rectangular buttons were most probably affixed at the same time across the joints. These buttons were later replaced by the present, larger ones which have been glued vertically along the joints. The stencilled label on the reverse (ODK) has not been identified.[9]

During treatment at the Hamilton Kerr Institute the raised paint flakes running along the edges of splits were realigned and secured using gelatin adhesive and a warm spatula. Losses at the tail end of the two left hand splits were filled. Where white putty or ground was exposed by flaking losses or along splits it was retouched using tempera. Laropal K80 varnish was stippled into these retouches. Finally the painting was reframed, avoiding any constriction of the painting.

Infrared examination with a vidicon television

Fig. 1 Gert van Lon, *Madonna in the Rosary* (King's College Chapel, Cambridge)

Fig. 2 Gert van Lon, *Madonna in the Rosary* from the *Altarpiece of the Holy Kinship*, Münster (Westfälisches Landesmuseum für Kunst und Kulturgeschichte; Leihgabe des Westfälischen Kunstvereins)

system has shown the underdrawing done by Gert van Lon (fig. 3). The artist's first idea was to paint angels in the four corners to enhance the heavenly character of the scene as well as to integrate the oval composition harmoniously within a rectangular space. The lower pair of kneeling angels can be clearly seen, their hands held up in front of them in a devotional attitude.[10] More surprising, perhaps, is the degree of definition in these hands; for the angel on the right they have been clearly sketched, but for that on the other side, they are represented according to a most elementary and schematic formula. The underlying drawing is not without elegance: Gert van Lon has indicated the forms with firm but subtle outlines and a few hatchings. In size and compositional importance, the two angels recall the donors painted by Gert van Lon in the lower part of the *Madonna in the Rosary* (fig. 2) from the *Sippenaltar* now in the Westfälisches Landesmuseum in Münster.[11] There, the outer panel of the right wing which shows the Virgin and Child has the donor raising his parted hands piously in front of him while his wife clasps hers together in a more traditional way. The Münster painting shows the *Madonna in the Rosary* against a brocade. The King's College panel, however, has a heavenly setting even if the four angels originally planned were in the event reduced to two. Instead of the lower pair, Gert painted two nuns reciting the rosary wearing brown vestments and white head-dresses; they are presumably the patrons[12] and they probably commissioned the painting in the second decade of the sixteenth century.[13]

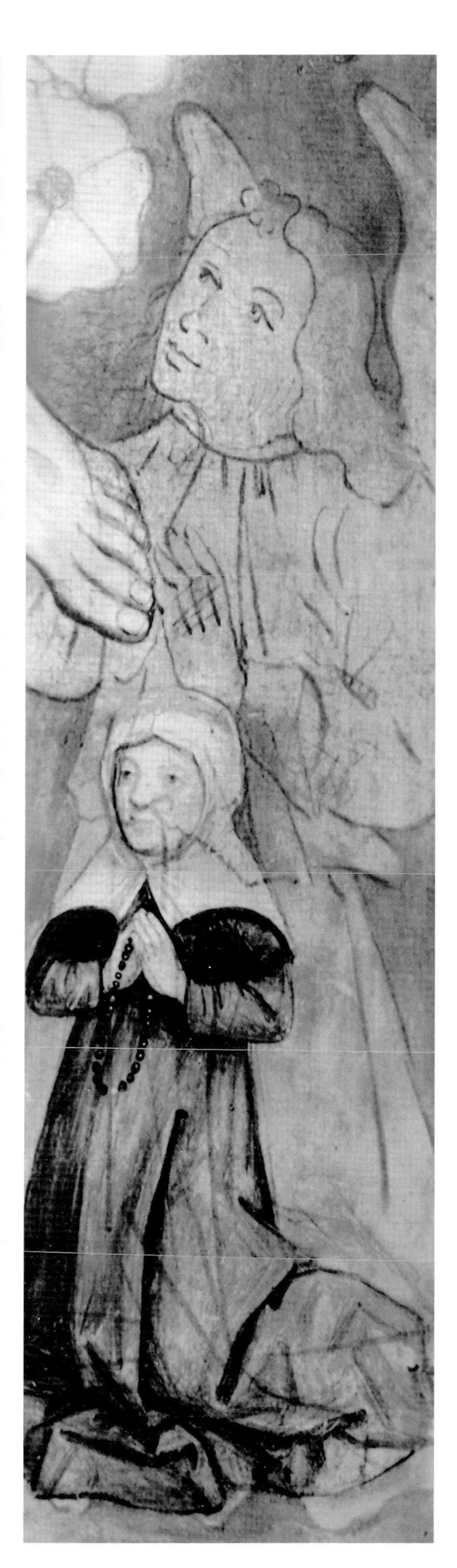

Fig. 3 Infrared reflectograph of the *Madonna in the Rosary*, King's College Chapel, Cambridge: Details of bottom left and right corners.

Notes

1. Bibliography: *Verzeichniss der Gemälde-Sammlung des Geheimen Regierungs-Rathes Krüger zu Minden*, Minden 1848, p. 14 no. I.33, (republished by R. Fritz, 'Der Katalog der Gemäldesammlung Krüger zu Minden', *Westfalen*, XXIX, Münster 1951, p. 89); London, Christie and Manson, *Catalogue of pictures not required for the National Gallery, consisting chiefly of a portion of the Krüger Collection*, Saturday, February 14, 1857, p. 6 no. 17; *Catalogue of the Plate, Portraits and other Pictures at King's College, Cambridge*, Cambridge 1933, p. 91; N. Pevsner, *Cambridgeshire*, Harmondsworth 1954, p. 93; Royal Commission on Historical Monuments, *An Inventory of the Historical Monuments in the City of Cambridge*, I, London 1959, p. 128; W. Koenig, *Studien zum Meister von Liesborn*, (Quellen und Forschungen zur Geschichte des Kreises Beckum, VI), Beckum 1974, pp. 76–77 no. 33, pl. 110; M. Wessing, *Gert van Lon. Ein Beitrag zur Geschichte der spätgotischen Malerei Westfalens*, Frankfurt am Main etc. 1986, pp. 77–80 and 151–152, fig. 23.
2. For the life of Gert von Lon, see M. Wessing, *op. cit.* in n. 1 above, pp. 8–16 and 248–249; for the documents, see pp. 231–247 and 251–262.
3. Provenance: *Nonnenkloster* in Soest; Collection Carl Wilhelm August Krüger; bought by the National Gallery, London, in 1854; resold at Christie, on 14 February 1857. Bought by Mrs. H. S. Ashbee in 1886 or 1887 in a sale of bankrupt stock in Cheapside; coll. C. R. Ashbee, Sevenoaks; in 1931 given by him to King's College, Cambridge. Ashbee also designed the oak frame; on his life, see A. Crawford, *C. R. Ashbee, Architect, Designer and Romantic Socialist*, New Haven and London 1985. For the Krüger Collection, M. Levey, *National Gallery catalogues. The German School*, London 1959, pp. 112–114.
4. For the *Madonna in the Rosary* and its iconography see E. Wilkins, 'Rosenkranz', *Lexikon der christlichen Ikonographie*, III, Rom . . . 1971, col. 568–572; Cologne, Erzbischöfliches Diözesan-Museum, *500 Jahre Rosenkranz*, 25 Oktober 1975–15 January 1976, Cologne 1975. For the early representations, see also F. H. A. van den Oudendijk Pieterse, *Dürers Rosenkranzfest en de ikonografie der duitse rozenkransgroepen van de XVe en het begin der XVIe eeuw*, Amsterdam . . . 1939.
5. For the symbolism of cherries, see H. Friedmann, *The Symbolic Goldfinch. Its History and Significance in European Devotional Art*, Washington 1946, p. 95; I. Bergström, 'Disguised Symbolism in "Madonna" Pictures and Still Life', *Burlington Magazine*, XCVII, London 1955, p. 304. In the Münster painting, Christ is holding strawberries.
6. Cologne, *op. cit.* in n. 4 above, p. 162. The Mass of Saint Gregory and the Madonna in the Rosary were also painted by Gert van Lon on the outer wings of the Crucifixion altarpiece in the St Nicolaikirche in Lippstadt; Wessing, *op. cit.* in n. 1 above, pp. 59–64 and 168–171, pl. 18–19.
7. See above, n. 4.
8. This essay incorporates the conclusions of the condition and treatment reports by Ian McClure and Ella Hendriks.
9. An old label indicating that the panel came from a *Nonnenkloster* in Soest is mentioned in the *Catalogue of . . . Pictures at King's College*, *op. cit.* in n. 1 above, p. 91; this label, now lost, must have been an extract from the *Verzeichniss der Gemäldesammlung . . . Krüger*, *op. cit.* in n. 1 above, p. 14, which claims that the painting came 'Aus einem Nonnenkloster in Soest'.
10. See for example M. Baxandall, *Painting and Experience in fifteenth Century Italy*, Oxford 1972, pp. 65–67.
11. P. Pieper, *Die deutschen, niederländischen und italienischen Tafelbilder bis um 1530*, (Westfälisches Landesmuseum . . . Bestandskataloge), Münster 1986, pp. 293–298.
12. Wessing, *op. cit.* in n. 1 above, p. 79, has shown that the costume does not correspond to that of either Dominican or Augustinian nuns; the painting, therefore, does not seem to have been painted for the women's convents of Paradies or Sankt Walpurgis in Soest; for these houses, see L. Schmitz-Kallenberg, *Monasticon Westfaliae*, Münster (Westfalen) 1909, pp. 74–75, nos. 2 and 5; these convents, incidently, were dissolved in 1809 and in 1811 respectively. Pevsner, *op. cit.* in n. 1 above, p. 114, and the volume of the Royal Commission . . . , *op. cit.* in n. 1 above, p. 128, mention that the panel came from an Ursuline Convent in Soest; that Order however, had no convent there: Schmitz-Kallenberg, *op. cit.* above, p. 101. Obviously, the panel might have been made for another house before being transferred to a Soest monastery (if we believe the *Verzeichniss . . .*, *op. cit.* in n. 1 above, no. 1.33, which records such a provenance). There were other monasteries in Soest. The Tertiarierinnen des heiligen Dominikus (Third order of St. Domenic), had a convent (Mariengarten) which was founded, circa 1300, as a hospice for widows (Versorgungshaus); for this foundation, see Schmitz-Kallenberg, *op. cit.* above, p. 87 no. 8. For a Beguine convent also in Soest, *ibidem*, pp. 75–76, no. 6.
13. Wessing, *op. cit.* in n. 1 above, p. 149, dated it in the 'Mittlere Zeit, ca. 1512–1520'; this is also the dating proposed for the *Sippenaltar*.

The examination and restoration of El Greco's *El Espolio*

Ann Massing

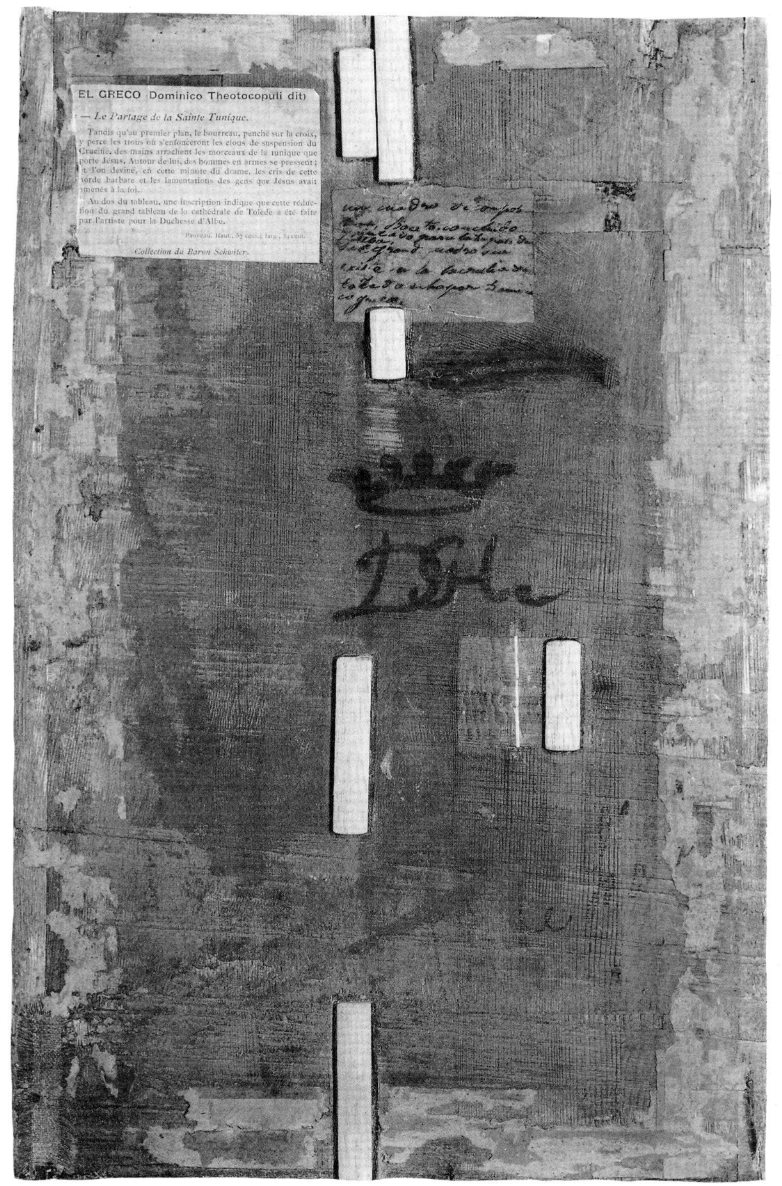

Fig. 1 Back of panel before restoration

El Greco (1541–1614)
El Espolio
oil? on panel, 55.6 × 34.7 cm
National Trust, Upton House

The panel from Upton House is a small version of the painting representing the disrobing of Christ in the sacristy of Toledo Cathedral, painted c. 1577–79.[1] Several studies and repetitions of the cathedral picture are known[2] and questions arise over their authenticity and chronology; especially tantalizing is the possibility that one of the versions may be the painter's model and the others later replicas. After removal of the discoloured varnish from the panel from Upton House, there is no doubt that the execution is entirely by the hand of Domenikos Theotokopoulos (1541–1614), the famous Spanish painter known as El Greco (plate 55, p. 85). Examination of the painting while it was being restored at the Hamilton Kerr Institute has provided information concerning this artist's painting technique.

Preliminary examination

When the painting was brought to the Hamilton Kerr Institute for restoration, preliminary examination was hampered by a thick layer of discoloured varnish. The varnish was scratched, and runs or dribbles had hardened in the varnish at the top of the painting. A number of discoloured restorations and a few minute losses were visible, but the general condition of the paint layer as well as the quality of the painting was difficult to assess. The results of the X-radiograph and the infrared reflectograph were slightly confusing (see below) before removal of the thick layer of surface dirt and varnish.

Support

The support is a wooden panel;[3] the thickness varies between 5 mm and 7 mm. The original panel consists of three members joined vertically. Two later additions are attached along the right and left edges. Several old splits are accompanied by signs of previous repair; there are also two original insets let into the panel before painting began, presumably because of defects in the wood. The larger has split independently from the panel and has been repaired from the back (see fig. 1).

The splits and joints appeared stable and no treatment of the panel was necessary. Although

Fig. 2 X-radiograph assembly

Fig. 3 After removal of varnish, before repaint removal

the strips of wood on either side were not original, they are covered by the frame, and were not removed. The frame however required adjustment to accommodate the movement of the panel, whose slight permanent convex set varies with changes in relative humidity.

The monogram surmounted by a coronet on the reverse of the panel is the mark of Don Gaspar de Haro y Guzmán (1629–1687), a 17th century collector and patron of Velázquez, whose collection which included over 1,800 paintings was dispersed after his death in 1687.[4]

X-radiograph (fig. 2)

The joints and splits as well as the repairs to the panel are clearly visible and correspond to what one expects to see. Losses in the original paint layer are also clearly visible.

The most puzzling area is the sky. There is a total absence of correlation between what one sees on the X-ray and what one sees with the naked eye. Areas that one would expect to show clearly on the X-ray are only faintly visible, while other areas in the sky show forms that one does not see on the painting. The contours of the sky around the heads is lower in places than on the X-ray. Further investigation clarified these differences. Minute samples taken of the paint layer indicated that a thicker underlayer containing lead white was used for blocking in the sky. The figures were then coloured, overlapping the lead white underlayer. Then the top layers of the sky were painted, followed by the spears etc. The sky which one sees on the painting is not visible on the X-ray because it is very thin, while the thick lead white underlayer, which includes a different cloud configuration, shows strongly.

Infrared reflectograph (fig. 4)

The infrared reflectograph reveals a considerable amount of underdrawing which is very firm in handling and corresponds closely to the finished composition (fig. 5). Closer inspection does show a number of small changes in the following areas:

– as in the X-ray, the sky does not correspond to what one sees,
– the outline of the heads against the sky is slightly different,
– the top of the head of Mary Magdalene as well as her left hand has been changed,

Fig. 4 Infrared reflectograph assembly

Fig. 5 Infrared reflectograph: detail right side

– the end of the cross in the lower right corner was straightened.

These slight alterations indicate that although El Greco may have been working from an established composition, he still made changes.

Restoration

After removal of the surface dirt and the upper layers of thick discoloured varnish, a thin layer of unpigmented varnish, undoubtedly very old, remained which was not removed. A small cleaning test showed this varnish layer was soluble in relatively mild solvents, but could not be removed without affecting the extremely thin original paint underneath. This thin yellow transparent layer does not mute the striking effects of El Greco's bright pigments. The repaints which were uncovered, however, were unevenly applied, thick, discoloured, and generally disfiguring (fig. 3).

Two layers of considerably discoloured blue repaint were removed in the sky, uncovering a coarse brown layer of repaint extending down both sides, covering the additions and extending over onto the original paint layer. This brown layer was slightly modelled to extend the composition on both sides, but covered much undamaged original paint. The repaint was removed up to the edge of a painted black strip which became visible during cleaning. The black strip, about 1 cm wide, encloses the painting on all four sides. It is more soluble than the rest of the original paint layer, and the brown repaint on top of it could not be safely removed. To compensate, the slip in the frame was altered, and adjusted to cover the edges which were intended to be black.

This black strip was on top of the edges of the original paint layer (never under), but nothing was found to disprove its originality. In fact other panels by El Greco have similarly painted black edges.[5] Also, it serves an important function by enclosing the tightly packed composition.

Chipping of the upper layer(s) of paint occurs over most of the painting (plate 59, p. 86), but only in the sky do the small losses seriously affect the composition. Many very small paint particles are missing from the clouds, confusing the transition between cloud and sky, and the form of the clouds is lost in places. The damages are minor compared to the general condition of the panel which is still very good. Although obvious losses and some missing glazes have now been restored, the appearance of the sky remains slightly more colourful than intended by the artist, due to former harsh treatment; some of the upper layers are missing as well as the very thin early layer of slightly yellow varnish.

Overpaint

Several samples were taken in the sky before removal of varnish and overpaint. In all these samples two blue layers of overpaint were found on top of a thick brown layer of overpaint, composed of brown ochre, a little red ochre, carbon black, and lead white probably in an oil medium. The blue paint layers on top of the brown contained a fine blue pigment mixed with varying amounts of lead white. The blue in the lower layer was recognizable microscopically as smalt. This was confirmed by the presence of silicum and cobalt in the microprobe analysis. When this layer is treated with NaOH it falls apart, indicating an oil medium. The top layer was similar, but finer. Between the blue layers was a thin layer of varnish indicating they were not from the same period. Smalt was used frequently from the 16th until the 19th century; the discolouration of the repaint as well as the discolouration of the varnish on top suggest that the repaint could have been 19th century or earlier.

Both the blue layers as well as the brown layer were later additions; they covered original paint and losses in original paint, as well as the wooden strips attached to either side of the panel.

Varnish

Before varnish removal a small paint sample was taken from Christ's left foot. On top of the pale opaque layer of flesh paint, two layers of varnish were found showing some dirt in between. The dirt indicates a time gap between the application of the two layers, thus the thick top layer removed during restoration is confirmed as a later addition. The varnish layer closest to the paint is a thin yellow transparent layer, not pigmented. No dirt was found between this thin layer and the paint surface underneath. This does not prove it is an original varnish, however. In fact it is more likely that it is a varnish put on after an early cleaning, leaving no time for dirt to settle. In some paint samples, the original paint surface looks rubbed as if by too harsh a cleaning.[6] As stated earlier, this varnish layer could not be removed safely, and in any case, it does not dampen the brilliance of El Greco's pigments.

El Greco's painting technique

Several very small paint samples were taken from areas of damage to help distinguish between the original paint and the overpaint, and to provide a record of the overpaint. Paint samples were also taken to gather information about the painter's technique. Due to the small size, delicacy, and relatively good condition of the painting, samples were kept to a minimum; therefore many questions especially concerning El Greco's painting medium could not be answered.

Areas such as the yellow cloak of Mary Magdalene show craters in the paint layer which are not characteristic of an oil medium, but of a water-based medium (plate 58, p. 86). El Greco's use of tempera or an oil-egg emulsion is a much debated question which it might have been possible to answer had the necessary sample size not been too large to be justified.[7] The small samples taken from the edge or next to damages were treated with NaOH to get an indication of the medium. One sample which included the brown underlayer indicated that the sketch was not in oil. Tests for medium on a sample from the Virgin's blue cloak point in the direction of oil. The opaque highlights (plate 56, p. 86), usually containing lead white, were not tested. Because of the lead white, these highlights would have dried faster than the more transparent layers to which they were applied, even if both mediums were similar. This alone could be the reason why the top layer of paint has flaked off in places. If the opaque highlights were in tempera, or were an oil emulsion, this change of medium would provide an even better explanation for the flaking of the upper paint layer.

Examining the yellow hat with grey-blue shadows of the man on the extreme left, it is clear that both the yellow and the grey-blue paint are very lean; although they are sitting next to and on top of one another they do not mix as when painting wet-in-wet (plate 60, p. 86). This can also be observed in a cross-section taken from this area. On top of the white ground a thin layer of organic red pigment with particles of azurite spread over it was found, then a thicker layer in lead-tin yellow. In the hollows of this layer, particles of azurite, embedded in some medium or varnish, are covered by another varnish layer (plate 61, p. 86).

Paint layer

Flesh Another conclusion which may be drawn from samples such as the one from Christ's left foot was that El Greco did not glaze the paint layers; the opaque highlights were the final stage of painting. Shadows in the flesh were made by allowing the brown underlayer to show through.

Blue sky The blue sky is painted in two layers (plate 62, p. 86). The underlayer, used to block in the sky at an early stage, is composed of lead white and some pinkish particles (too few for identification). Only a trace of blue is present, perhaps because the sample was taken in a damage. The visible blue layer is thinner and consists of azurite mixed with a little lead white (plate 63, p. 86).

Blue cloak Samples from the Virgin's blue cloak show a rather thick layer of azurite under a layer of dark blue overpaint.

Blue-grey The blue-grey dress of Mary Magdalene is made from a mixture of azurite and red lake.

Green The green shirt of the man of the right of Christ is made of copper resinate. On top of the green transparent layer of copper resinate, opaque highlights contain a mixture of copper resinate, lead white, and a little chalk. These opaque highlights containing lead white would have dried more quickly than the underlayer. Probably it is because of El Greco's unstable technique that this area is especially damaged.

Orange Orange from the sleeve of the green shirt consists of lead white and red lead. The light orange and blue clothing of the man on the right in the foreground is azurite applied directly on the gesso with a layer of lead white and red lead on top.

Yellow The yellow of Mary Magdalene's cloak and the yellow hat of the man on the extreme left are lead-tin yellow.

Monochrome underlayer

A sample taken from near the edge in the yellow cloak of Mary Magdalene shows that the yellow overlaps the blue of the Virgin's cloak. The layer of azurite lies directly on the white gesso ground. On the other half of the sample, a brownish transparent layer containing small particles of black lies directly on the ground. Other samples confirm that this is the monochrome sketch visible on the painting in many of the areas in shadow, where this brown tone corresponds to the tone the painter wished to achieve in the final painting (plates 57, 64 and 65, p. 86).

Ground

A white gesso ground (calcium sulphate or gypsum) was found in all the samples. In most places it was pure white, unstained by absorption of discoloured varnish, indicating that the original paint must have been rather lean, otherwise the medium would have been absorbed also. In any case, no imprimatura layer was used to make the ground less absorbent or to have a toned working surface.

Summary

The composition was sketched onto a white ground using a thin brown paint (black pigment in a brown medium) strengthened with thicker black brush strokes which are clearly visible in the infrared reflectograph and in places even with the naked eye. The sky was then blocked in with a purplish blue. Colour and details were added, but the underlayer was often retained in the shadows. Highlights were applied in a thicker dryer paint. El Greco painted a second layer of bluish paint in the sky on top of which he painted the white clouds.[8]

The line of heads against the sky is a very revealing area. One can see the second layer of blue sky painted around the heads, in places failing to cover completely the first blue layer and the monochrome underlayer. As a result of this technique, the painting gives the illusion of being solidly painted although in fact a minimum of pigment was extremely skillfully applied and the execution was undoubtedly very rapid.

It has been suggested that the panel from Upton House may have been used as a *modello* prepared by El Greco for his painting in the sacristy of Toledo Cathedral, and not simply a later repetition made for clients. The underdrawing revealed in the infrared reflectograph appears to delineate rather than compose the forms, suggesting that the artist was working from an already established composition. However, this does not eliminate the possibility that the panel was used as a *modello*. In fact, closer inspection reveals an underdrawing so vigorous and assured that it only confirms the high quality of the painting. Another possible use of the panel was as a *ricordo*. Pacheco writes that El Greco kept 'originals of all he had painted in his life, painted in oil on small canvases and kept in a room that he instructed his son to show to me'.[9] Perhaps the Upton panel had the same function.

Acknowledgement

The analysis presented in this article was done by Karin Groen, the preliminary examination by Pamela England.

Notes and references

1. For the previous history of the panel see the entry in: *Upton House The Bearsted Collection: Pictures*, The National Trust, 1964, pp. 80–82. See also the more recent entry in *The Golden Age of Spanish Art from El Greco to Murillo and Valdés Leal: Paintings and Drawings from British Collections*, Nottingham University Art Gallery, 1980, p. 11; and H. Wethey, *El Greco and His School*, Princeton New Jersey 1962, pp. 55–56.
2. A brief foray into the literature on El Greco resulted in at least 13 versions, not all by El Greco's own hand. The painting closest to the panel from Upton House is the Contini-Bonacossi version, now in the Stanley Moss Collection, New York. For a discussion of the Contini-Bonacossi version see: *El Greco of Toledo*, an exhibition organized by the Toledo Museum of Art, Boston 1982, pp. 232–233.
3. In the literature the panel is said to be pine. During the restoration the identification was not confirmed microscopically due to the difficulty of finding a suitable sample area on such a small panel.
4. E. Harris and H. Lank, 'The Cleaning of Velázquez's Portrait of Camillo Massimi', *The Burlington Magazine*, cxxv, 1983, pp. 410–415. This article discusses a painting on canvas from the same collection.
5. A colour transparency of the Contini-Bonacossi version, kindly given to the Hamilton Kerr Institute by William B. Jordan and Edmund Pillsbury also shows the composition framed by a black line. The *Adoration of the Name of Jesus* in the National Gallery, London also seems to have a similar black strip on all four sides.
6. For example in a sample taken from the blue-grey

dress of Mary Cleophas the surface of the paint layer looks abraded and a few particles of azurite have floated up into the varnish, indicating that the paint layer was rather loosely bound initially or became so during an early cleaning.

7. There are many references to El Greco's use of tempera, but few are based on scientific analysis. The best of the articles on El Greco's painting technique: H. von Sonnenburg, 'Zur Maltechnik Greco's, in *Münchner Jahrbuch d.b.K.*, IX, X, 1958/9, pp. 243–255.
8. Francisco Pacheco (1564–1638) was a painter and the author of a monumental treatise on the theory and practice of painting, *Arte de la Pintura*. Pacheco knew El Greco and refers to Domenico Greco in his treatise. In Book III Chapter 5 Pacheco refers to a *bosquexo* or *bosquejo* which he considers a kind of underpainting that is more than a loose sketch in oil, but less than a finished painting, and which seems similar to the technique described in this article about the Upton Panel:

   HOW TO MAKE THE BOSQUEXO.
   Let us assume that everything to be painted has been drawn correctly with accurate profiles and that we wish to begin the *bosquexo*. This is done in various ways. Some paint it with black and white, or with white mixed with carmine and Italian umber. This is an easy and comfortable way . . . [but] it is best to begin the *bosquexo* in colors for the heads and flesh of the figures, and especially if they are taken from life. For fair flesh, use white and vermilion and a little light ochre; for flesh that is not so fair, use red earth of Levante and ochre, adding more or less according to the variations of the shadows. The appropriate tints are made with bone black, Italian umber, lamp black, spalt, and red earth, and carmine is used as well for some darks. For rosy flesh, use vermilion and carmine, and for those that are less rosy, mix the vermilion with red earth. THE BEST BOSQUEXO. Some make the *bosquexo* very complete and leave it as finished; others just paint it with blotches of colors and leave it confused . . . Thus, the flesh colors are the first to be painted in the *bosquexo* and the last to be retouched and finished. After the *bosquexo* is completed and washed with a sponge and water, the skies should be finished first, then the distances, the buildings and fields, and all that serves as ornament to the figures. Then the figures should be dressed in their appropriate colors, according to what we shall say, and the finishing of the faces and flesh waits until last.

   The translation is from: Z. Veliz, *Artist's Techniques in Golden Age Spain*, Cambridge, 1986, pp. 69–70.
9. *Ibid*., p. 40.

The examination of a tabernacle altarpiece

Karen Ashworth

Fig. 1 Paolo di Stefano, *Tabernacle Altarpiece*

Paolo di Stefano known as Paolo Schiavo (1397–1478)
Madonna of Humility: a tabernacle panel
142 × 69 × 16.2 cm (largest dimension)
Fitzwilliam Museum

This tabernacle altarpiece is an unusual example of an almost completely intact original structure (fig. 1). Early Italian altarpieces have often been reframed, or in the case of polyptychs, dismantled and reframed so that their original appearance has been completely changed. In examining the altarpiece the aim was to determine its construction, whether it had been altered and to assess its original appearance.

Born in Florence, Paolo di Stefano matriculated in the Arte di Medici e Speziali in 1429. It is thought that his early training was in the workshop of Lorenzo Monaco but he was soon influenced by Masolino of whom Vasari suggests he was a pupil. His best known works are the frescoes in the Collegiata at Castiglione d'Olona painted between 1429 and 1436. He decorated a small tabernacle by Donatello (Victoria and Albert Museum). In 1448 he worked in Pistoia on frescoes in the Capella d'Assunta and is mentioned in documents as active in Pisa around 1462. He died there in 1478.

This examination of the Fitzwilliam altarpiece is primarily concerned with the structure and decoration of the framing elements, however, the iconography is of considerable interest. On the main panel the Madonna is seated on the ground as an image of humility. Above are four angels, derived from Fra Angelico's *Linaiuoli* altarpiece; on the pilasters SS Francis, Mary Magdalene, Jerome and Bernard; the predella shows a funeral scene with members of a Confraternity of Flagellants and on the console is the *Fall of Man*. Unfortunately the coat of arms, now defaced, has not been identified. The altarpiece was probably commissioned as a dedication to a dead brother of the Confraternity and the damaged shields on the bracket may have originally displayed the arms of the family of the deceased.[1]

The tabernacle, was therefore, intended for a side wall or chapel for intimate devotional purposes. This is reflected in its three-dimensional sculptural design in contrast to the elaborate yet basically two-dimensional polyptychs of high altars which were intended to be viewed from a distance. Many-storeyed high altarpieces reflect cathedral design, the painted panels being divided by colonnettes and surmounted by arches and finials reminiscent of the external buttressing of contemporary churches. Tabernacle altarpieces, however, have design elements which are closer in derivation to tomb sculpture. The wall tomb of a gentleman of the Bardi Family in S. Croce, Florence[2] provides a typical example. The projecting sides and canopy supported by spiral columns are paralleled in the Fitzwilliam altarpiece, the rear wall is painted and angels depict the soul being carried heavenwards. The tomb on the floor beneath the canopy probably once carried an effigy just as the predella scene of the dead brother lies above the base of the tabernacle.

Florentine tabernacle altarpieces are frequently found with similar design elements although usually they are less three-dimensional. Amongst works attributed to Paolo di Stefano in fresco and on panel,[3] of particular interest is the small painted relief after Donatello with a painted frame by Paolo di Stefano dated c. 1435–40, in the Victoria and Albert Museum.[4] The design of the frame, although small in scale, has a similar three-dimensional conception with projecting sides and angled inner edges. The lower curved console which is particularly unusual in such altarpieces, provides a transition from the projecting base to the wall surface.

Preliminary examination

The altarpiece was first examined visually in order to assess the extent of original carpentry and decoration. Detailed measurements were taken and recorded, its overall height being 142 cm and width 69 cm.

The initial examination revealed some areas of damage and overpaint such as the upper surface of the plinth and the curved side sections of the console, but generally the painted decoration appeared to have been only modified, supporting the theory that the structure was largely original.

A more detailed examination of the gilding was carried out using the stereo microscope with the intention of differentiating original gilding from repairs, and since most of the structural elements are gilded, thereby assessing which parts of the altarpiece are original and which, if any, are later additions.

The main panel was examined first since apart from some abrasion exposing the red bole layer there appeared to have been no major repairs. Brushstrokes of paint overlap the gold leaf, especially obvious in the Child's hair, further indicating that this is an area of original gilding and providing a standard with which to compare the gilding elsewhere.

The gold on the main panel is continuous onto the arch and the side panels. A crack has developed in the layer of gesso between the panel and arch members showing it to be a continuous layer applied after the altarpiece was assembled.

The gilded elements of the altarpiece consist of the background to the figurative panels, the carved arch moulding, the twisted columns and the front plane of the base and border of the bracket decoration. Most of the gold appears to be original with repairs of leaf gold obvious as brighter patches on an abraded surface. The gilding is missing from the upper part of the side sections behind the columns indicating a possible alteration. The lower edge of the console may be a replacement since it is completely covered with gold paint.

The original gilding examined under ×60 microscopic magnification is smooth in texture containing many tiny fractures revealing the dark red bole beneath. This is found in all parts of the altarpiece except for the twisted columns and capitals which seem to be in suspiciously good condition. Here there is an absence of fine cracks in the gold leaf, and a much brighter orange bole showing through in areas of abrasion on the outer profile of the columns, similar to bole in obvious areas of repair on the main panel.

Further information was necessary in order to prove that the twisted columns were in fact later additions. Microscopic analysis was carried out to compare the ground and bole on the columns with the rest of the altarpiece. Cross-sections were made from tiny samples taken from damages in the original gilding next to the letters on the base, from the arch moulding considered to be original and from the left column. Tiny scrapings of ground and bole were also taken.

All the samples of ground were found to consist of calcium sulphate with some differences in particle shape between the column and other samples. The cross-sections and crushed samples of bole on the arch moulding and base were very similar. Viewed under ×1250 microscopic magnification the bole consisted of a single layer of fine bright red particles with some larger darker red particles (plate 66, p. 87). A cross-section from the bole on the column showed two layers, the lower consisting largely of fine pale orange particles with some darker red and the upper layer paler with more white particles (plate 67, p. 87). A sample of the bole crushed and viewed in transmitted light was paler and more transparent than the other samples.

Since the bole on the twisted columns is different from that found elsewhere, it is probable that they have either been completely regilded or are replacements for damaged original columns.

Construction

When it was established that the frame was largely

2

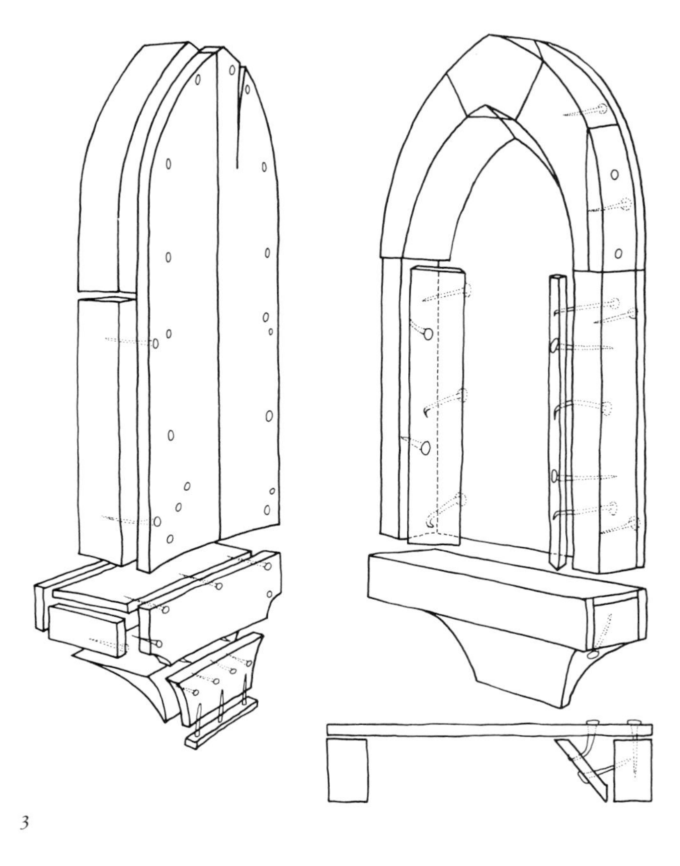

3

Fig. 2 Composite X-radiograph

Fig. 3 Line drawing of the reverse and front

original a detailed examination of the construction of the altarpiece was begun using X-radiography as the principal technical means.

The wall-mounted X-radiograph facilities at the Hamilton Kerr Institute necessitated the construction of a frame of slotted right-angle steel sections to safely support the altarpiece on an easel. The altarpiece was X-radiographed from the back in sections[5] and the processed film joined to give a composite image (fig. 2).

Information drawn from the X-radiograph included the position of joins, direction of woodgrain and orientation of nails. Of particular importance is the differentiation of irregular hand-worked nails and modern machine-made ones which would indicate a later repair. Comparing visual evidence, such as the position of stopping concealing a nail head with the angle and orientation of a nail in the X-radiograph, the location and function of an individual nail could be identified.

The structure of the altarpiece was determined in this manner. From the back of the altarpiece, the main panel of 3 cm thickness is in two sections with a join running slightly to the left of centre (fig. 3). The X-radiograph (fig. 2) reveals a reinforcement of this join with rectangles of fine cloth applied to the front surface and concealed beneath a thick gesso ground. The major arch and side elements are attached directly onto this panel (fig. 3). The arch is in two sections 9.5 cm in depth, joined at the centre with an insert at the point of the arch attached by two nails and a join at the right side, the small additional piece being secured by two hand-beaten 9 cm long nails driven laterally into the main section.

The solid arch has an angled inner edge, the profile being continued in the side sections by

continued on p. 93

Plate 55 El Greco *El Espolio* The Disrobing of Christ, National Trust, Upton House, after restoration

Plate 56 Detail of figure, back row centre. Detail shows the dryness of application of the highlights.

Plate 57 Detail of figure behind and to the left of Christ. Detail shows the highlights over the monochrome underdrawing.

Plate 58 Detail of yellow cloak in foreground. The small 'craters' in the upper paint layer are uncharacteristic of oil paint.

Plate 59 Detail of Christ's red tunic. The pinkish highlights in Christ's red tunic are thicker and more opaque than the dark red rather transparent layer underneath. The thicker layer is chipped away around the edges.

Plate 60 Detail of yellow hat with grey-blue shadows, background left side. Detail shows monochrome underlayer.

Plate 61 Cross-section of yellow hat
d. Varnish covering a few particles of azurite. The layer of azurite is worn; blue pigment particles remain only in the hollows of the layer of lead-tin yellow underneath.
c. Lead-tin yellow (yellow hat)
b. Azurite and red lake (grey-blue shadow of yellow hat)
a. Gesso (calcium sulphate)

Plate 62 Detail of figure in background, left side. Detail shows two layers of blue sky and underdrawing.

Plate 63 Cross-section of same detail
c. Azurite and some lead white (sky)
b. Lead white mixed with a bright purplish pigment (underlayer, visible in the X-ray, used to block in the sky before painting the figures)
a. Gesso

Plate 64 Detail of head directly behind Christ. Detail shows yellowish white ground, underdrawing, and more thickly painted highlights.

Plate 65 Cross-section of head directly behind Christ
c. Thin layer of lead white containing fine black pigment particles (highlights)
b. Fine bone black pigment particles, also ochres and lead white in a brown matrix (monochrome sketch)
a. Gesso

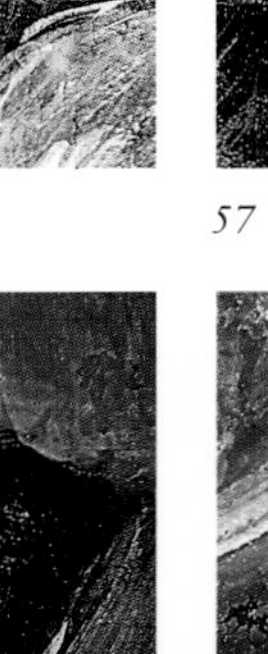

56

57

58

59

60

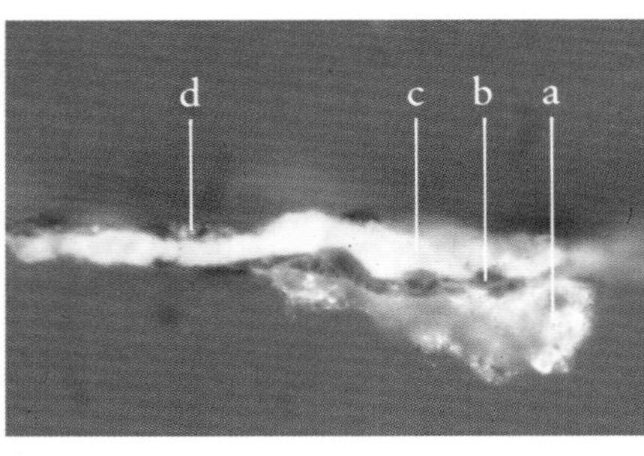

61

62

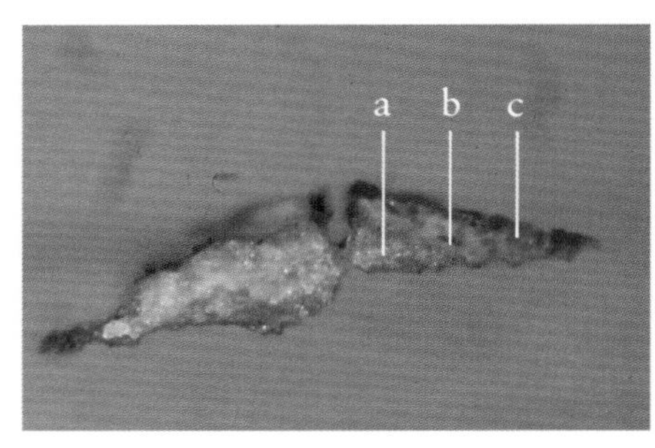

63

64

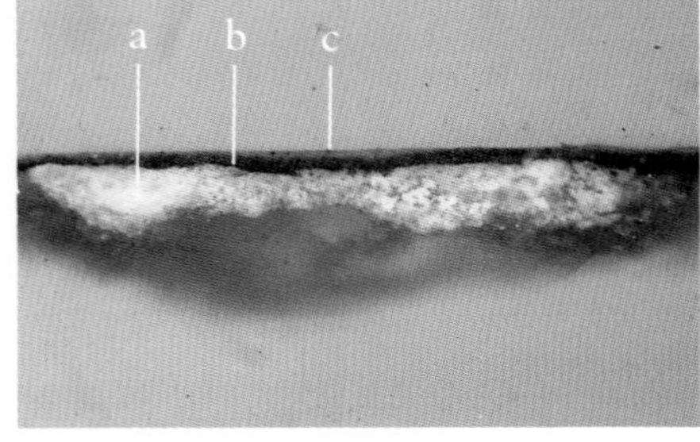

65

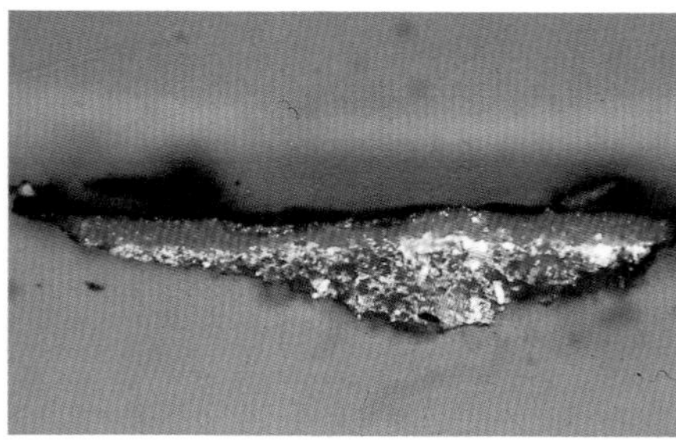

66

67

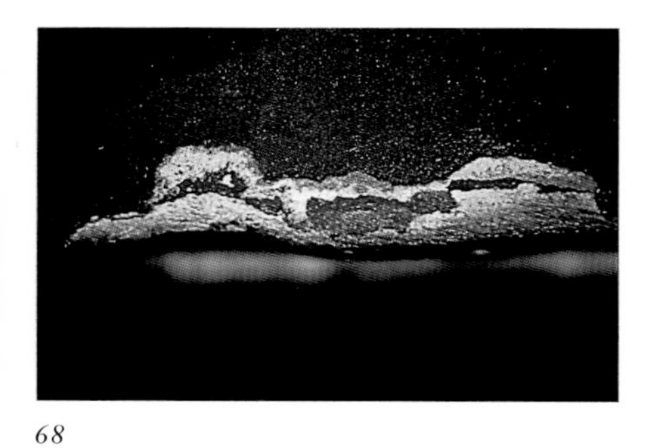

68

Plate 66 Paolo di Stefano, *Tabernacle Altarpiece:* cross-section showing original bole layer from arch

Plate 67 Cross-section showing bole layer from replacement columns

Plate 68 Cross-section showing repainted arch in smalt over the original azurite layer

Plate 69 Reconstruction, suggesting original appearance

69

70

71

Plate 70 Canaletto, *Campo SS. Giovanni e Paolo*, detail, the lantern above the dome, which lies above the painting of the sky

Plate 71 Detail, the windows on one of the righthand buildings

72

73

74

75

76

77

Plate 72 Detail, the dome, showing how the end of a brush was scored into the wet paint to define the ribs

Plate 73 Detail, the *trompe l'oeil* on the walls of the Scuola di S. Marco

Plate 74 Detail, the façade of the church, showing the paint texture

Plate 75 Detail, the base of the monument to Bartolomeo Colleoni

Plate 76 Detail, a foreground figure which is painted over the architecture

Plate 77 Detail, the gondolier in the foreground

Plate 78 Cross-section from the sky, showing a deep blue pigment, identified as Prussian blue, lying above the double ground

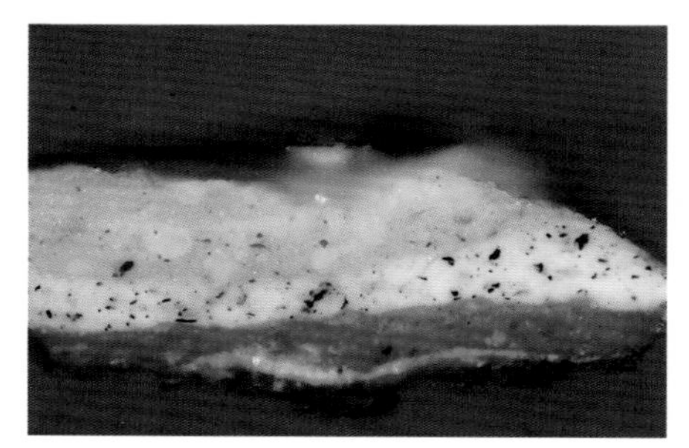

78

Plate 79 Orazio Gentileschi, *Joseph and Potiphar's Wife* (Her Majesty the Queen), after restoration

Plate 80 Detail of right slipper. The 'bituminous' craquelure corresponds to the dark shadow of the bedcover.

Plate 81 Detail of right slipper. Craquelure is visible in the red stripes, but the thickly applied lead-tin yellow has prevented the formation of further cracking. (Sample taken near damage, lower centre.)

Plate 82 Cross-section of right slipper.
f. Traces of discoloured varnish
e. 2–3 layers of lead-tin yellow (stripe of slipper)
d. Red lake and vermilion (stripe of slipper)
c. Translucent greenish brown layer, with a little lead-tin yellow and lead white (shadow of bed-cover)
b. Lead-tin yellow, lead white, and verdigris (bedcover)
a. Lead white and charcoal black (second ground layer, first layer missing)
Layer c. is possibly a slow-drying bituminous layer which has pushed up the layers above, causing cracks in the yellow highlights.

80

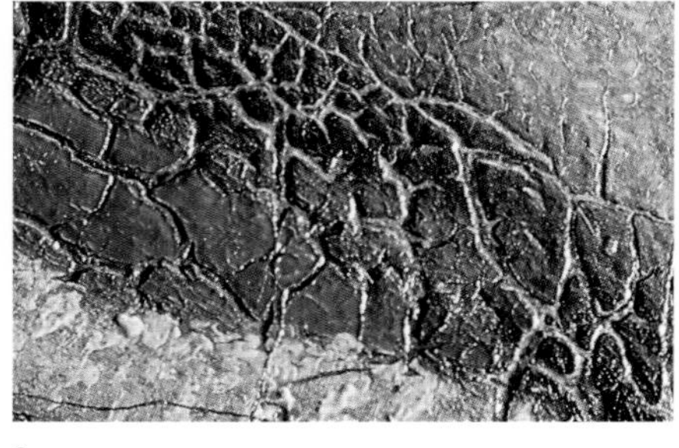

81

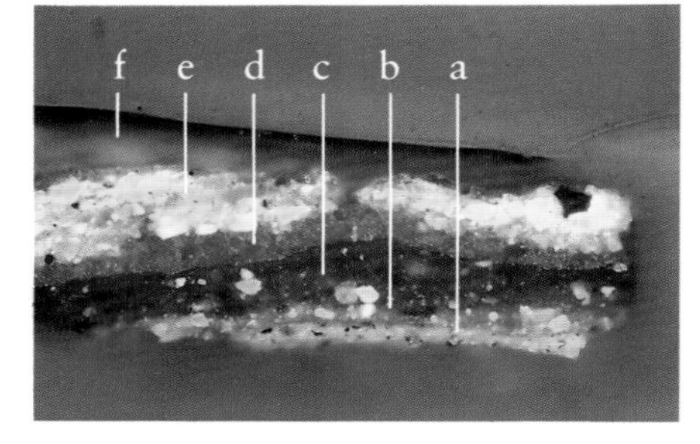

82

Plate 83 Detail of dark green bedcover. The 'bituminous' craquelure is less severe where the paint layer was covered by the frame.

Plate 84 Detail of dark green bedcover. Same detail in higher magnification.

Plate 85 Cross-section of dark green bedcover.
e. Pigmented varnish
d. Translucent brown layer, similar to layer c., but with fewer particles of lead-tin yellow and lead white
c. Translucent brown layer with lumps of lead-tin yellow and lead white and crystals of verdigris (bedcover)
Doubleground:
b. Lead white and charcoal black
a. Red ochre
On the painting layer d. shows bituminous-like craquelure. However bitumen tends to dissolve in the paint medium, therefore pigment particles are not visible in a cross-section.

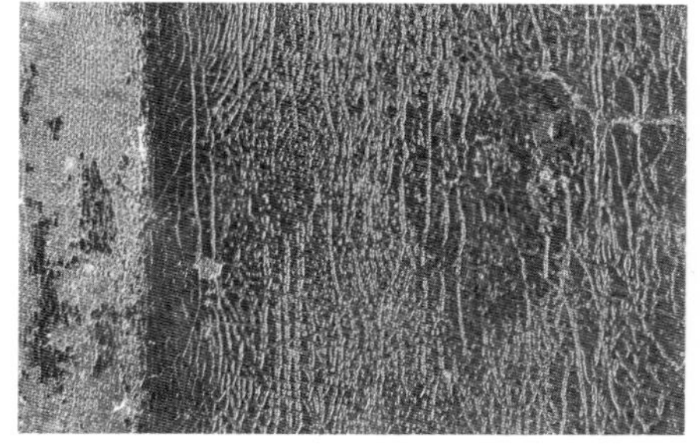

83

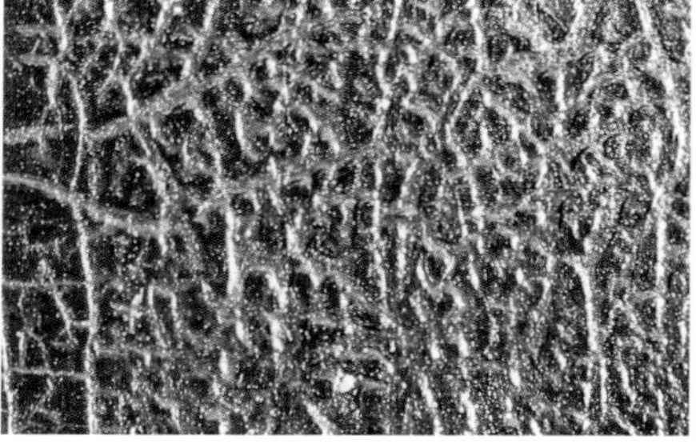

84

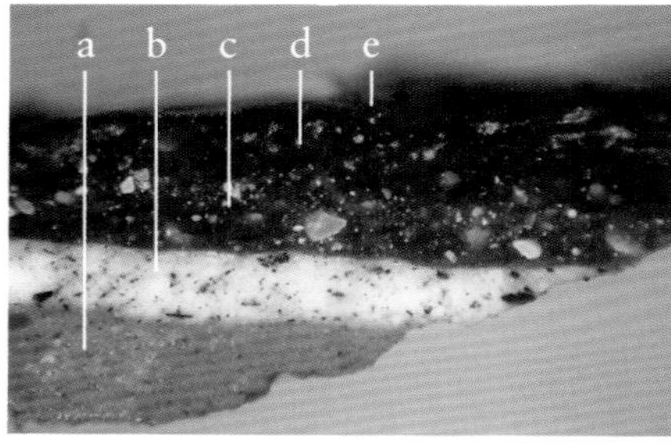

85

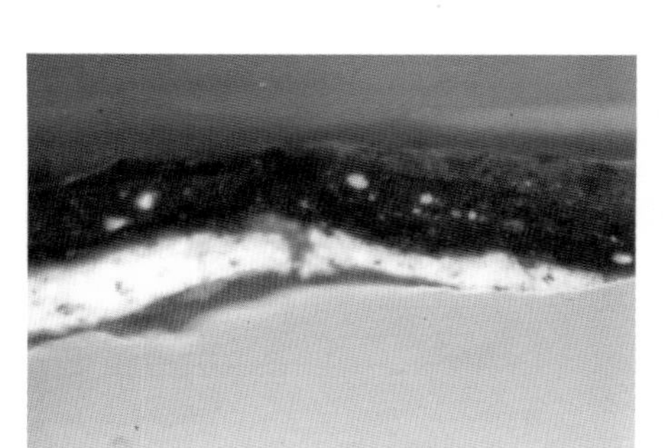

Plate 86 Cross-section of background near left edge. A bituminous paint layer is above and below a layer of red lake, indicating that the red curtain originally came much lower down before Gentileschi overpainted it (fig. 2, p. 100).

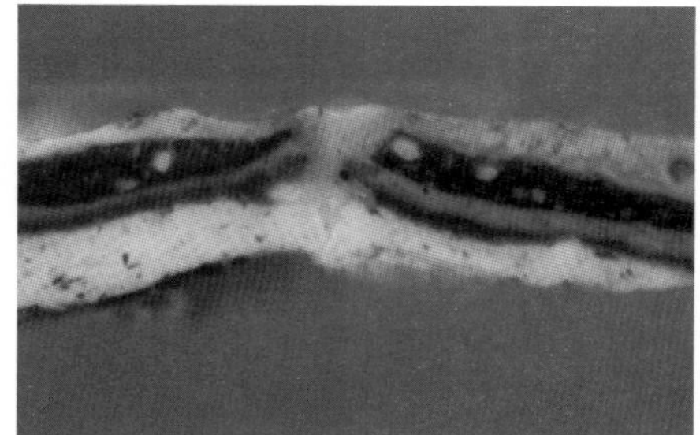

Plate 87 Cross-section of background near left edge in ultraviolet light. The overpaint fluoresces and continues down into a crack in the paint layer.

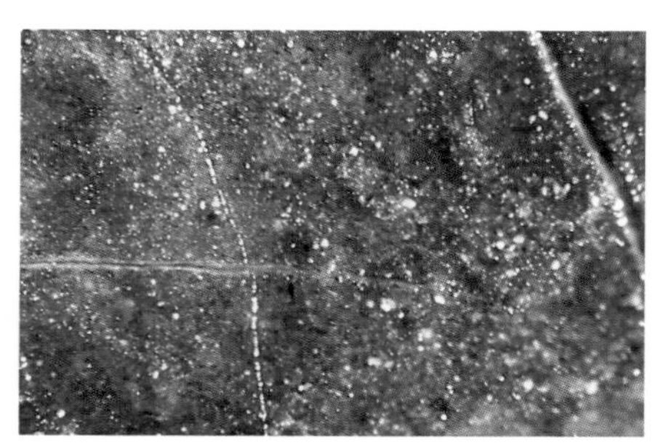

Plate 88 Potiphar's wife's blue dress. Ultramarine and lead white.

Plate 89 Detail of Joseph's tunic, after cleaning, before restoration. Small damages along the original seam in the canvas are filled with white chalk putty.

Plate 90 Detail of black braid of Joseph's tunic. Lead-tin yellow highlights on top of black (bituminous?) underlayer.

Plate 91 Cross-section of black braid.
e. Lead-tin yellow (highlights on black braid)
d. Finely ground carbon black (black of braid)
c. Red lake Joseph's tunic
Doubleground:
b. Lead white and charcoal black
a. Red ochre

89

90

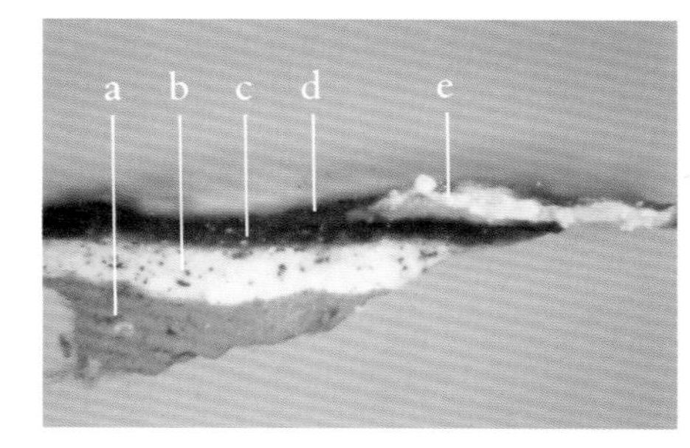

91

Plate 92 Godfried Schalcken, *Self-Portrait*, unframed. Where the paint layer was protected by the rebate of the frame, the colour of the blue background and of the sitter's red jacket is unchanged.

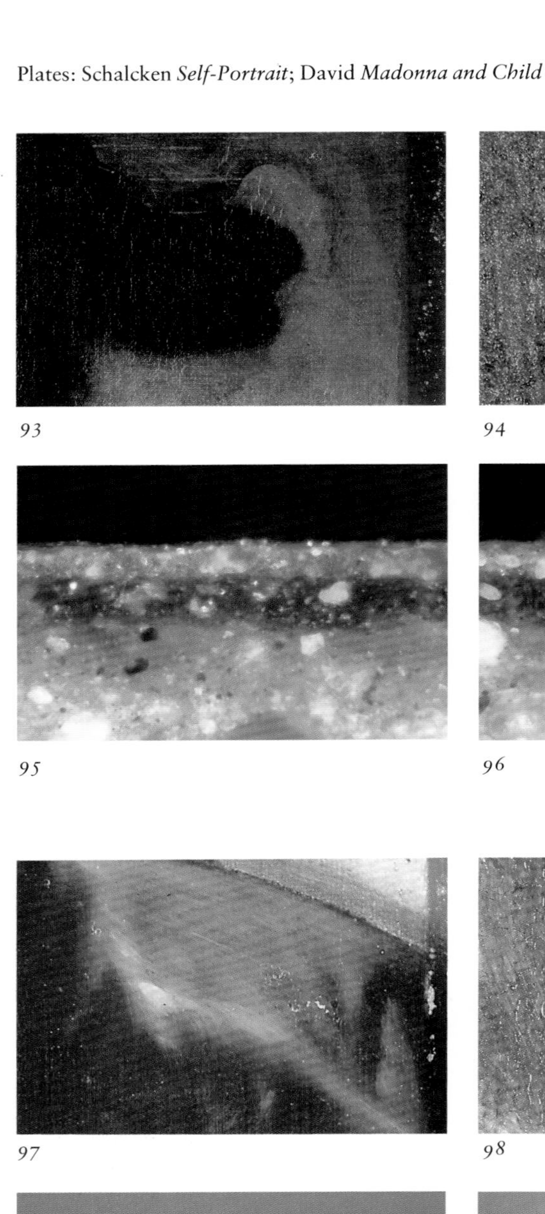

93

94

Plates 93 and 94 The colour of the blue background has changed considerably where it was not protected by the rebate of the frame.

Plates 95 and 96 There are two blue layers. Indigo and smalt are mixed to give the blue colour; the upper layer contains more lead white. The ground layers are composed of lead white, chalk and a little umber. Despite the considerable difference in the colour of the background, the cross-sections look very similar. Although fading of the pigment particles may have occurred (plate 95), chalking of the paint layer must account for most of the change in colour.

95

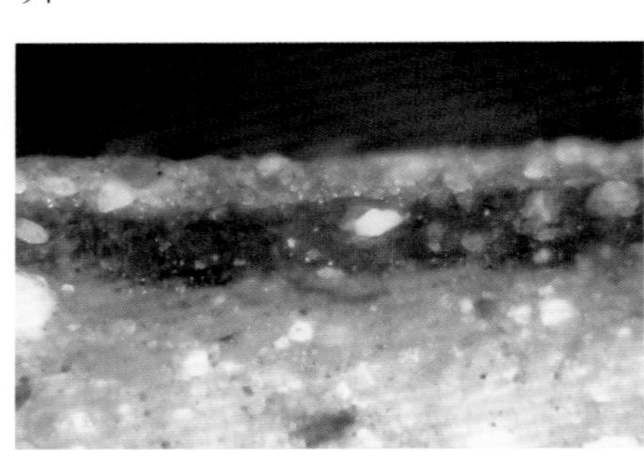

96

97

98

Plates 97 and 98 The red lake of the sitter's garment has faded where it has not been protected by the rebate of the frame.

Plates 99 and 100 In plate 100 the red lake has faded; the red ochre and bone black underlayer is unchanged. The ground layers are missing in plate 99. Both cross-sections show a clear varnish layer on top of the red lake.

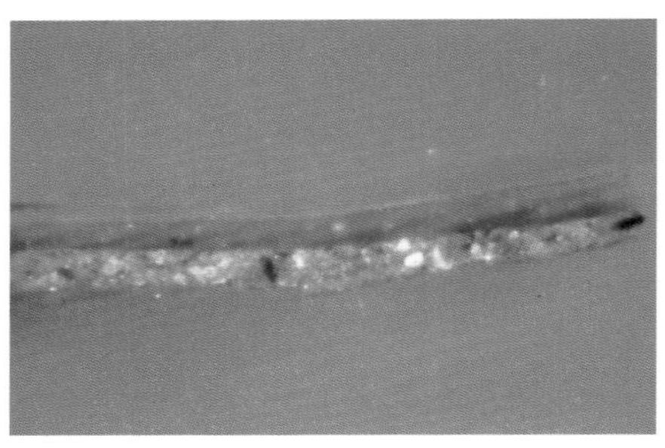

99

100

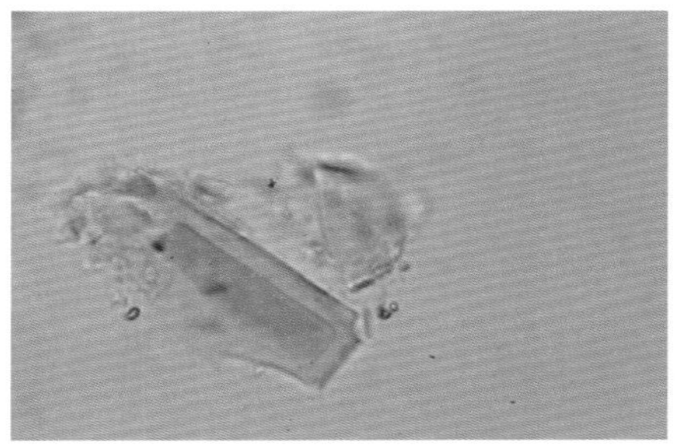

Plate 101 A particle of smalt viewed in transmitted light. Smalt is often found with a discoloured edge surrounding an unaltered core.

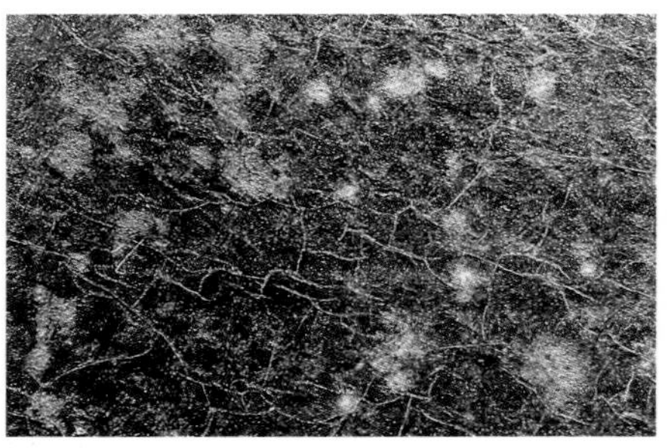

Plate 102 Detail, tip of the hat right side. Deposits on the paint surface have a chalky appearance.

Plate 103 Gerard David, *Madonna and Child*, detail during cleaning, before the removal of the added crown

continued from p. 84

rectangular pieces of wood of the same thickness as the arch element, nailed to the main panel from the back (fig. 3). Angled panels are placed against the inner edge and attached to the side pieces with two nails 9–10 cm in length driven sideways (fig. 3). Three nails have been inserted from the back into these sections. The X-radiograph shows the nails to be distorted: their hooked profile was created when the end of the nail penetrated through the panel and was hammered flat.

A section of wood 1.4 cm in thickness is attached to the front edge of the arch onto which the carved and gilded decoration is tacked. The panel is in three sections with an insert at the point and the grain on either side lying in the direction of the arch. Presumably it would be a structurally more stable base for the delicate carved arch moulding.

A Florentine fleur-de-lys has been stamped on the reverse of the base, possibly when the object was exported from Florence. The construction of the base and its attachment to the back panel are shown in fig. 3. All of the nails appear to be original apart from the three 4.5 cm long machine-made nails attaching the lower strip of wood to the edge of the bracket, providing further evidence that this is a later addition or restoration.

Strips of moulding conceal the join between side and arch, running from the outer edge around the section above the column capital to the inner surface. Moulding is also applied to the edges of the base. Small nails 3 cm in length are used to attach these strips.

The twisted columns running the length of the side elements are of one piece and show no structural damage or woodworm holes, further suggesting that they are later additions. Further examination of the wood structure by microscopic analysis of thin sections taken with a scalpel from the back of the panel and an exposed edge of the capital helped to confirm this. The sample from the column showed the characteristics of softwood and the sample from the panel had the characteristics of hardwood consistent with an identification of poplar. It is unlikely that the original columns would have been softwood; however, similar surviving altarpieces demonstrate that it was usual to have spiral columns in this position, so they are likely to be replacements, rather than additions.

The altarpiece was, therefore, quite crudely made. Since the object was to be covered with gesso, gilding and decoration which would conceal the joins and protruding nails, precise carpentry would be considered unnecessary.

Decoration

A detailed examination of the decoration of the frame was carried out to ascertain the extent of alteration and to assess its original appearance. Damages were examined under magnification and several tiny paint samples removed, made into cross-sections and examined under the research microscope. Further technical analysis was carried out where necessary.

The gilded surfaces have already been discussed. Whilst the figurative imagery is not being studied it is interesting to note changes in pigments which alter the visual effect, notably a darkening of the coarse azurite in the Madonna's drapery and a discolouration to brown of the copper based green pigments, for example in the grass and lily.

Arch

The front plane of the arch behind the gilded moulding was originally a bright blue azurite over a dark under-layer containing white and black particles, applied before the moulding was attached. This has been overpainted with gesso and an upper layer of pale blue glass-like particles extending only to the edge of the moulding (plate 68, p. 87).

The pale green recessed edge beneath the arch moulding consists of a transparent copper pigment over a gesso ground. Similar pigment particles found in the centre of layers of obvious overpaint in a sample from the inner arch moulding indicate that it is a later addition. Since no other pigment layers are present, and on the evidence from other altarpieces, it is possible that a line of moulding, perhaps cusped tracery, has been lost from here.

Outer arch and sides

The decoration consists of a stylised floral pattern in dark red with a dull yellow background covering the sides and arch plane (fig. 4). The design is reminiscent of brocade patterns, sometimes found on the drapery in contemporary pictures.[6]

A cross-section from a sample taken from the red area shows a layer of translucent red glaze over the gesso ground. Thin-layer chromatography of this red lake and a sample of original red glaze from the Madonna's sleeve gave the same results, indicating that the side decoration is original. The insect-derived organic red shows most similarities to kermes.

Cross-sections and electron microprobe analysis of the dull yellow ochre coloured background show it to consist of a single layer of orpiment (arsenic sulphide). Charcoal particles found beneath the layer may relate to the laying out of the design and the dull appearance to dirt particles embedded in the surface of the originally bright yellow paint layer.

There is evidence of some orpiment on the lower side of the base in an area of possible overpaint. Although this may be the remains of original decoration, further analysis is necessary to confirm this.

The strips of moulding at the point where the arch springs from the sides are overpainted with a mixture of smalt and gesso. Investigation with the

Fig. 4 The left side of the altarpiece

stereo microscope proved that the bright red and yellow brocade pattern was originally continuous over this moulding.

Console

The upper surface of the console appears originally to have been decorated with bright red vermilion but surface dirt, insect and other damage obscures any possible remaining pattern.

The lettering scraped from a layer of pigment applied over the gilding (*sgraffito*) on the front plane of the base consists of a mixture of coarse azurite, iron-oxide red, black and a small amount of white. Since azurite is a major component it may originally have appeared more blue in colour.

The sides of the base are overpainted with a layer of gesso and pale blue smalt as found on the arch. Examination of damages under magnification revealed evidence of an original layer of bole then gold with a very thin black layer above. Within a cross-section this layer appeared to be slightly metallic under ×1250 microscope magnification.

The side edges of the bracket were covered with a similar layer of overpaint which itself was fairly damaged. Possible fragments of the original decoration could be seen when examined under magnification and although the altarpiece was not being restored it was decided to remove a small area of the overpaint to give some idea of the whole design. The later additions of gesso and smalt were easily removed under the stereo microscope using a scalpel and acetone with a few drops of water.

Although one section was lost due to damage by a wall support, a substantial part of the original decoration was uncovered (fig. 5). The black curved stems and foliage with incised lines lie over a layer of gold and were originally surrounded by a slightly overlapping layer of coarse azurite of which most has flaked off to leave the underlying bole. This inner triangle is surrounded by gilding covered with a thin black layer resembling that on the side of the base. A silver test carried out on tiny scrapings of the black layer from the side and bracket was positive, proving this to be oxidised silver.

Placing silver over gold seems unusual so the intended effect is difficult to assess, however, the original bracket decoration would have been very delicate: silver foliage with incised details against a deep blue blackground and a silver border complementing the central Adam and Eve panel. The side panels and moulding would also have been silver over gold, although it is uncertain whether there is any other decoration.

Conclusion

The examination was carried out as thoroughly as possible given the limitation that the altarpiece was not being restored. Although some questions concerning the original state of the decoration could not be answered, much has been discovered about the structure and the original appearance of the frame.

In the construction of the altarpiece, there is a notable absence of sophisticated carpentry, elements being crudely nailed to one another with joins and nails concealed beneath layers of gesso and surface decoration. The structure is relatively unaltered with only minor changes such as the replacement of the twisted columns and the

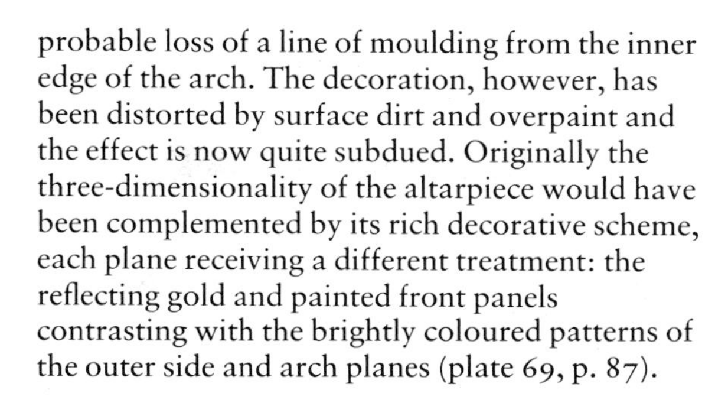

probable loss of a line of moulding from the inner edge of the arch. The decoration, however, has been distorted by surface dirt and overpaint and the effect is now quite subdued. Originally the three-dimensionality of the altarpiece would have been complemented by its rich decorative scheme, each plane receiving a different treatment: the reflecting gold and painted front panels contrasting with the brightly coloured patterns of the outer side and arch planes (plate 69, p. 87).

Notes

1. Fitzwilliam Museum Catalogue of Paintings, ii, Italian Schools, 1967, p. 124.
2. Panofsky, *Tomb Sculpture*, 1964, fig. 339.
3. R. Freemantle, *Florentine Gothic Painters*, 1975, pp. 525–6, 528–9, 532.
4. J. Pope-Hennessy, *Catalogue of Italian Sculpture in the Victoria and Albert Museum*, i p. 83 and iii p. 67, 1964.
5. The frame was X-radiographed with 30 kv for 100 seconds and the panel was given 20 kv for 60 seconds.
6. Masolino *Annunciation*, National Gallery of Art, Washington.

Fig. 5 Detail of the left side of the console showing decoration concealed by overpaint

Canaletto: *Campo SS. Giovanni e Paolo*

Keith Laing

Giovanni Antonio Canal, called Canaletto (1697–1768)
Campo SS. Giovanni e Paolo
Oil on canvas, 46.4 × 78.1 cm
Her Majesty the Queen

This painting (fig. 1) is one of the many Canalettos originally owned, and probably commissioned, by the wealthy merchant in Venice, Joseph Smith, and acquired by George III in 1762. It was engraved by Visentini, and published in the 1742 edition of the *Prospectus*.[1] Although of similar dimensions to the series of twelve views on the Grand Canal at Windsor which date from the mid 1720s, this picture is thought to have been executed c. 1735. It brings to a culmination all the technical skills explored in the earlier series, and compares stylistically with the very best of them.

The view is of the west front of the church. The Scuola di S. Marco is on the left, and the monument to Bartolomeo Colleoni in the centre. Preparatory drawings for this composition[2] do not include the Scuola, and are from a nearer standpoint. These drawings were presumably carried out on site, and transferred to the canvas in the studio. The present view is, in fact, impossible from one position, but is rather an amalgam of two viewpoints. The Scuola, however, can be seen from neither, which perhaps explains its absence in the drawings. Such licence is not uncommon in Canaletto's work: he often creates a composition from a number of given topographical elements.[3]

The painting was cleaned, relined, and restored in 1980 at the London studio of the Hamilton Kerr Institute. The following technical data were amassed from a detailed examination of the paint surface, together with X-radiography and microscopic and microchemical analyses of paint samples.

Above the glue-sized canvas lies a double oil ground: a red-brown ochreous layer below a grey layer of lead-white and charcoal. This combination is typical of paintings examined from the earlier half of the 1730s.[4] Above this grey layer, Canaletto loosely blocked in his composition, establishing the areas of sky, buildings, and canal. In the earlier views on the Grand Canal, the artist had become increasingly dependent upon mechanical instruments as a guide to the perspective and architectural details. This painting is equally reliant on such aids. Lines incised into the ground or the top layers of paint, the use of a compass, and thick, ruled lines can all be noted with the naked eye. Where ruled, the paint builds up along the edge of the rule to create a high relief. The X-radiograph detail (fig. 2) shows the clear incised lines defining the church and the windows, the latter achieved with the use of the compass. These lines were made in the ground; the top layers of paint can be seen to flow into them.

After the main compositional elements were blocked in, the silhouettes of the buildings and minor architectural details were added. Thus the lantern above the dome is seen to lie over the lively impasto of the sky (plate 70, p. 87), as is much of the skyline, including the chimney pots. Many lines can be seen which have been scored into the top layers of paint while it was still wet; these act as a guide to the perspective of the doors and windows. In the articulation of the two first-floor windows on one of the right-hand buildings (plate 71, p. 87) the scored lines can be seen running between the windows. They are now skilfully camouflaged as edges of the stonework. The black lines are added free-hand following the guidelines laid down. This black always appears to be mixed with some white, creating varying intensities of shadow, and also providing greater covering power than pure black.

The incision is generally made with a fine point, but there are examples of the use of a blunter instrument, possibly the end of a brush, seen, for example, in the ribs of the dome (plate 72, p. 88). Curiously, there are no indications of incised lines in the perspective of the pavement or in the detailed *trompe-l'oeil* on the ground floor walls of the Scuola di S. Marco (plate 73, p. 88).

Canaletto excels in the ability to convey surface texture, achieved through skilful brushwork. In the wall of the church façade, the impasto is thick and crisp, creating the illusion of coarseness (plate 74, p. 88). Small globules of paint in the windows of the south transept successfully convey the decoration of the latticework. For the creamy highlights on the pavement in the foreground, the paint is less viscous, and in the shadows it is at its most smooth and fluid. Such versatility illustrates how completely Canaletto understood the rheology of his paint. It would be interesting to know the exact composition of the medium, and discover whether this varied in different areas, depending on the consistency of the paint.

1

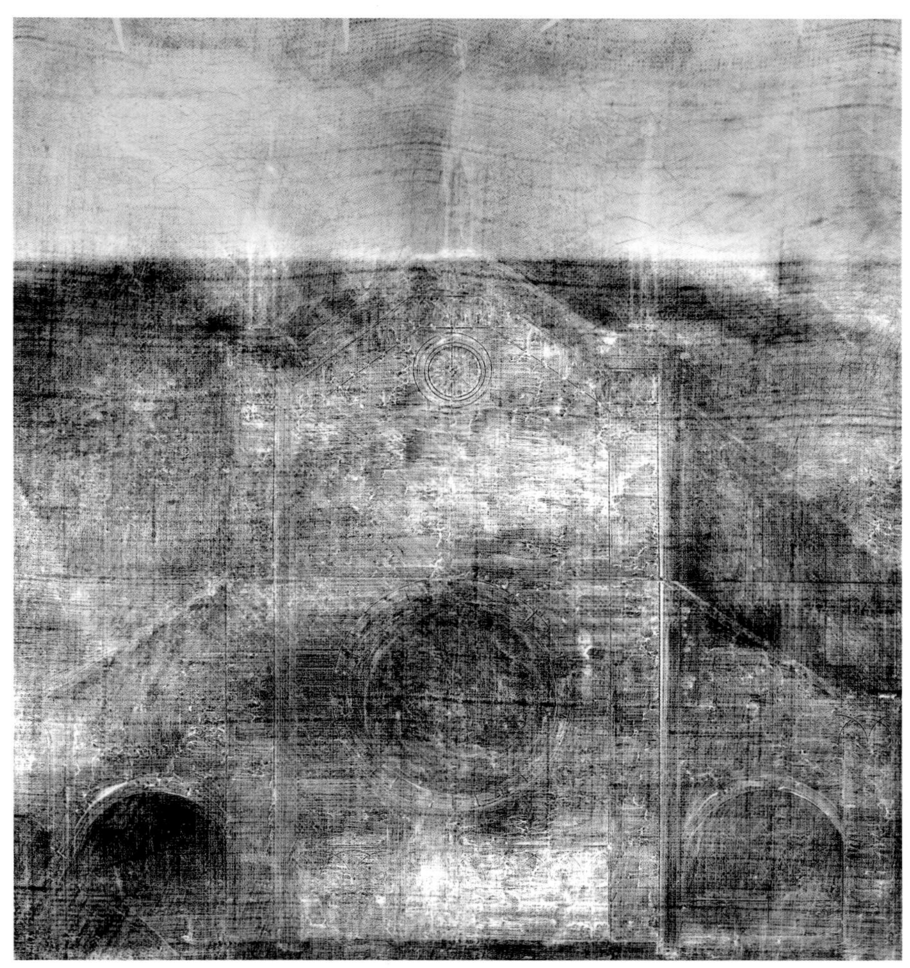

2

Fig. 1 *Campo SS. Giovanni e Paolo*, whole, after cleaning and restoration

Fig. 2 X-radiograph, detail, showing incised lines, and the use of a compass in the round windows and arches of the façade

Unfortunately, analyses of paint media cannot yet detect the presence of driers or other trace elements.

The base of the monument illustrates all the technical details discussed above (plate 75, p. 88). Incised and ruled lines define the basic shape. The impasto on the capitals and the relief decoration create a quasi-three-dimensional quality. Short, crude lines scored into the wet paint with the end of a brush articulate the side of the monument. The smooth flowing paint of the shadows forms the final detail.

The composition established and all the architectural details applied, the scene was now set for the figures and gondolas. These are the final details to be applied. Plate 76 (p. 88) shows clearly how the figure lies over the incised and raised lines of the steps. He is painted with great economy of detail: a few confident strokes suffice to convey the face and the play of light on his shirt and voluminous cloak. Such economy is characteristic of all Canaletto's figures. The white shirt of the gondolier is another example of the artist's dexterity (plate 77, p. 88): the thick impasto is built up working wet in wet, with the shadows roughly scored into the wet paint, producing a remarkably tactile effect. Canaletto must surely have worked with some speed, as so much of the effect depends upon the paint remaining soft.

Paint samples were limited, owing to the picture's fine condition. The blue pigment of the sky is Prussian blue (plate 78, p. 89), an early example of this synthetic colour first manufactured in 1704. It has been found on all the examined works by Canaletto.[5]

Notes

1. *Prospectus*, published in Venice by G. B. Pasquali, 1735.
2. T. Pignatti, *Il Quaderno di Disegni del Canaletto alle Gallerie di Venezia*, Venice, 1958, fols 50v.–52r.
3. O. Millar, *Canaletto: Paintings and Drawings*, The Queen's Gallery, 1980/81, in which he cites many examples of such skilful adjustments to reality.
4. P. England, 'An account of Canaletto's painting technique', in O. Millar's catalogue, *op.cit.* n. 3 above.
5. P. England, *op.cit.* n. 4 above, and D. Bomford and A. Roy 'Canaletto's "Venice: The Feastday of S. Roch"', *National Gallery Technical Bulletin*, vi, 1982, p. 40.

Orazio Gentileschi's *Joseph and Potiphar's Wife:* a 17th century use of 'bituminous' paint

Ann Massing

Orazio Gentileschi (1563–1639)
Joseph and Potiphar's Wife
oil on canvas, 201 × 262 cm
Her Majesty the Queen

The restoration of *Joseph and Potiphar's Wife* by Orazio Gentileschi was one of the first major treatments undertaken at the Hamilton Kerr Institute (plate 79, p. 89). While restoration was in progress, careful examination of the paint surface combined with judicious sampling helped to resolve problems of restoration, especially the detection of layers of overpaint, as well as providing information on Gentileschi's painting materials and technique.

Orazio de G[iovanni] Batista Lomi was born in Pisa in 1563 where he was trained as a painter in the Florentine tradition by his half-brother Aurelio Lomi. By 1576–78 he had gone to Rome where he took the name of a maternal uncle 'Gentileschi' and where his acquaintance with Caravaggio is well documented.[1] In 1621 Gentileschi left Rome and travelled to Genoa, then to Paris, and finally to England where he settled in London in 1625–26 as Court painter to Charles I. He remained in London until his death in 1639.

Gentileschi's large painting of *Joseph and Potiphar's Wife* illustrates an episode from Genesis xxxix, 2. Joseph was carried off into Egypt where he was bought by Potiphar, a court official. He resisted the advances of Potiphar's wife, and as a result she contrived to have him cast into prison.

Presumably the painting was commissioned by Charles I, as it was in the Royal Collection by 1633–34 when it was among pictures framed.[2] Other than the document relating to its framing little is known of the painting's history, although there can be no doubt of its authenticity. An inscription on the back: HORATIVS GENTILESCVS FECIT was revealed after removal of the lining canvas (fig. 1).

The painting was described by G. F. Waagen, the first director of the Berlin Museum, who published the diaries he kept after his two trips to England.[3] He mentions *Joseph and Potiphar's Wife* in 1837 and again in 1854 as part of his impressions of the visits made to Hampton Court. In his first diary published in German in 1837 he writes:

Orazio Lomi, gen. Gentileschi. Von diesem florentinischen Maler, der zur zeit Carl's I in England malte und starb, ist hier ein Hauptbild, der keusche Joseph und Potiphar's Weib, ganze, lebens grosse Figuren. Er hat diesere Vorgang im Costum und sonst ganz in seine Zeit übertragen, doch ist die Malerei sehr fleissig, die Färbung kräftig, die Wirkung sehr schlagend.

Fig. 1 Inscription on reverse, revealed during restoration

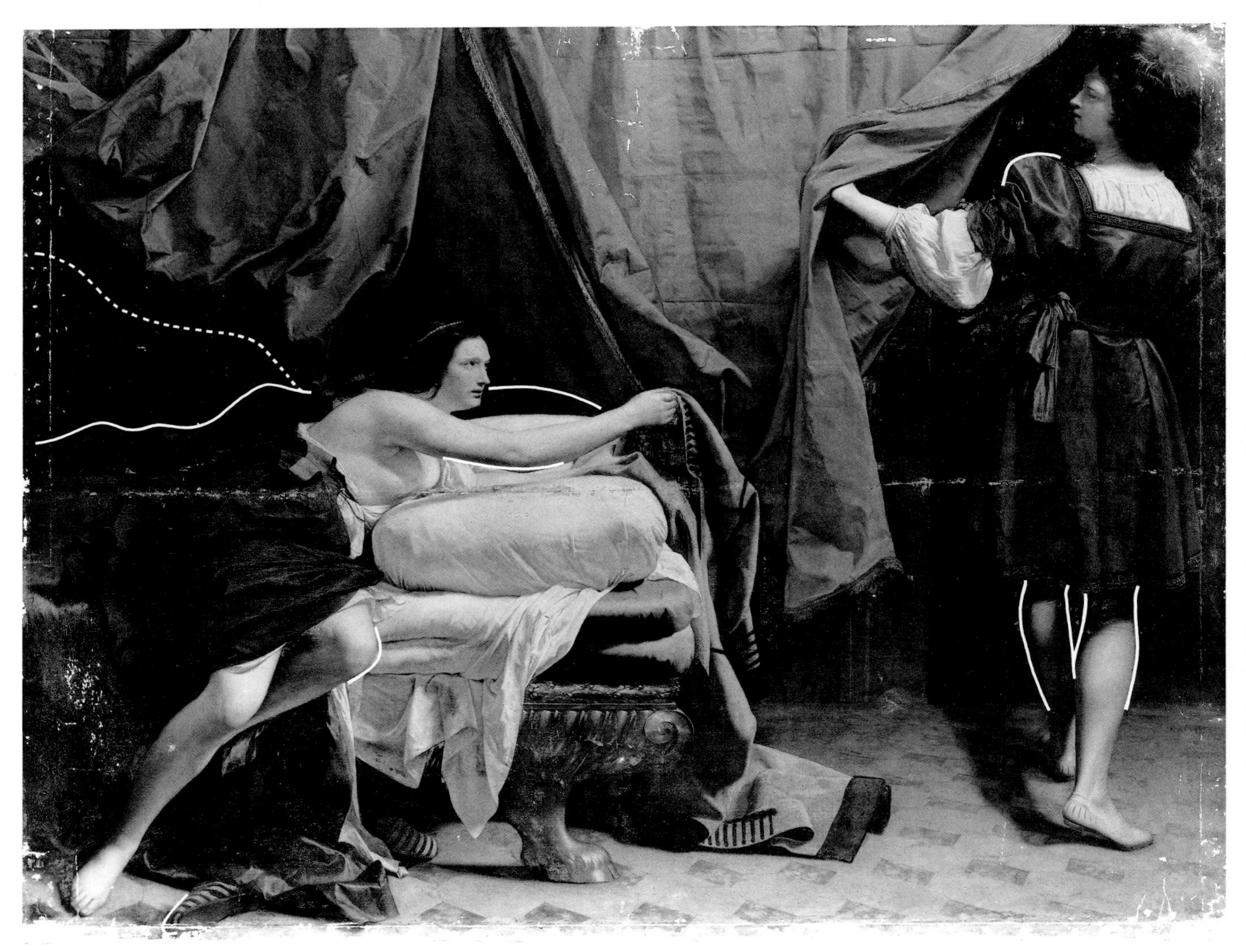

Fig. 2 After cleaning, before restoration. The damages in the paint layer are filled with white chalk putty prior to restoration. Pentiments, the artist's changes in composition, are indicated by white lines.

By 1854 the painting had been placed in the King's Drawing Room, and given the number 165. Waagen's account was published in London and he writes:

165 Orazio Lomi called Gentileschi – Joseph and Potiphar's Wife

This painting belongs to those later Florentine masters who, in contradistinction to the idealising tendency of the Florentine School of the 16th century, adopted a realistic style. Thus both of the personages are rendered with a portrait-like character and with the costume of the painter's own time. This picture which was originally of warm and harmonious colouring and striking effect, has unfortunately, by over-cleaning acquired a motley and hard appearance.

From Waagen's entry we assume the painting was restored between 1837 and 1854, and that the restoration was not pleasing to Waagen. The appearance of the painting would not have improved with the years and by the 1970s the painting was so obscured by multiple layers of discoloured varnish and repaint that it was impossible to appreciate the clarity of colour and the precision of detail which are so characteristic of Gentileschi's painting technique.

Restoration

During the restoration of Orazio Gentileschi's *Joseph and Potiphar's Wife* flaking paint was re-adhered, the glue lining was removed and replaced by a wax resin lining (unbleached beeswax and MS2 resin), and over a century's accumulation of layers of discoloured varnish was removed. While removing the overpaint, however, problems concerning the differentiation of overpaint from original paint occurred which necessitated close collaboration between the restoration studio and the analytical laboratory. The results led to interesting insights into Gentileschi's painting materials and techniques, and it is this aspect of the restoration, as well as the information gathered during restoration relating to the history of the painting, with which this article is concerned.

Repaint removal and detection of overpaint

In the early stages of varnish removal it was found that large areas were covered by repaint. On removal of some of this repaint it became evident that original paint had previously been removed completely down to the grey ground layer. The most significant areas include the hair of Potiphar's wife and the shadow area of Joseph's cloak which is lifted up by Potiphar's wife. In some areas, the difficulty of distinguishing repaint from original and removing the repaint was uncomplicated: large areas of repaint were removed from the red curtain, the right side of the tiled floor, and over the juncture of the two canvases, revealing relatively small losses and much undamaged original paint.

It was suspected moreover that several areas of brown/black bituminous-like paint were overpaint, but in order to ascertain if there was original paint underneath, and if indeed they were later additions, small samples were taken and made into cross-sections to study the layer build-up.

Bitumen and asphaltum are different terms for the same material; bitumen is the Roman name, asphalt the Greek. 'Bitumen' refers to a substance containing essentially no organic or mineral matter but a high proportion of hydrocarbon solvent-soluble components.[4] When prepared with a drying oil bitumen can absorb any amount of oil, and the result is a rich transparent brown paint pleasing to use but which never dries completely, and the paint layer forms drying cracks which may continue to develop into abnormally wide cracks. Similar pigments equally difficult to identify, such as mummy (parts of Egyptian mummies, ground with a drying oil) or Van Dyck brown (from peat deposits near Cologne) were also used in paintings. To the restorer, a deep brown-black paint layer with pronounced drying cracks, which is soluble in relatively weak solvent mixtures, is considered 'bituminous'. In this article, we have referred to bitumen although a definite identification of bitumen has not been made.[5]

The green bedcover on the far left and the black background above it and to the left of Joseph were analysed. Also the black braid on Joseph's tunic was extremely soluble in mild solvent mixtures and was therefore suspected of being a later addition. After studying the cross-sections and examining the painting more closely with the stereo microscope, it became obvious that most of these bituminous-like layers were original, albeit sometimes covered with repaint of a similar bituminous character.

The green of the bedspread was painted with a mixture of verdigris and lead-tin yellow, the proportions being varied to produce a more green or yellow hue. The yellow highlights are in thick, pure lead-tin yellow. The yellow of the slipper is also lead-tin yellow and the deep red is a pure red lake used as a glaze. In places the red runs over the yellow and elsewhere the yellow over the red showing that Gentileschi worked rather freely in the details of his composition. In places, there are two upper layers of yellow with the top one being slightly paler due to the presence of lead white with the yellow.

The most obvious proof that the bituminous-like craquelure of the green bedcover is due to an original paint layer is in fact visible with the naked eye. The illustrations of Potiphar's wife's right shoe (plates 80–82, p. 90) show that the bituminous cracks in the dark shadows of the green bedcover continue across the shoe. The shoe was painted on top of the green bedcover, and the craquelure in the shoe is caused by the bituminous layer in the bedcover underneath. Since the shoe is obviously original, the bituminous layer underneath is original also.

In the cross-sections of the green bedcover on the left (plates 83–85, p. 90), the ground layers are covered by the green paint layer of the bedcover, yellow and green pigment particles in a darker matrix. On top of this is a dark brown layer with only a few pigment particles in a dark brown medium. There was not a definite division between the two layers in the cross-section. Because of the similarity of the two layers in solubility and because of the rough texture of the paint, removal of the upper layer was not considered.

The area between the red curtain and the female figure on the left side of the picture was thought to be overpainted with green-black paint. Also, part of the curtain appeared to have been covered up at some stage and it was necessary to be able to distinguish between overpaint and pentiment. Samples taken from the background near the left edge (plates 86 and 87, p. 90) show the bituminous layer above and below a red layer similar to that of the curtain behind the bed: Gentileschi made a slight change in his composition and painted over part of the curtain, raising the level significantly. On top of these layers, the overpaint fluoresces in ultraviolet light and runs into a crack in the paint layer, indicating that the overpaint was applied after the original paint layer had cracked, thus confirming that it is a later addition. In addition, X-ray electron microprobe analysis showed the presence of the element barium in the top layer. Barium was not used as a pigment or as an extender until the 19th century. After confirmation that this green-black layer was overpaint, it was removed. Small damages were revealed along the edges which indicate that a change in the dimensions of the painting had been made (see fig. 4 and the discussion which follows).

The originality of the braid around the bottom of Joseph's tunic was doubted after the black was found to be susceptible to mild solvent mixtures. However a cross-section taken through the braid clearly demonstrated that the black was covered by two layers of yellow, the first a dull yellow and the second a bright lemon yellow. (plates 89–91, p. 91). If the yellows could be shown to be original then the authenticity of the black could also be confirmed. Therefore the following areas of yellow paint were sampled and analysed with the X-ray microprobe:

- yellow decoration on black braid of Joseph's red tunic,
- yellow fringe of the red curtain,
- Joseph's yellow coat,
- yellow in Potiphar's wife's shoe,
- yellow in the leg of the bed,
- yellow highlights of the green bedcover, here mixed with a small amount of green.

All the yellows tested proved to be lead-tin yellow with the same impurities of silicon, aluminium and calcium. Therefore it was concluded that the black of the braid was original. Its solubility may be due to the use of a medium other than drying oil. Dry heating tests of this black paint suggest the presence of a resinous substance mixed with drying oil.[6]

Gentileschi's use of bitumen is regrettable for it has not aged well. The green bedcover has especially suffered. The paint layer is so badly broken up due to the formation of extremely wide drying cracks that the form in the darker areas to the left of Potiphar's wife's legs is almost completely lost. It is interesting to note that where the paint surface was protected by the frame the drying cracks have not formed. Areas of repaint have also prevented their formation (on plate 83, p. 90, the area with fewer drying cracks had been covered with thick overpaint). Highlights of lead-tin yellow in Potiphar's wife's shoe and in the bed leg also seem to have prevented the formation of drying cracks in the paint layers underneath. The highlights seem to cover the cracked underlayer, as a later repaint often seems to do, but here all layers are original (plate 80–82, p. 90).

Historical use of bituminous paint

Bitumen is popularly considered to be a pigment which was used extensively from the mid-18th century especially in Britain. Sir Joshua Reynolds used bitumen and his paintings often display drying craquelure similar to those on the green bedcover of this painting by Gentileschi.[7] There are earlier recorded instances of its use, however, including treatises from the period. The most important in relation to this painting is *Pictoria Sculptoria* by Théodore Turquet de Mayerne.[8] Positive identification of bitumen as a pigment requires very sensitive techniques of high resolving power. In 1979, the National Gallery in London acquired a gas- chromotography – mass-spectrometry system which is well suited for such identification. In a few instances a positive identification has been made for paintings from the 17th century (see note 4).

Original dimensions

During the restoration it was discovered that the size of the original canvas had been reduced by stretching it onto a slightly smaller stretcher at some time in the past. Perhaps the painting was reduced to fit a smaller frame, or a certain position on the wall of the King's Drawing-room. Such alterations were then commonplace, and indeed the present-day restorer is often involved in returning a work of art to its original dimensions. During removal of repaint, lines of paint loss were uncovered 7 cm from the original turn-over edge on the left side and 6 cm from the original edge on the right side; also tack holes about 3 cm apart and 4 cm from the edge were uncovered (see fig. 2). Along the top and bottom edges 3 cm of original paint were still turned over the edge of the stretcher. Because the lower 3 cm include the tip of the shoe of Potiphar's wife, it was decided to enlarge the present stretcher and frame during relining although this change in dimensions necessitated extensive puttying and retouching of losses along the bottom edge.

Gentileschi's painting technique

There are two layers of priming; a red layer (ochres and carbon black) covered by a greyish layer (charcoal[9] and lead white); both ground layers cover the entire canvas and are visible in the cross-sections reproduced. Where samples included all the paint and priming layers down to the canvas surface, canvas fibres are occasionally included with traces of a gluey material surrounding them. This suggests that the canvas was first prepared with a glue sizing which was normal procedure.[10]

Gentileschi appears to have begun his composition by blocking in the main areas. The floor and the floor tiles were painted before the figures. A cross-section shows that the yellow of the bed leg runs over a layer of grey-beige which is the paint used for the floor tiles. Also, because with age the oil becomes increasingly translucent, the meeting of the floor and the background can just be seen underneath Joseph's stockings. The craquelure system of the paint layer also changes because of the difference in the underlayer.

After the floor, the main figures were added. The bed was painted before the female figure judging from the pentiments in the right shoulder; that the bottom of the bed was painted before the untucked sheet is also indicated by pentiments. A greenish layer which is probably the bedcover is present in several samples from that area indicating that it originally covered an area much larger than that of the present bedcover.

There are many other pentiments, some of which reveal major changes in the composition, for instance, the perspective was considerably

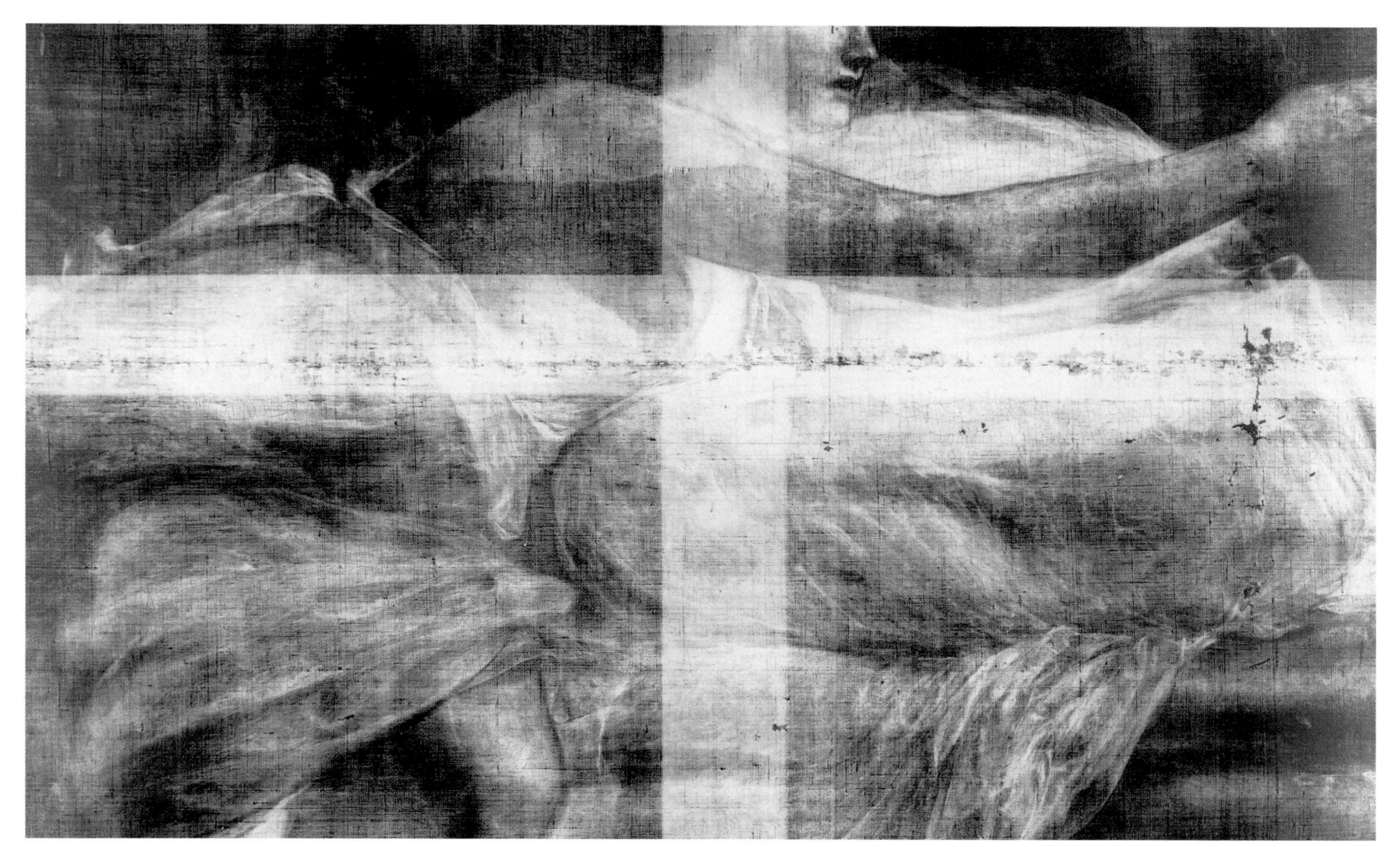

Fig. 3 X-radiograph assembly: detail

Fig. 4 Detail during cleaning

changed by lowering the far side of the bed. Pentiments of the bed coverings are visible since removal of the repaint in the background, and a cross-section of the red curtain near Potiphar's wife's chin reveals Gentileschi's indecision about this change. The texture of the red curtain immediately above the white pillow is rather different from elsewhere on the curtain, as it overlaps a layer of pure lead white representing a previous position of the pillow. The white gives the red a deep luminosity. Under the white is a pale pink (flesh?) under which is another red glaze (curtain?). This layer build-up suggests that a number of changes were made in the area; this is supported by the evidence in the X- radiograph (see discussion below). The red curtain was much lower (a pentiment is visible in the dark background and other cross-sections confirm red pigment much lower still). There are several other minor pentiments including a change in the position of Joseph's legs (fig. 2).

The yellow of Joseph's coat was painted directly onto the grey of the second priming layer. The red of his tunic was painted in a single layer of pure red lake. In places this has been rubbed and worn so that the grey priming shows through. The red tunic has a dull yellow sash which is painted with a yellow glaze on top of a beige underlayer which rests directly on the red of the tunic.

The pale mauve of the bedcover is underpainted with a thin layer of pale blue; a mixture of lead white and blue verditer. The top layer is lead white with a little red lake and blue verditer. Underneath these two layers is yellow-green paint, exactly the same as was used for the bedcover. This may represent a previous positioning of the bedcover.

A small sample was taken from the flesh of Potiphar's wife's wrist. The top layer is painted in almost pure lead white with the addition of small amounts of red lake and carbon black. This is underpainted with a much darker paint, a deep pink mixture of the same pigments.

Potiphar's wife's blue dress is painted in two layers of bright blue paint, the main component of which is ultramarine. There is little difference between these two layers although the lower has a slightly purple hue due to the presence of a little red lake mixed in with the ultramarine. The blues are underpainted with a pale grey (plate 88, p. 90).

X-radiograph (fig. 3)

The X-rays of the figure of Potiphar's wife show the pentiments mentioned above: the changes in the height of the pillow and in the outstretched right arm. Also, in the X-ray only one breast of the nude figure is visible, in the final version both can be seen.

Dark areas indicating losses along the original canvas seam are visible within the light band caused by the stretcher bar on the back of the canvas.

Conclusion

Despite the apparent clarity of conception of Gentileschi's composition, he appears to have begun rather freely, blocking in the main areas, then placing the figures, and making several changes before arriving at the final form.

Acknowledgement

The analysis included in the article was done by Pamela England; parts of her analytical report have been included in this article.

Notes and references

1. Gentileschi was involved in a libel suit in 1603 brought against him by the painter Giovanni Baglione in which Caravaggio states that he has not seen Orazio for 3 years.
2. M. Levey, *The Later Italian Pictures in the Collection of Her Majesty the Queen*, London 1964, p. 82.
3. G. F. Waagen, *Künstwerke und Künstler in England*, Berlin 1837, I, pp. 391–392; and *Treasures of Art in Great Britain: being an account of the chief collections of paintings, drawings, sculptures, illuminated MSS, I–III*, London 1854, p. 359.
4. For a discussion and bibliography on bituminous pigments see: R. White, 'Brown and Black Organic Glazes, Pigments and Paints', in *The National Gallery Technical Bulletin*, 10, 1986. pp. 58–71; also J. S. Mills and R. White, *The Organic Chemistry of Museum Objects*, London 1987, pp. 48–59.
5. In view of the recent advances in the identification of painting mediums, Karin Groen has proposed further research on this painting to be reported at a later date.
6. see note 8.
7. Sir Joshua Reynolds' use of bitumen is frequently referred to; for a recent reference, see pp. 63–65 of the catalogue of the Reynolds exhibition at the Royal Academy of Arts, edited by Nicolas Penny, London 1986.
8. T. Turquet de Mayerne, *Pictoria Sculptoria et quae subalternarum artium*, 1620, reprinted Audin Imprimeurs Lyon.

   Théodore Turquet de Mayerne (1573–1655), court physician to the King of England, wrote a manuscript on painting technique, now in the British Museum, London, in which he mentions his contemporaries: Rubens, Van Dyck, Gentileschi and others. In folio 92 De Mayerne suggests using 'spalte' or 'aspalathum' for shadows, specifying it must be chosen 'pur, très noir, et friable.'

   De Mayerne mentions Gentileschi several times in his manuscript. In several places (folios 9, 10, 146, and 150), he speculates that Gentileschi used 'Amber Varnish from Venice' mixing it with his colours on the palette. Amber varnish was used for varnishing lutes, but De Mayerne assures us that the reddishness does not ruin the colour, and that it allows the painter to work when he wishes without waiting for the paint to dry completely.

   De Mayerne also mentions other aspects of painting technique which correspond to what was found on *Joseph and Potiphar's Wife.* He describes the common practice of giving the canvas a priming of glue made from leather cuttings. Then when the glue is dry he suggests to prime lightly with brown red or English red brown, then flatten with a pumice stone. A second and last coat of white lead and charcoal 'well chosen' is then applied.
9. The carbon black is here identifiable as charcoal because of the splintery nature of the pigment particles and because a few fragments show the remains of wood structure.
10. see note 8.

A self-portrait by Godfried Schalcken

Ann Massing and Karin Groen

Godfried Schalcken (1643–1706)
Self-Portrait
Oil on canvas, 61 × 50 cm
Fitzwilliam Museum

Godfried Schalcken studied with Samuel van Hoogstraten in Dordrecht and with Gerard Dou in Leyden. He painted mainly genre scenes and portraits but also biblical and mythological subjects. In 1692 he came to London, where he became a successful portrait painter. When Thomas Platt, the British Commissioner, ordered a self-portrait from Schalcken for the Medici Portrait Gallery of Cosimo III in Florence, he described the artist as 'un pittore olandese assai famoso'.[1] After a stay in England of about five years, Schalcken returned to Holland to work in the Hague.

Schalcken's *Self-Portrait* is a rare example of a 17th century painting still unlined and probably unaltered by restorations. However, despite this, significant changes to the paint layer have taken place due to the artist's use of poor quality materials, and because the painting has not been kept in a stable environment.

Preliminary examination

The pictorial quality of Schalcken's *Self-Portrait* is matched neither by the materials nor by the construction of the support. The canvas is stretched onto a narrow (4.5 × 1 cm) fixed wooden stretcher which cannot be altered to accommodate changes in the tension of the canvas due to variations in relative humidity. The corners of the stretcher are half lap-joined and secured with three nails in each corner. The four members are roughly cut and the construction poorly made. Because there is no bevel on the stretcher, the canvas rests directly on the stretcher bars (fig. 2). Before treatment, while the painting was on view in the Fitzwilliam Museum, the canvas formed a significant bulge in the lower half of the painting.

The canvas is unlined and has suffered no accidental damage, but it is a plain weave of poor quality. There are large knots and the thickness of the threads is very variable, some being almost five times thicker than others (The weave count is c. 13 threads/cm^2).

The turn-over edges of the canvas are fixed onto the stretcher with the original tacks that are now rusty, and in many places the canvas underneath them has deteriorated leaving the canvas unattached. In addition to the tacks there are pinholes along all four sides (which are probably original). One pin is still in place (fig. 3).

The painting was primed with a brownish ground before being stretched onto the stretcher. The tacking edges along the lower and right sides were cut after the priming was applied (fig. 3). Along the top and left, they are unprimed; the ground stops slightly before the turn-over edge and the paint layer extends over onto the bare canvas. Cusping of the canvas weave coinciding with the tack holes is noticeable along both the top edge and the left side (fig. 5).

The outline of the sitter and the craquelure show on the reverse of the canvas. Especially in the lower half of the canvas the ground has been pushed through the canvas weave, looking like accretions deposited on the surface. Microscopic analysis of one of the small particles shows that it is pigmented similarly to the ground layer.

Although the paint has not suffered from lining or from overcleaning, considerable changes in the appearance of the paint layer have occurred. A very strong craquelure system, which is raised and distracting, has developed in the centre of the painting where the canvas was not adequately tensioned. Around the edges, where the canvas was resting on the stretcher bars, the paint layer has not cracked (fig. 1). The spiral craquelure near the artist's chin is the result of a former knock.

The paint has begun to flake very slightly near the right edge on the sitter's shoulder as well as just under the rebate of the frame. The loose paint was readhered with gelatin and the small losses retouched during restoration. An interesting change made by the artist himself is his signature in the bottom right corner. In raking light, one can see two signatures; Schalcken painted over his first signature, moving it slightly up and to the right (fig. 4). There are other pentiments; the right tip of the hat and the contour of the sitter's left shoulder have been altered.

The varnish is extremely thin and only slightly discoloured. However there is a disturbing whitish opacity, especially in the area covering the sitter's dark curly hair where it falls over his shoulder; other areas include the right corner of the hat and much of the background. It was difficult to determine the cause of this whitish appearance and whether it was confined to the surface coating or if the deterioration extended also to the paint

1

2

layer. Since it appeared to be mainly in the varnish, it was decided to recommend removal of the varnish, which indeed made some improvement.

Deterioration of the paint layer

The most striking alteration in the appearance of the paint layer is the marked change in the blue background. The area protected by the rebate of the frame is still a deep dark blue, but where the paint layer was exposed to air and light, the colour is considerably lighter. The red drapery is also lighter in colour than when it was first painted (plate 92, p. 91).

The blue consists of two blue layers both containing a mixture of indigo, smalt and a little lead white; the upper layer contains more lead white. The ground layer is composed of lead white, chalk and a little umber. For the red drapery a red lake was used, i.e. an organic red dye precipitated onto an inert base. The red could not be identified with certainty, but thin layer chromatography suggested a type of red wood.[2] The inert base is aluminium oxide. The red lake is painted onto an under-layer of red ochre and bone black, which remains unchanged.

Indigo is derived from plants of the genus *Indigofera* and is one of the more stable organic pigments. Smalt is made by crushing blue-coloured glass, which has its blue colour from the addition of cobalt oxide to the glass while in a molten state. Although smalt is an unstable pigment, its instability is not due to the action of light but to a chemical reaction, with cobalt acting as a catalyst in the oxidation of the paint medium. The reaction is not limited to a pure phase boundary catalysis and the change in colour also depends on the reactivity of the glass. In paintings smalt is often found with a discoloured edge surrounding an unaltered core (plate 101, p. 92). In Schalcken's painting the smalt particles from the faded and the non-faded areas could not be distinguished microscopically, and cross-sections from the faded and the non-faded blue did not show a significant difference (plates 93–96, p. 92). If the indigo had discoloured at all under the influence of light, the effect would be seen only in a few microns at the top of the sample. In the background, the discolouration caused by exposure to light, especially ultraviolet radiation, does not seem to be so much a result of the fading of a pigment but of erosion of the medium causing chalking. Some of the small whitish areas look like deposits on the surface (plate 102, p. 92). Gas-chromatographic analysis of the paint medium showed that the medium used for the ground in the painting was simply drying oil. The blue paint layer, however, showed a suppressed peak for azelate, indicating that a mixture of oil and egg was used.

The cross-sections made from samples from the faded and non-faded red show a distinct difference

Fig. 1 Raking light. Surface deformations have formed in the paint layer because of the unsatisfactory original support.

Fig. 2 Reverse. The outline of the sitter and the craquelure show on the reverse of the canvas. On the lower half of the canvas, the ground has been pushed through the canvas weave.

Fig. 3 Reverse detail. The canvas was primed with a brownish ground before painting began. On the right the tacking edge is unprimed; along the bottom, the edge was cut after the priming had been applied.

Fig. 4 Signature photographed in ultraviolet light. Changes in an artist's signature are usually later alterations; here Schalcken himself overpainted his first signature, moving it up and to the right.

Fig. 5 Raking light detail. Cusping of the canvas weave, coinciding with the placing of the tacks, is noticeable along the top edge. This is an unavoidable result of stretching the canvas and a definite indication that the painting has not been trimmed to reduce its size.

3

4

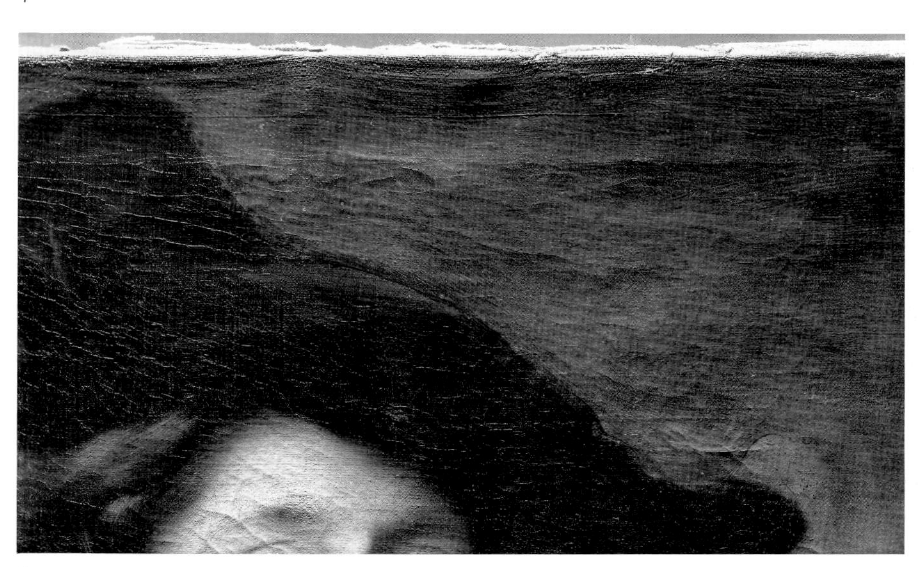

5

Fig. 6 During restoration. The painting was stretched onto a loom to keep the canvas under slight tension while the paint film gradually relaxed.

(plates 97–100, p. 92) as many red lake pigments are indeed very sensitive to light. The sample taken from under the frame shows discolouration only on the very top of the red glaze, suggesting that the entire painting must have been exposed to light for some time during its history. In the sample from the faded area, the discoloration is much more pronounced; all the red has disappeared except in the bottom of the paint layer. Organic pigments can undergo photo-chemical reactions not only under the influence of ultraviolet but also under visible light due to their ability to absorb light at these wavelengths. The surroundings of the pigment (substrate, medium, moisture, oxygen) also play a part in the fading. It is impossible to assign a certain mechanism to the reaction resulting in the fading of the pigment particles. In this particular case one can only go so far as to say that the chromophore has been destroyed.

Restoration

A painting of the 17th century which has not been lined or altered in any way by previous restorations is an extremely rare object, and any interference with the object should be restricted to the absolute minimum. To readhere the flaking paint, then simply return the painting to a controlled museum environment, was considered but ultimately rejected; it was decided that some further treatment was necessary to prevent further physical deterioration. The surface deformations which had formed were due to the unsatisfactory original support, therefore in order to arrest the deterioration it was decided to replace the original support by a stretcher with bevelled edges which could be lightly tensioned.

The original canvas, although fragile, is strong enough to support the picture, but in order to restretch the painting onto a new stretcher, strip-lining was necessary. Fine quality cambric was slightly fringed then attached to the tacking edge of the original canvas with Beva 371 film. As this article goes to press, the painting is being kept taut on a temporary loom (fig. 6) which keeps the original canvas under light tension while the paint film gradually relaxes. Moisture treatment to reduce the raised craquelure is envisaged before restretching the painting onto a new stretcher.

Notes

1. The portrait is now in the Uffizi Gallery. For this information see: Petra Ten-Doesschate Chu, *Im Lichte Hollands, Holländische Malerei des 17. Jahrhunderts aus den Sammlungen des Fürsten von Lichtenstein und aus Schweizer Besitz*, Kunstmuseum Basel, Zürich 1987, pp. 234–235; for further reference to Schalcken's self-portraits, see n. 13.
2. Thin-layer chromatography as in W. A. Th. Roelofs, *Thin-layer Chromatography, ICOM Committee for Conservation, 3rd Triennial Meeting* Madrid, 1972, pp. 18–19. Madder lake, cochineal and kermes were absent.
3. According to R. Giovanoli and B. Mühlethaler, 'Investigation of Discoloured Smalt', *Studies in Conservation* 15, 1970, pp. 37–44, there is a change in coordination of the cobalt ion, with the cobalt coordinated to an organic compound of unknown constitution. In silicate glasses this coordination is predominately fourfold tetrahedral, the cobalt producing an extremely intense purplish blue. In the six-fold coordination the cobalt ion is only slightly pink to colourless depending on the type of glass.

The conservation of *The Family of Henry VIII*: preliminary report

Herbert Lank

Unknown artist
The Family of Henry VIII
141.0 × 355.0 cm
Her Majesty the Queen

Henry VIII is seated placing his right hand on Prince Edward; Jane Seymour is seated on the King's left. On the left of the group stands Princess Mary and on the right Princess Elizabeth. Through the archways at each end of the colonnade are glimpses of the Great Garden at Whitehall Palace. The painting can be dated c. 1545[1] (fig. 1).

On the night of 31st March 1986, Hampton Court Palace was severely damaged by fire. Miraculously the Hampton Court Salvage Company, trained against just such an eventuality by the Superintendent of the Royal Collection at Hampton Court, Mr Joe Cowell MVO, rescued virtually everything. Six works suffered water damage as well as the effects of heat and smoke.

This painting was severely affected by water. The Cartoon Gallery in which it hung was badly damaged (fig. 2).

Water, trapped at the back of the stretcher, loosened paint along the bottom edge. This was secured on site in the days following the fire. Subsequent examination revealed that the severe blanching visible on the surface had damaged varnish and paint layers (fig. 3).

Laboratory analysis of the paint medium showed that some of the water miscible components of the aged linseed oil medium had been leached out.[2] This left micro-fissures which scattered light, destroying the intended optical effect and leaving the paint with a chalky white appearance.

After removal of discoloured varnishes a grey fatty layer was found to be present over much of the paint surface. This had shielded the paint to some extent. Subsequently, further treatment was carried out to retrieve optical coherence.[3]

Notes

1. Oliver Millar, *The Tudor, Stuart and Early Georgian Pictures in the collection of Her Majesty the Queen*, London, 1963 cat. no. 43 pp. 63 and 64.
2. Medium analysis was carried out by Raymond White at the Scientific Department of the National Gallery, London.
3. It is intended to publish a detailed account of the Institute's laboratory analyses, treatment and technical findings in the next issue of the *Bulletin of the Hamilton Kerr Institute*. The research work is still in progress.

Fig. 1 Before the fire

Fig. 2 The Cartoon Gallery after the fire (COI: Crown Copyright)

Fig. 3 Detail, showing water damage

The catalogue

This section of the Bulletin covers the second part of the exhibition and is a survey of the work undertaken by the Institute in its first ten years. The paintings are not selected simply to demonstrate particularly successful conservation treatments, but to show the range of paintings worked on, as well as demonstrating the many different factors that are involved in conservation. Paintings badly damaged in the past dictate particular approaches to treatment, as in the *Triptych* by Lippi and the *Portrait of a Woman* by Gheeraedts. Sometimes such defects are reversible, as in the relining of *Lady Downing* by Gainsborough. Sometimes such dramatic improvements to the surface appearance are not possible, or the treatment would be unjustifiably hazardous as in Stubb's *Gimcrack*. Finally, there is a group of paintings largely untouched by restoration, where the restorer's duty is to do only that which is sufficient to ensure their survival and present them free of distorting layers of dirt and discoloured varnish. Lining has been avoided in Zoffany's *Woodley Family* for this reason. In other cases removal of the discoloured varnish has revealed works in exceptionally good condition, requiring little or no restoration.

Many of the entries mention the varnish applied after restoration. The varnishes used on the paintings are Ketone resin 'N', Laropal K80 and MS2A. All are synthetic cyclohexanone resin varnishes and are soluble in white spirit with a high aromatic content. Ketone resin 'N' was manufactured by BASF until 1979, when notification was given of a change in product name to Laropal K80. MS2A is a reduced, hydrogenated resin based on the condensation of a cyclic ketone with formaldehyde. It is no longer commercially available, but has been manufactured specially for British conservators by Laporte Industries under laboratory conditions, and is available only in small quantities. The gloss of the film can be reduced by the addition of Cosmolloid Wax 80H, a synthetic microcrystalline wax which is non-yellowing, neutral and stable.

Gerard David (active 1484–d. 1523)

Fig. 1 Before restoration

Fig. 2 After restoration

Mentioned as Master of the St. Luke guild in 1484, he was the most important figure in the flourishing centre for arts that Bruges remained despite its declining economic importance from the beginning of the sixteenth century. He looked for inspiration to Jan van Eyck and Roger van der Weyden. It is possible that David moved to Antwerp in 1515, where his contemporary, Massys, was working. His works were widely imitated by contemporaries but by the mid-seventeenth century he was virtually forgotten. Research in the Bruges archives in the second half of the 19th century revealed his existence and his oeuvre was established at the beginning of the twentieth century.

1. *Madonna and Child*
Oil on oak panel, in late 19th century gothic frame; panel 15.7 × 12 cm, frame 28 × 17 × 2 cm deep
National Trust, Upton House

The original appearance of the frame
The painting, a rectangle with a semi-circular top, is set into a gothic style gilt frame with a triangular gable and finials on the sides (fig. 1). The original frame must have been a simple moulding, with a semi-circular top like the painting, and a sloping sill.

At the back the panel was carved out to provide a recessed painting surface as part of the original design. At the front the original framing survives only as a groove in the panel around the painted surface. The bottom sill is preserved, but the sides and arched top have disappeared. The frame may well have been carved as part of the panel. It was probably removed to make way for the modern frame.

Although the back of the painting had five layers of red marble overpaint, examination under the microscope revealed that the original paint-layer was meant to look like porphyry. It consisted of a fine black underlayer covered with red, pink and white splashes and a glaze of red lake which in turn was covered with pink and white dots. Unfortunately, this porphyry paint-layer is not sufficiently well preserved to be uncovered.

The front edge of the painting shows minute remains of red paint which are difficult to interpret. A porphyry frame with a gold moulding edging the painting would make more sense. Possibly there was a line of 'porphyry' edging the painting to separate the gold ground from the frame. The painting is probably one half of a diptych with the portrait of the donor on the other half.

Cleaning
The painting, although generally in very good condition, had a number of darkened retouchings, mainly in the

Child's face, the Virgin's robe and the white garments of the two angels. The original gold ground was entirely covered with a later layer of oil gold. The Virgin's crown proved to be a later addition, added with the oil-gold layer (plate 103, p. 92).

Removing the oil gold revealed the original gold ground. In place of punched ornament the gold ground was covered in countless small blue stipples centering like rays on the Virgin and growing denser towards the edges of the painting, as if gold light was emanating from her. Removal of the retouchings from the Child's face revealed a bad scratch and damages due to separation of the paint-layer from the enamel-like white imprimatura underneath. These losses were due to tiny flakes which had splintered off along the vertical cracks when the wood had shrunk during periods of low relative humidity. However, the imprimatura layer is intact almost everywhere and it covers the underdrawing. There were also losses in the Virgin's and angel's robes (fig. 3).

The delightful expression on the Child's face emerges undisturbed from the underdrawing (fig. 4); the serene eyes, the round cheeks and pointed small chin, the smile in the corners of his mouth and the shadow under his round lower lip.

The somewhat dotted appearance of the underdrawing can be seen as an indication that the composition was transferred to the panel by means of a punched cartoon. The outline of the drawing on the cartoon would have been punched with a needle. The cartoon was then placed on the gessoed panel and dabbed with a small porous bag filled with carbon powder. The black powder went through the punch-holes and left the outline of the drawing on the panel. These outlines were then drawn out with a brush and black paint in an aqueous medium such as gum arabic.

Although the underdrawing is complete, it was not possible to reconstruct the same delightful expression on the Child's face when retouching the damages. Gerard David had inevitably and unconsciously made minute changes during the painting process.

Renate Woudhuysen-Keller

Fig. 3 Detail, after cleaning, before restoration

Fig. 4 Infrared reflectogram assembly of Child's face

Fra Filippo Lippi (1406–1469)

Born in Florence, Lippi was placed in the Convent of the Carmine as a boy and became a monk in 1421. Much influenced by Masaccio, with whom he may have worked in the Brancacci Chapel, Lippi's first dated work is the *Tarquinia Madonna* of 1437. He is recorded in Siena in 1428 and was working in Padua by 1434. He is thought also to have visited Venice about that year. In Florence he worked on the *Coronation of the Virgin* for Sant'Ambrogio between 1435/36 and 1441. In 1452 he began to work in Prato. In 1456 he abducted Lucrezia Buti from the nunnery of S. Margherita in Prato where he was chaplain, and his son by her, Filippino Lippi, was born in 1457. In 1461 Pope Pius II granted him a dispensation to marry. In 1465 Lippi completed his painting in the Cathedral at Prato and from 1467 until his death there in 1469 he worked in the Cathedral of Spoleto.

Fig. 1 Before restoration

2. *The Virgin and Child with a donor, St John the Baptist and St George*
Central panel 42.3 × 26.8, wings 11.7 × 43.5 cm (average measurements)
Fitzwilliam Museum

Berenson in 1950 considered that this and the painting of the same donor about to be presented to the enthroned Virgin and Child in the Cini collection in Venice might be *modelli* for larger works. Although this hypothesis does not seem very likely, an attribution to Lippi himself, proposed independently by Philip Pouncey and confirmed by Marchini in his monograph on Lippi (1975), is now generally accepted. The date remains uncertain. The influence of Masaccio, particularly evident in the figure of St John, implies an early date and certainly one before 1437.

Fig. 2 After restoration

Cleaning (figs. 1 and 2) removed the doubts over the attribution to Lippi. The framing of the triptych, although regilded, was found to be largely original. The central panel was covered with linen before the gesso was applied. A repair to the panel itself has caused the linen to be slightly buckled lower right. The gesso layer of the wings is applied directly to the wood. The wings on the reverse have been toned brown. Traces of a paint layer beneath remain, but are too fragmentary to indicate whether any decoration was present. Both wings proved to be in very much better condition than the central panel. The panels were gilded before painting; the darker band down the right side of St George shows where the paint significantly overlaps the gilding. This practice was generally avoided as paint layers tend to flake from a gilded surface. The central panel had suffered extensive loss to the gilding and to the Madonna's robe. Indeed, after the removal of overpaint and putties there were only traces of red modelling above the Madonna's lap. These were identified as the organic red, kermes. The lake glaze here had been applied to the gesso. Kermes mixed with lead white was used for the mid tones and was identified in St George's cloak. After several experiments with neutral toning, a schematic rendering of the Virgin's robe was effected in thin tempera over the bare ground. Elsewhere retouching was confined to toning the bare gesso in the background and on the halo, and spot retouching of losses throughout.

Ian McClure, Anna Sandén

Luis de Morales (c. 1520–1586)

Morales lived in Estremadura, where he was probably born. He is thought to have studied with the Flemish artist Pedro de Campana who worked in Seville c. 1537. Campana's work combined both Flemish and Italian traditions and similar influences, particularly that of Leonardo's followers, can be noted in Morales' work. Morales was official painter to Juan de Ribera, Bishop of Badajoz. In 1564 his *Via Crucis* was given by Philip II of Spain to the Monastery of S. Jeronimo at Madrid and he may have worked at the Escorial. In 1576 he painted a retable for the cathedral at Elvas in Portugal. He died at Badajoz in 1586.

3. *Pietà*
Oil on panel, 85 × 66.5 cm
Church of SS Peter and Paul, Ospringe, Kent

The painting is one of the most elaborate of Morales' compositions. It was taken from Spain during the Peninsular War by Marshal Soult and later was part of the Stirling Maxwell collection. It was first lent to the museum at the instance of St John's College by the Parish Council of the Church of SS Peter and Paul, Ospringe, Kent, to whom it had been given by Captain Hastings Weber in memory of Elizabeth Townsend Weber.

Before cleaning (fig. 1) the painting was covered by at least two thick varnish layers, which had developed heavy craquelure patterns and were extremely discoloured. Cleaning revealed the remarkable condition of the painting (fig. 2). Removal of extensive retouches on the hair and veil of the Magdalen revealed that the transparent veil had been mistaken for a varnish defect, and partially cleaned away with the hair, and the milky glaze of the veil where it passed over the green robe was obliterated. Special care was taken in cleaning the vulnerable area of silver or tin gilded hatching on St John's tunic.

The panel was prepared with a gesso layer of gypsum. Some undermodelling in brownish and greyish tones was executed under blue, green and red areas, often slightly modified – with azurite and copper resinate under Elizabeth's gown, for example. The robe of the Virgin was painted in azurite – no ultramarine was found. Shadows were worked with an organic red glaze in a brown medium and are now probably strengthened by the darkened medium. The green proved to be copper resinate, the pink shawl built up with a layer of organic red mixed with lead white: the organic red is probably Brazil wood.

Various pentimenti were visible in Mary's hand and in other more minor adjustments of contours, in the right shoulder of both Mary and Christ and in the fingers of Mary's left hand.

Retouching of losses was carried out in egg tempera with Laropal K80 resin glazes. Thin glazes were also used to soften the line of transition between Christ's jawline and beard where lost glazing and the increasing transparency of the paint layer caused the underlying light imprimatura to become obtrusive.

Ian McClure, Ella Hendriks

Fig. 1 Before restoration

Fig. 2 After restoration

Marcus Gheeraedts the Younger (1561/2–1636)

Born in Bruges, he was brought to London by his father Marcus the Elder, painter and engraver, to avoid religious persecution. A pupil of De Heere, his career prospered; from 1609 he was commissioned to paint royal portraits, and by 1618 he was referred to 'as picture drawer to his Majesty'.

4. *Portrait of a Woman* (1601)
Oil on Panel, 113.7 × 83.8 cm
Her Majesty the Queen

When examined before treatment the paint was flaking in some areas, the varnish was noticeably discoloured, and retouchings were dark and unsightly and covered much of the original paint. The removal of the old discoloured varnish and retouchings revealed large losses, particularly in the woman's left sleeve (fig. 1).

The pattern on the cloth of the dress was complex and it was not possible to re-create with certainty the design over these large losses. The reconstruction would, therefore, be to some extent conjectural. It was decided that the retouchings should be made so that they were indistinguishable from the surrounding original paint at a normal viewing distance but clearly not original on close examination. This effect was achieved by first painting a base-colour (in egg tempera) which was slightly lighter than the surrounding original paint. Then, using ×4 magnification, tiny lines in a darker shade or the same colour were painted on top. These blended with the base-colour when seen from a normal viewing distance. The dark red pattern was painted in the same way (fig. 2). Small losses, where there was no doubt about the reconstruction, were more closely matched (fig. 3).

Sara Lee

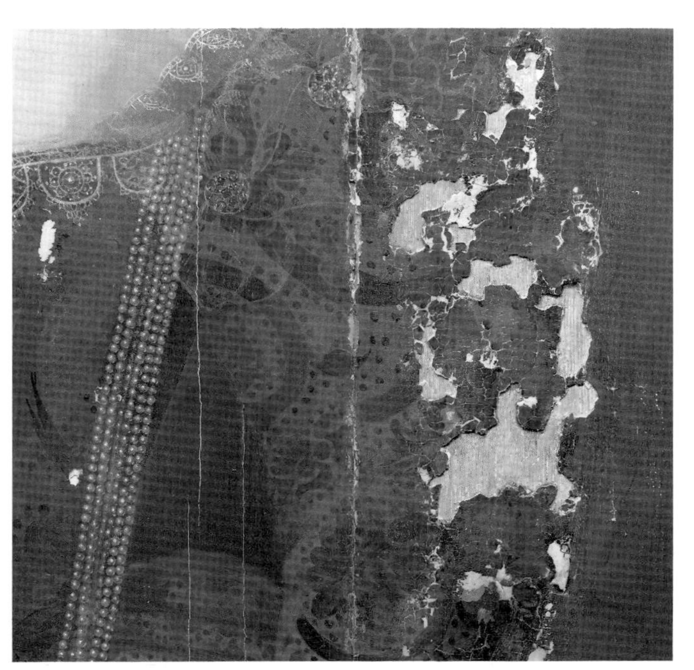

Fig. 1 Detail of sleeve after cleaning

Fig. 2 After cleaning, before restoration

Fig. 3 After restoration

Robert Peake (c. 1551–1619)

Peake painted portraits after the types developed by George Gower and Sir William Segar, based on the Hilliardesque portrait style. His career spanned the reigns of Elizabeth I and James I. In 1576-8 he was in the pay of the Office of the Revels. His name appears on a list of artists published by Francis Meres in the 'Palladis Tamia' (1598), indicating he was considered one of the most important painters practicing in England. The only signed painting known at present is a portrait of an unknown military commander dated 1593. In 1604 he was appointed painter to Henry, Prince of Wales. In 1607 he is recorded as holding the 'Office of Sergeant Painter' jointly with John de Critz. He seems to have been succeeded by Isaac Oliver as the 'picture-maker' to the Prince of Wales shortly before the death of Prince Henry in 1612. Peake died in 1619.

5. *Prince Charles, Duke of York* (1613)
Oil on canvas, 158 × 87.4 cm
The Old Schools, University of Cambridge

Charles, son of James I and younger brother of Henry, Prince of Wales, was created Duke of York in 1605, and Prince of Wales in 1616 after his elder brother's death in 1612. He succeeded his father to the throne in 1625. In 1649 he was executed.

The portrait commemorates the Duke of York's visit to Cambridge in 1613. It is the only documented painting by Peake. Payment was made to the painter on July 13th 1613 of £13.6s.8d. 'in full satisfaction for Prince Charles his picture'.

The painting shows the young Duke of York in a pink garment standing beside a table with a green velvety table cloth. The dark background is seen through the parted yellow curtains. His white hat ornamented with pearls and golden jewels is lying on the table. A piece of paper showing a Latin inscription is pinned to the curtain on the left. The inscription, translated into English, reads as follows:

Charles, we the Muses, since you deigned to agree to both, have both welcomed you as our guest and painted you in humble duty. Visiting the University in the 10th year of his father's reign over England, on March 4, he was enrolled in the ranks of the Masters and admitted in this Senate House by Valentine Carey Vice-Chancellor. (J. W. Goodison: *Catalogue of Cambridge Portraits,* Cambridge 1955 pp. 16–17).

When the painting was cleaned at the Institute (fig. 1), examination under the microscope showed the presence of another painting underneath the thin grey priming layer of the visible painting. In raking light the impasto of ornaments on the tablecloth and highlights in the curtains are visible, which do not correspond with the ornaments and highlights on the surface.

Whereas changes in paintings and whole areas being overpainted is not uncommon, it is very rare to find an entire painting completely covered with a new ground before a second series of paint layers. The colouring of the first and second painting seems to differ considerably: underneath the yellow curtains the colour of the first painting was red glazed on black, underneath the pink breeches, brushstrokes in yellow ochre and red were found.

In addition to the differences in colours an X-radiograph of the head showed another head beneath, slightly lower and on a slightly larger scale (fig. 2). An X-radiograph of the whole painting would provide more interesting information about the underlying painting. Was a painted canvas re-used by Peake or was the portrait of Charles extensively reworked? The different scale might suggest that the sitter was first painted three-quarter length or seated.

Renate Woudhuysen-Keller, Karen Ashworth, Sally Thirkettle

Fig. 1 After restoration

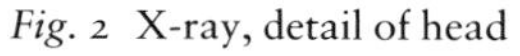

Fig. 2 X-ray, detail of head

Jan Brueghel the Elder (1568–1625)

The son of Pieter Brueghel the Elder, born in Brussels, he was commonly known as 'Velvet' Brueghel. He studied with Pieter Goedkindt and in 1589/90 went to Italy. He was in Naples in 1590 and Rome from 1592 to 1595, and then in Milan, patronised by Cardinal Federico Borromeo. Later he visited Germany and was in Prague in 1604. In 1609 he was appointed Court Painter to the Archduke Albert and the Infanta Isabella at Brussels, although Brueghel continued to live in Antwerp. A friend and collaborator of Rubens, he was particularly renowned for his landscapes. Apart from his sons his only pupil was Daniel Seghers who specialised in flower-painting. Brueghel died in Antwerp.

6. *A Vase of Flowers*
Oil on panel (oak), 60.3 × 42.2 cm
Fitzwilliam Museum

Klaus Entz expressed doubts in his entry on the painting in Vienna (no. 558) in the catalogue *(Bruegel: Une dynastie de peintres*, Brussels, Palais des Beaux Arts, 1980, no. 126) as to the autograph status of this picture which he considers a replica of the painting in Prague. The Prague painting (Ertz, *Jan Brueghel der Ältere*, Cologne 1975, no. 166) is not signed. Although it is larger than the Fitzwilliam painting, the quality judged from photographs does not seem quite so exquisite. There are several differences between the two paintings, although the distribution of flowers is closely similar. Most notable is the presence at the top of the Fitzwilliam painting of a tulip and a snow-drop, whereas these are replaced in the Prague picture by an iris. There are more insects scattered through the Cambridge picture, and on the shelf the ring and jewellery are replaced in Prague by a strawberry.

The cleaning of the painting has revealed it to be of first rate quality (fig. 1) and it is likely that the painting in Prague depends on the Fitzwilliam picture rather than *vice versa*. Before treatment the surface was covered with a layer of discoloured varnish. The paint layer proved to be in excellent condition with only slight abrasion to some of the lake glazes and fine detail such as the legs of insects. Extensive overpaint was found to cover the loosely painted 'imprimatura' layer behind the bouquet. This was removed. Examination with infrared reflectography revealed the presence of underdrawing probably on top of the imprimatura layer, although this is not clear in cross-sections. The drawing is sketchy (fig. 2) – shapes of flowers merely indicated, and the painting departs considerably from the drawing.

Ian McClure, Sarah Murray

Fig. 1 After restoration

Fig. 2 Detail of infrared reflectograph assembly

Sir Anthony van Dyck (1599–1641)

Born in Antwerp, Van Dyck studied with Hendrik van Balen and was registered as a master in the Guild of St Luke in 1618. Much influenced by Rubens, who referred to him as 'the best of my pupils', van Dyck first visited England in 1620. From 1621 to 1627 he was in Italy, mostly in Genoa but also travelling as far as Sicily. He returned to Antwerp to establish his studio there and by 1630 was described as painter to the Regent, the widowed Archduchess Isabella. In 1632 he went back to London and later that year was 'Principal Painter in Ordinary to their Majesties'. Charles I knighted him and granted him an annual pension in 1633. Van Dyck amassed a fine collection of paintings including nineteen Titians. Apart from a visit to Flanders from 1634 to 1635 and again late in 1640, with a journey to Paris early in 1641, van Dyck stayed for the most of his life in England. He married Mary Ruthven in 1640 and died in France 1641.

Fig. 1 After restoration

7. *William Laud, Archbishop of Canterbury*
Canvas, 121.6 × 97 cm
Fitzwilliam Museum

Laud (1573-1645) was the son of a Reading draper. Educated at Oxford, he was patronized by the Duke of Buckingham. In 1621 he was Bishop of St David's, in 1626 of Bath and Wells, in 1628 of London and in 1633 he became Archbishop of Canterbury. An anti-Puritan, he was a sound and practical administrator, devoted to the King and dedicated to enforcing uniformity of worship in the English Church. He was impeached in December 1640, imprisoned in the Tower and beheaded in 1645. A fine Hebrew scholar, he collected Oriental manuscripts which he presented to Oxford; he was Chancellor of the University and had the Canterbury quadrangle at St John's built at his expense. Michael Jaffé has shown (in 'Van Dyck Studies I: The Portrait of Archbishop Laud', *Burlington Magazine* vol. cxxiv, October 1982, p. 600 ff.) that the likely date of this portrait is 1635, and that the composition is inspired by Titian and dependent on Van Dyck's own portrait of *Cesare Scaglia, Abbate di Staffada* of 1634 (collection of Lord Camrose).

Cleaning revealed the superior quality of the portrait, which had previously been dismissed by scholars (apart from its former owner Charles Ricketts) as a good but secondary version of the painting now in the Hermitage.

The cleaning and restoration of the painting (fig. 1) provided the opportunity for a thorough examination of the painting technique. The existence of the version of the portrait in the Hermitage, Leningrad and of another in Lambeth Palace, London, made this of particular interest.

The result of the examination may be summarized as follows: the portrait was painted on a canvas covered with a streaky light grey ground over a light pink priming. On this luminous surface the features of the face and hands were laid out in broad sketchy brushstrokes in various gradations of brown. The flesh was then painted wet-in-wet almost totally alla prima, including the underpainting for the ruff. Osias Humphrey described Van Dyck employing this procedure. In the draperies, however, a rough underpaint is visible which must have been reasonably dry before the next paint layer was applied, since the brush strokes lie undisturbed under the second paint layer. The handling of the paint indicates a certain speed and assuredness; the slight changes made during the course of painting to the ruff, the sitter's left sleeve and the outline of the sitter's right hand suggest that this portrait was spontaneously painted from the life rather than copied from an existing painting. The sketch for a portrait of a bearded man wearing a wheel ruff in the Ashmolean Museum, Oxford (fig. 2) shows that Van Dyck did paint the face wet-in-wet to the finished stage during the first sitting, leaving the surrounding draperies to be painted later in the studio. This technique was probably employed in this portrait. The head, ruff and hands were painted first in a single sitting, the paint being applied wet-in-wet without preparatory layers. The draperies and background consist of an underlayer and later alla prima modelling.

This explains the apparent inconsistency between the face being one paint layer applied wet-in-wet and the background being several layers, as the background was worked up later in the studio without the sitter, using studio props. In the portrait of Cesare Alessandro Scaglia, Van Dyck used the same column and curtain as background.

The mastery evident in this painting is in the economy of means. The painter did not have to repeat his brush strokes to make a feature more precise. The precision and confidence of the brushwork is a very striking characteristic of this portrait and shows the very skilled hand of a self-confident painter rather than the necessarily more reluctant hand of a copyist.

Renate Woudhuysen-Keller, Karin Groen

Fig. 2 Portrait of a Bearded Man in a Wheel Ruff (Ashmolean Museum)

Jan Steen (1626–1679)

After restoration

Taught by Nicholas Knüpfer, Adrien van Ostade and his future father-in law Jan van Goyen, Steen became one of the founder members of the St Luke's Guild in Leiden in 1648. He leased a brewery between 1654 and 1657. He settled in Haarlem in 1661 and entered the guild. He returned to Leiden in 1670 on the death of his father. In 1672 he opened an inn and remarried in 1673 after his first wife's death in 1669. Steen was a productive painter who produced portraits, history and religious subjects as well as the interior scenes with which he is so closely identified.

8. *The Burgher of Delft and his Daughter* (1655)
Oil on canvas, 82.5 × 68.6 cm
Private collection, United Kingdom

Cleaning confirmed that this painting is in a good state of preservation. However, there was a fine network of cracks over the entire surface, emphasised by the fact that the paint was thin and often very worn along the edges of the cracks. This was possibly the result of a previously insensitive lining, but was more probably caused by harsh cleaning when the paint surface was badly cupped. This network of cracks, with adjacent wearing through to the salmon-pink ground, gave the picture a flat appearance and destroyed the perspective.

Keith Laing

Pieter de Hooch (1629–1684)

Fig. 1 After restoration

Born in Rotterdam, de Hooch is mentioned as a pupil of Nicolaes Berchem, presumably at Haarlem. In 1653 he is mentioned as a servant and painter working for Justus de la Grange, a cloth-merchant who lived at Delft and Leiden. De Hooch married in Delft in 1654 and entered the Delft guild in 1655. By 1661 he had moved to Amsterdam where he remained until his death in 1684.

9. *Courtyard with an Arbour and Drinkers 1658*
Oil on canvas, later marouflaged, 68 × 57.5 cm
Private collection

Previously owned by the Empress Josephine, this is one of de Hooch's finest paintings (fig. 1). None of his pictures is dated earlier than 1658, but his earliest genre interiors seem to be in the style of the Haarlem and Amsterdam barrack room painters. The paintings of 1658 and those painted immediately before and after are in the new Delft style initiated by Carel Fabritius, which finds its greatest expression in the work of de Hooch's Delft period and of Vermeer. The scene is

Fig. 2 In raking light

Fig. 3 Detail in infrared

probably a composite invention: the wall at the right assembles sections of the Old Town Hall, the glimpse through the alley suggests a site on the Oude Delft or the Binnenwatersloot and the inscription on the plaque over the archway, which reappears in the *Courtyard in Delft* of the same year in the National Gallery (no. 835), originally hung over the entrance of the Hieronymusdael Cloister in Delft and still survives in the garden behind no. 157 Oude Delft. It reads: 'This is in St Jerome's vale, if you wish to repair to patience and meekness. For we must first descend if we wish to be raised, 1646.'

The canvas has been stuck to an oak panel. Viewed in raking light (fig. 2) the grain of the panel appears in addition to the texture of the canvas. It seems likely that the painting was not lined before this operation was carried out and that the gluing was done with light pressure as the impasto is wonderfully preserved and there is a pattern of craquelure which has not been pressed down. The discoloured varnish had only been partially removed in a previous restoration, leaving areas such as the highlights in the woman's dress toned down. Further application of varnish which had subsequently discoloured had rendered these highlights darker than the mid-tones, thus rendering many passages of the painting flat. Cleaning revealed the painting to be in superb condition with only a few spot losses. Retouches to worn glazing on the foliage and to reduce pentiments were removed, as was the strengthening of outlines on the furniture visible through the window on the left. Retouching was confined to retouching losses and glazing leaves where traces of a green glaze still remained. Infrared photography revealed a number of alterations. In addition to a balustrade now painted out, visible through the courtyard, the seated figure to the left had several adjustments made to his pose, and the position of the glass in the woman's hand was changed (fig. 3).

Ian McClure

Jan Asselijn (c. 1615–1652)

Asselijn was born either at Dieppe or at Diemen, near Amsterdam, about 1615. Probably the pupil of Jan Martens the younger, between 1635 and 1642 at the latest he went to Rome where he was made a member of the Netherlandish artistic colony, the Bentveughels, with the nickname Krabbetje (little crab), a reference to a deformity of his left hand. On his return from Italy he worked in France and Antwerp and by 1647 he was back in Amsterdam.

10. *Italian coast scene*
Oil on copper, 12.7 × 25.1 cm
Fitzwilliam Museum

An unusually small painting on copper by this gifted Italianising landscape painter. Influenced to some extent by Pieter van Laer and aware of the work of both Jan Both and Claude Lorrain, Asselijn in his turn had a marked influence on other Netherlandish artists who painted in the Italian idiom, notably Adam Pijnacker, Karel Dujardin and Nicolaes Berchem.

The thin panel had several raised bumps, particularly on the lower edge, which may have occured when the panel was fixed into the frame with nails. There was a crooked scratch in the sea through the prow of the boat in the centre. The varnish layer appeared to have been partially removed and the tower and foliage on the left were extensively overpainted. A line is visible, in some places more deeply indented than in others, running around the edges of the panel, probably due to framing the picture before the paint layer was completely dry.

The most prominent distortions in the panel where paint had been lost were levelled as far as possible. After varnishing losses were filled and retouched in egg tempera with synthetic resin glazes.

Ian McClure, Sally Thirkettle

After restoration

Jan Griffier the Elder (c. 1652–1718)

Jan Griffier was born in Amsterdam between 1652 and 1656 and was trained there by Roelandt Roghman who specialised in landscapes. Griffier began his career as a flower-painter but soon abandoned this for landscape. He studied the works of Salomon van Ruysdael and Johannes Lingelbach and was most influenced by Herman Saftleven. Griffier came to England soon after 1666 and had considerable success with his topographical views. He died in London.

11. *A View on the Rhine*
Oil on copper, 34.3 × 25.2 cm
Fitzwilliam Museum

A characteristic example of Griffier's decorative landscapes. This river and mountain landscape shows the clear influence of Herman Saftleven to whom the painting was at one time attributed. It was probably painted in the first decade of the eighteenth century and is stylistically comparable with a picture at Dresden (no. 1675) which is signed and dated 'J. Griffier 1708, London'.

Painted on a copper panel 1 mm thick, the painting has a slight S-curve in the vertical profile and has also been slightly twisted across the diagonal, possibly through poor handling and fitting into the frame. Apart from minor losses, principally about the lower edges, the painting is in good condition. In refitting the panel care was taken not to flex the panel as movement and local pressure could lead to paint loss.

Ian McClure, Larry Keith

After restoration

Johann Zoffany (1733–1810)

Johannes Josephus Zauffaly was born in Germany near Frankfurt. After an apprenticeship in Regensburg and further studies in Rome (where he may have been a pupil of Mengs), he came to England in the 1760s and began signing his works Zoffany. Johann Zoffany became an English artist by adoption and excelled in the art of conversation pieces or 'family pieces'. This type of portraiture was extremely popular in the 18th century; Hogarth and Gainsborough painted many such group portraits. Zoffany's conversation pieces, such as this portrait of the Woodley family, are painted with meticulous attention to detail, and although the setting and grouping of the family members are obviously artificial, the result is one of lively animation.

Fig. 1 After restoration

12. *Group Portrait of the Woodley Family*
Oil on canvas, 114 × 168 cm
National Trust, Kingston Lacy

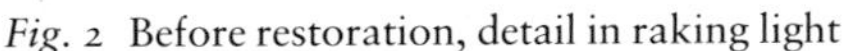

Fig. 2 Before restoration, detail in raking light

Fig. 3 Detail of the original stretcher

Zoffany's portrait of the Woodley family is of special interest because it is exceptionally well preserved. It is unlined, and apart from a very few minor repairs, practically untouched by previous restorations, (fig. 1). However, years of benign neglect had finally allowed the condition of the painting to deteriorate to the extent that some treatment was necessary in order to prevent further physical deterioration. There was a considerable layer of surface dirt and a thick discoloured varnish, and in addition the craquelure system was sufficiently raised to be very disturbing. Bulges and buckles had formed in the corners of the painting and there was a small tear near the dog's hind legs (fig. 2). Since an unlined painting of the 18th century is very rare, the structural treatment was kept to the absolute minimum and the painting was left unlined.

The original 5-member stretcher was very crudely made: roughly hewn pine members of slightly unequal length (± 3 cm) were half-lap joined and secured with three nails in each corner (fig. 3). The wood had split in places and had warped. Only the exterior sides of the centre cross-bar were chamfered; otherwise there was no bevel and the canvas rested directly on the stretcher bars. Since the stretcher was fixed it could not be keyed out when the canvas slackened as a response to changes in relative humidity.

The canvas is finely woven (20 threads/cm^2) and obviously extremely sensitive to injury and changes in relative humidity. Various irregular craquelure patterns remain as evidence of former injuries. The spiral craquelure, for example, to the right of the dog is the result of a knock. Due to the poor quality of the support and the variable climatic conditions to which the painting was exposed, the paint layer has cracked noticeably. Only where the paint layer was protected by the stretcher bars is there relatively little craquelure.

In addition to the prominent raised craquelure, the painting is covered completely but irregularly with minute lumps (unrelated to the painted form). Analysis proved the lumps to be calcite crystals in the chalk of the first ground layer. There are three ground layers: the first and second are white, composed of lead white and chalk; the third is grey, charcoal and some yellow ochre having been added to the lead white and chalk. The ground layers are very powdery, with poor adhesion to the canvas. The tacking edges are narrow and slightly frayed. In addition to the tacks, there are pinholes along the tacking edges and also on the front of the painting along the edge just under the frame. Some of these holes had caused local damage to the paint layer and had been retouched.

Removal of the varnish layer revealed the paint layer in excellent condition, undamaged by lining or previous cleaning. The impasto of the highlights, uncrushed by lining, causes the silk dresses to glitter. Yellowish stains in the sky remained, however, possibly the artist's 'oiling out' during painting. Also, a thin glaze or varnish layer extended over the entire foreground stopping 1 cm before the turnover edge, and so not covering the thin band of paint underneath the frame. This layer was not removed. The slight unevenness in the sky was lightly glazed with MS2A resin during restoration.

After the painting had been removed from its stretcher, thick cakes of tightly packed dirt and straw could be scraped off the back of the canvas. This foreign material, which was causing protrusions in the canvas, had become so tightly lodged behind the lower stretcher bar that previous attempts to dislodge it had been unsuccessful. The narrow tacking edge of the original canvas was reinforced and lengthened with a fringed band of linen canvas adhered with Beva 371 film. The canvas was of sufficient length that it could be used to prestretch the painting onto a loom. With the canvas tautly stretched on the loom, the Willard's low-pressure table was used to provide the humidity and slight warmth necessary to relax the canvas and paint. The paint film relaxed significantly and the painting was stretched immediately onto a conventional keyed stretcher with bevelled edges. In order to protect the painting from fluctuations in relative humidity which might occur in a country house, a canvas coated with two layers of Laropal K80 'matt' varnish (which contains a very high proportion of Cosmolloid 80H wax) was first fixed onto the new stretcher. This loose lining in addition supported and protected the delicate original canvas without adhesion.

The loose paint around the small tear was secured with isinglass (fish glue) before beginning treatment. While the painting was stretched on the loom the threads were relined and pressed, then welded together with droplets of a polyamide resin applied with a hot needle. No further consolidation or patch was necessary. The painting was varnished with MS2A resin and restored with egg tempera underpainting and glazes in MS2A resin on top of chalk/gelatin fillings.

Ann Massing

Thomas Gainsborough (1727-1788)

Born in Sudbury, Suffolk, Gainsborough was sent to London as a pupil of Gravelot c. 1740. He returned to practise in Sudbury in 1748. In 1759 his increasing reputation as a portrait painter led him to try his fortune in Bath. This proved successful and his move to London in 1774 reflected his high status as portrait painter. From 1781 he received many royal commissions.

13. *Lady Margaret Downing*
Oil on canvas, 127 × 101 cm
Downing College, Cambridge

This portrait has recently been re-attributed to Gainsborough (fig. 1). It is very close in composition to the portrait of Mrs William Leyborne in Bristol Art Gallery which can be dated to 1763. Previous restoration had considerably distorted its appearance. The surface was lumpy and uneven and the background uniformly overpainted to give the image a flat appearance. The exuberant modelling of the dress was concealed by a very discoloured layer of varnish.

The painting had been lined with a glue-paste lining. However, this was very poorly executed. A large number of blister-like lumps were visible, distorting the paint surface. Some of these were single, others in arched chains, one beside the other. Close inspection revealed that the distortions were not just in the paint-layer, but that they affected the canvas as well (fig. 2).

Whatever the cause of the lumps, they had to sit between the original and the lining canvas. It was decided to remove the relining canvas. After the painting had been cleaned, and all the putties and previous retouchings removed from the surface, a facing of eltoline tissue was applied with carboxy-methyl cellulose paste. Once the canvases were removed from the stretcher, the relining canvas was peeled away in narrow strips, as the adhesion of the old lining paste was still very strong. It was then seen that the lining paste had not been applied evenly, but in broad irregular brush-strokes (fig. 3). In some areas the brush had left particularly thick ridges, and large drops of paste that had fallen off the freshly-dipped brush had not been spread out. During drying these thick layers of paste developed considerable tension, because the paste contracted due to loss of volume as the water evaporated. Thus strong cupping developed at the back of the canvas, which showed as lumps at the front. As the adhesion was so strong, the original canvas and paint-layer had to

Fig. 1 After restoration

Fig. 2 Detail showing distortions to paint surface

follow the distorting movement.

After the old glue had been removed, the original canvas was stretched on a loom and with humidity and gentle heat relaxed, and the lumps levelled out. The painting was then relined, using a mixture of beeswax and synthetic resin as an adhesive.

During cleaning a pentiment, which had been covered by earlier retouchings, came to light. At first, Gainsborough had portrayed Lady Downing with her left arm still slightly raised holding the rose in front of her as if she had just been smelling it, as in the portrait of Mrs. Leyborne. In the final version he altered the arm holding the rose, placing its pink petals and green leaves against the white and pearly grey of the lace dress.

Renate Woudhuysen-Keller

Fig. 3 Detail showing application of glue-paste in previous lining

George Stubbs (1724–1806)

Born in Liverpool, he was largely self taught as both a painter and engraver. A brief stay in Rome, 1754–6, made little impression apart from his 'Lion Attacking a Horse' series based on an antique marble in the Palazzo dei Conservatori. After establishing himself in London after 1760, he became known as a painter of horses and wild animals. His interest in anatomy was paralleled by his interest in paint media and supports. Many of his paintings as a result are exceptionally vulnerable to cleaning solvents and heat. His collaboration with Josiah Wedgwood to produce paintings in enamel on ceramic plaques produced a durable medium: an example, *Una and the Lion*, hangs in the Fitzwilliam Museum.

14. *Gimcrack with John Pratt up on Newmarket Heath* (c. 1765)
Oil on canvas, 100 × 124 cm
Fitzwilliam Museum

Gimcrack was one of the most famous race-horses in England in the 18th century. He began his career at Epsom in 1764 and in 1765 first ran at Newmarket,

Fig. 1 After restoration

winning his first victory there in the colours of William Wildman, a Smithfield sheep salesman for whom this picture was painted. The jockey, John Pratt, was Lord Bolingbroke's riding groom, but the colours he is wearing are Wildman's. Bolingbroke bought the horse from Wildman and it was for him that Gimcrack won his most famous victory, a match for 1,000 guineas against Sir James Lowther's Ascham.

Stubb's painting technique and the unusual painting media he used often present the restorer with problems. The painting had developed a pronounced craquelure pattern with a very cupped surface (fig. 1). This type of crack pattern is due to tension in the ground-layer containing too much medium. For the painter a strongly bound ground had the advantage of being quite hard and could be polished to an enamel-like smoothness. It was also less absorbent to the oil-paint and allowed a more fluid brush-stroke.

The ground in this painting has a pinkish colour. This plays an important part in the changing hues of the clouds. The cracks in the ground run as an even rhythm all over the painting, indicating the position and width of the original stretcher-bars and the points of impact where subsequent concentric crack-patterns have formed. Such patterns, due to the painter's preparation of the ground, if exhibited sympathetically are acceptable to the present-day viewer. This pattern was completely painted out and cupping filled with a thick layer of varnish in a previous restoration. It would be even less obtrusive if the surface was not cupped (figs. 2 and 3). The painting has been relined, probably in an attempt to reduce the cupping. The adhesive is glue-paste. Even though the unevenness of the surface does not present any risk to the paint-layer, it is aesthetically slightly disturbing. Attempts to improve matters by slightly relaxing the cupping with water vapour and very gentle heat (40°C) under slight vacuum pressure were only partly successful, as the glue-paste must have taken the shape of the cupped canvas during the relining process and was now holding it in that shape. The only way to solve this problem would be to remove the relining canvas and adhesive before again trying to relax the original canvas and ground. However, since the paintings by Stubbs are invariably very delicate and as there is at present no danger to the paint-layer, it was decided that the possible aesthetic gains would not justify the potential risks to the painting during a second relining procedure.

There is a second system of craquelure visible in the painting which is also indirectly caused by the ground, and which appears in the dark areas only. The paint-layer forms wide cracks exposing the light colour of the ground. Early drying cracks are formed as a consequence of an excess of oil and its shrinking during the drying process. Since dark pigments absorb much more oil than light ones during the paint-making process, early drying cracks tend to form in dark areas unless the oil is absorbed by the ground. Since the ground in this painting is not very absorbent, drying cracks have appeared in the horse and the foreground. Areas were retouched to reduce the cracks to the width of the ordinary craquelure. Making them disappear altogether would have caused dark patches in the even rhythm of craquelure.

Fig. 2 Detail of cupping before treatment

Fig. 3 Detail of cupping after treatment

Renate Woudhuysen-Keller

Marie-Louise Elizabeth Vigée-Le Brun (1755–1842)

The daughter of a pastel painter, Vigée-Le Brun showed talent at an early age. Encouraged by her father, she was supporting her family by the age of 15. In 1776 she began to paint portraits of members of the royal family. A chance meeting, it is said, led to the many portraits of Marie Antoinette. The Queen's influence made her a member of the Academie Royale in 1783. She escaped to Italy after the revolution and thereafter travelled extensively, achieving recognition and success in Rome, Vienna, St Petersburg, Moscow, England and Switzerland, before returning in 1810 to settle in France, as her *Souvenirs* published in 1835 and 1837 recount. She exhibited at the Salon until 1824. After her death a gravestone carved with a palette and brushes was erected as she requested.

After restoration

15. *Self-portrait*
Oil on canvas, 103 × 84 cm
National Trust, Ickworth

The 4th Earl of Bristol and Bishop of Derry commissioned this version of the *Self-portrait* now in the Uffizi while in Naples in 1791; the portrait of Marie Antoinette which the artist is painting was prudently replaced in the Earl Bishop's version by a portrait of the artist's daughter. The lined painting was in generally good condition, although obscured by discoloured varnish. After cleaning it was noticed that a strip of unfaded red glaze on the artist's sash survived where protected by the frame rebate on the bottom edge. After cleaning the painting was varnished with MS2A and retouches effected with Paraloid B72, an acrylic resin.

Alec Cobbe

François-Xavier Fabre (1766–1837)

Fabre was born and trained in Montpellier. In 1783 he registered at the School of the Academie Royale in Paris as a pupil of David. In 1787 Fabre won the Grand Prix de Rome. He stayed in Rome until 1793 when he left the city for Florence because of the hostility of the Roman government towards the republican French. On Hubert Robert's advice Fabre did not return to Paris where the situation remained turbulent, but stayed in Florence, where he met Vittorio Alfieri and the Comtesse d'Albany who with Lord Bristol introduced him to several English patrons, notably Lord Holland. Fabre visited Paris in 1806 and 1809–10 but was based in Florence until 1826, two years after the death of the Comtesse d'Albany, when he returned to Montpellier. There he set up a Museum, the Musée Fabre, which was inaugurated in 1828. He died in Montpellier in 1837.

16. *Allen Smith contemplating Florence across the Arno* 1797
Oil on canvas, 70.9 × 90.5 cm
Fitzwilliam Museum

Of Allen Smith little is known. As a tourist travelling in Italy he must have been a man of means, as he commissioned no fewer than five paintings from Fabre. The Comtesse d'Albany in a letter to Lord Holland refers to these commissions. 'He [Smith] has made large purchases of paintings and ordered three from Fabre as well as two portraits, one large as life is the middle of the ruins of ancient Rome.' An oil-sketch in the Musée Fabre (inv. 837-1-156), clearly inspired by Tischbein's portrait of Goethe (Staedel, Frankfurt), is probably Fabre's first idea for the portrait of Smith. Neither that nor the completed painting shows the ruins of ancient Rome, and it is likely that both the changes in posture between the *modello* and the finished painting and the inclusion of the view of Florence (Rome was not the safest place for a Frenchman to visit in 1797) were ordered by Smith. A letter from Fabre to Lord Holland dated 24 August 1797 probably refers to this painting: 'As for the composition of M. Smith's picture, your guess is perfectly correct: the honour of the composition is entirely his. My only merit is in the execution.'

The discoloured overpaint covering an old tear, about 11 cm long, in the upper right quarter of the painting was removed during restoration.

Alec Cobbe

After restoration

Charles François Daubigny (1817–1878)

Daubigny first achieved fame as an engraver. From 1834 he began to paint in the outskirts of Paris and particularly in the Forest of Fontainebleau. His reputation was established by 1853 with the award of a gold medal at the Salon. Through his membership of the jury of the Salon of 1868 works by Pissarro and Monet were accepted. He recognised Cézanne's talent when they met in 1872.

17. *Villerville, Normandy*
Oil on panel, 25.1 × 41.0 cm
Fitzwilliam Museum

Villerville-sur-Mer was one of Daubigny's favourite sites on the Normandy coast, where he first painted in 1859. The looseness of handling and spontaneous appearance of this small sketch argue for it having been painted on the spot. The date, misread in the Museum catalogue as 1886 (eight years after Daubigny's death), probably reads 1876 although Robert Hellebranth (*C. F. Daubigny*, 1976, no. 623) reads it as 1874.

The painting is on a thin wooden panel and is made up of two pieces with the grain running horizontally. The panel is in good condition with hardly any warp. The paint is in a good state with only a few very minor paint losses restricted to the edges of the panel where the frame has caused some abrasions. In these areas a dark brown underlayer is visible.

The painting was brush varnished with MS2A resin and retouched using the same medium as the varnish. The painting was given a spray varnish of MS2A and a final coat of MS2A with a small proportion of Cosmolloid wax added.

Mary Allden

18. *On the River Oise*
Oil on panel, 24.5 × 46.3 cm
Fitzwilliam Museum

A characteristic late example of Daubigny's work on the Oise, probably painted in the late 1860s or early 1870s. From 1856 he had regularly worked from his floating studio 'Le Botin', exploring the River Oise and the Seine, often in the company of his son, Karl. The present painting has been made over an earlier painting, so that there are several pentimenti visible. These are especially noticeable in the sky where the dark shapes of tree trunks are now just discernible. In raking light textural changes, due to the painting underneath, are also visible. The first painting was obviously scraped down by the artist before he proceeded with the second and indentations in the paint surface, particularly in the sky, can be seen as a result of this.

During cleaning in 1986 a large retouching in the lower left corner was found to cover a red paint stamp with the words 'vente Daubigny'. This reveals that the painting was in Daubigny's studio at his death and was most likely subsequently sold at the sale after his death, on May 6th and 11th 1878, although there was also a smaller sale of his paintings on his widow's death on April 4th 1891.

Old, thick and discoloured varnish was removed in cleaning and also some small scattered discoloured retouchings in the sky. The 'vente Daubigny' stamp was left visible as being of historical interest. Other retouchings were made with MS2A resin as a medium and the painting was varnished with MS2A.

Mary Allden

Villerville, Normandy, after restoration

On the River Oise, after restoration

Gustave Courbet (1819–1877)

Jean-Désiré-Gustave Courbet was born in Ornans near the Swiss border. Throughout his lifetime he painted numerous landscapes of his native Franche-Comté, including many snow landscapes. *Winter Scene*, a late work by the artist, was given to the Ashmolean Museum in 1936.

After restoration

19. *Winter Scene*
Oil on canvas, 32.5 × 40 cm
Ashmolean Museum, Oxford

The condition of the paint layer is excellent. However in 1982 when the painting was brought to the Hamilton Kerr Institute for restoration it was covered with a thick layer of surface dirt and an uneven discoloured varnish. The canvas was slightly slack and buckled in the upper corners; there was a very small pin hole in the lower right corner and some cleavage of the paint layer in the sky. The incipient flaking was treated and the small hole repaired, but no further structural treatment was undertaken since the fixed stretcher proved to be original.

When the surface dirt and the discoloured varnish were removed, the full effect of Courbet's innovative portrayal of the luminosity of freshly fallen snow could be appreciated. Courbet covered an industrially prepared buff-coloured ground with dark, almost black paint. On top of this dark underlayer he applied white paint in varying thicknesses, often allowing the black to show through to create blue shadows. This technique of applying light paint on top of dark is known as scumbling, creating what is called the 'turbid medium effect'. A similar effect is the bluish haze created by white smoke in a dark room. Courbet was certainly not the only painter to have used this technique; another very famous French painter, Claude Lorraine, used a black ground to help create the delicate atmosphere and the sensation of recession in the distant landscapes for which his paintings are so admired.

Ann Massing

John William Inchbold (1830–1888)

After restoration

John Inchbold was born in Leeds in 1830 and trained in London and was influenced by the Pre-Raphaelites. He exhibited at the Royal Academy and elsewhere from 1849.

20. *Anstey's Cove, Devon* (1854)
Oil on canvas, 50.5 × 68.3 cm
Fitzwilliam Museum

This painting was submitted to the Royal Academy in 1854 when it was rejected. It forms one of a group of extensive landscape subjects painted between 1853 and 1856. Millais particularly admired it when he saw it at the Academy before its rejection and wrote to Holman Hunt that it was 'a lovely landscape with the sea and cliffs . . . quite original and exquisitely truthful and refined.'

Anstey's (or Anstis) Cove is a celebrated beauty spot on the east coast of Devon, just north of Torquay. It is remarkable for the variety and brilliance of the colour of its rocks, which Inchbold captures in detail against an azure sea.

The painting was cleaned and restored in 1985. It was felt necessary to do this as several small retouchings in the sky had become blanched and visible The natural resin varnish was also moderately discoloured. The painting is otherwise in good condition, with only some discoloured retouchings along the lower edge of the painting and one or two small retouchings in the rocks. The sea had been scumbled over in areas to disguise some wearing. After removal of the discoloured varnish and old retouchings the painting was varnished with MS2A and retouched in an egg tempera medium with MS2A resin glazes.

Mary Allden

Oscar-Claude Monet (1840–1926)

Monet was born in Paris. His parents moved to Le Havre in 1845 and it was there in 1858 that Monet met Eugene Boudin, whose influence was more important for his development than any formal training he received either at Le Havre or in Paris, where he went in 1859 to study at the Académie Suisse. With his fellow students at Gleyre's studio, Bazille, Renoir and Sisley, he worked at Chailly in the Forest of Fontainebleau in 1864. He first exhibited at the Salon of 1865. In 1874, at the first Salon des Refusés, his painting *Impression: Sunrise* earned the group the derogatory title 'Impressionists'.

21. *Sailing Boats near the Needle and the Porte d'Aval, Etretât*
Oil on canvas, 65 × 81 cm
Private collection, on loan to the Fitzwilliam Museum

To paint this particular view, Monet must have set up his easel on the cliff not far from the top of the Manneporte at the west of Etretât. Monet painted another view from the same position which is dated 1885 and was exhibited at George Petit's gallery in Paris in 1886. Monet was at Etretât from mid-September until 14th December 1885. In several of his letters he complained about the deplorable weather and expressed his anxiety that he would not be able to finish all his paintings. In a letter of 24th October to Alice Hoschedé he mentions that he had begun work on some *répétitions*, and this painting, clearly unfinished, not signed but stamped with the studio stamp, may be one of these.

The painting had been glue lined, appeared to have areas of overpaint and was much obscured by discoloured varnish when examined before cleaning in 1983. During cleaning it was found that a thin layer of pale green overpaint extended from the base of the cliffs and

After restoration

covered the upper half of the sea. The edges of the canvas had been overpainted where the original brush strokes did not completely cover the canvas. This restoration was probably done to give the canvas a more 'finished' appearance for sale. Small losses and embedded lumps of paint on the lower and upper edges probably correspond to the clamps of the easel bars when the picture was painted. The removal of varnish and overpaint restored the precipitous viewpoint of the composition. Never intended to be varnished, the painting was given a thin matt spray coating of Laropal K80 resin with Cosmolloid K80 wax which did not alter the surface quality. However, the glue lining has flattened the impasto appreciably.

Ian McClure, Karen Ashworth

John Singer Sargent (1856–1925)

Born in Florence of American parents, Sargent studied at the École des Beaux-Arts and was a pupil of Carolus Duran in 1874. In 1885 he moved from Paris to London. In 1897 he was elected to the Royal Academy. Sargent travelled extensively; he was influenced by the Impressionists, and studied Velasquez and Hals. Although his reputation was made as a portrait painter he also painted a considerable number of landscapes. Sargent died in London.

22. *Near the Mount of Olives, Jerusalem*
Oil on canvas, 66.5 × 97.7 cm
Fitzwilliam Museum

Sargent began to plan a second journey to the Middle East, to visit Syria and Palestine, in 1905. The likely reason for his visit was to research for his murals for the Boston Public Library: the six lunettes connecting the Pagan and Christian ends of the Library Hall which were installed in 1916 included a 'Sermon on the Mount' and for this he probably wanted to have first-hand experience of the topography of the Holy Land. He reached Palestine in the autumn of 1905 but his visit was cut short by news of his mother's death on January 21 1906.

The view is taken from near the Mount of Olives looking to the walls of Old Jerusalem. Sargent painted a number of water colours on this visit and the looseness of handling in this oil gives a brilliance of surface effect similar to that captured in his watercolours.

The painting is unlined. It was covered by a layer of surface dirt and discoloured varnish, but cleaning revealed it to be in virtually unblemished condition. Traces and 'pockets' of varnish were removed from the impasto using solvent and a small brush. The painting was very thinly varnished with a silk covered pad and a final matt varnish, MS2A with Cosmolloid 80H wax, left the work with an almost unvarnished appearance whilst protecting the surface.

Ian McClure, Sarah Murray

After restoration

Spencer Frederick Gore (1878–1914)

Gore was born at Epsom in Surrey. He studied at the Slade School 1896 – 99, a contemporary of Harold Gilman. In 1904 he met Walter Sickert in Dieppe and subsequently associated with him, Lucien Pissarro, Gilman and Charles Ginner. He helped found the Allied Artists' Association in 1908, in 1909 he was a member of the New England Art Club and in 1911 was co-founder and first president of the Camden Town Group. Influenced by the first Post-Impressionist exhibition, he exhibited at the second in 1912. In 1913 he exhibited with Gilman at the Carfax Gallery and became a member of the London Group. He died at Richmond, Surrey.

After restoration

23. *Nearing Euston Station*
Oil on canvas, 51 × 61 cm
King's College, Cambridge

The picture, which was bought by John Maynard Keynes from Michael Sadler's sale at Christie's (30 November 1928, lot 133) is a prime example of Gore's 'expressionist' colouring. It was severely discoloured by old varnish, and cleaning revealed the full authority of Gore's original tones. The picture must post-date the first Post-Impressionist exhibition (1910/11) and was probably painted in 1911. *The Nursery Window, Rowlandson House* of that year also depicts Euston Station. The removal of the varnish revealed no losses or damage to the paint layer, which was thinly revarnished for protection.

Ann Massing

Philip Wilson Steer (1860–1942)

Born in Birkenhead, after training at the Gloucester School of Art Steer studied in Paris for three years, after failing to be accepted at the Royal Academy Schools. The influence of Impressionism on his work appears later, after a series of exhibitions in London in the 1880s, although he recorded his admiration for Manet. He taught at the Slade School from 1895 to 1930 and was one of the founder members of the New English Art Club.

After restoration

24. *Hydrangeas* 1901
Oil on canvas, 85.4 × 112 cm
Fitzwilliam Museum

Probably a portrait of Miss Ethel Warwick, the illusion of a tour de force of alla prima painting is, as in much of Steer's work, a result of considerable reworking and adjustment of tones. The painting, which is unlined, had a discoloured layer of varnish. Although the craquelure pattern is raised, with a noticeable crack corresponding to the stretcher bar, lower centre, no structural work was deemed necessary. Several areas of the paint layer were found to be extremely soluble, for example, on the left side and details such as the cat, suggesting the presence of resinous glazes. A very thin layer of varnish, Laropal K80 with Cosmolloid K80 wax, was applied to retain the unvarnished appearance of the paint whilst protecting the paint layer.

Ian McClure

Ben Nicholson (1894–1982)

Kettle's Yard was given by Jim Ede to the University of Cambridge in 1966. Jim Ede's friends Winifred and Ben Nicholson inspired his interest in contemporary art, and many of their works are included in his collection now displayed at Kettle's Yard. *Still Life with Knife and Lemon*, 1927, an early work by Nicholson, hangs in the large extension to the original cottage, which was designed by Sir Leslie Martin and opened in 1970.

After restoration

25. *Still Life with Knife and Lemon*
Gouache (?) on canvas, 91.5 × 122 cm
Kettle's Yard, University of Cambridge

Twentieth century paintings are often in need of restoration even though no accidental damage has occurred, because contemporary painters are often careless or experimental with their materials or techniques. Several of Ben Nicholson's paintings from Kettle's Yard have been treated for flaking paint.

Still Life with Knife and Lemon was painted on a canvas which had been stretched onto the wrong side of the stretcher, ie the bevelled edge was facing out and the painting was therefore resting directly on the stretcher bars. Dust and dirt were lodged between the canvas and the stretcher bars and had caused distortions in the canvas. Because the stretcher bars were touching the back of the canvas, they had begun to mark through to the front of the painting; along the edges the paint layer had begun to crack.

The paint layer appears in relatively good condition, but closer inspection reveals losses, and the bare canvas or underlayers show through in several places. Areas such as the black plate on which the two lemons are sitting appear blanched. Very little restoration was undertaken; a small dent in the canvas was removed; the other defects, due to inconsistencies in technique, were left untouched.

However, in order to prevent further deterioration, the painting was removed from its stretcher and restretched onto the bevelled side. The painting was surface cleaned, using white spirit since the paint was water soluble, and then given a light spray coat of Ketone Resin 'N' matt varnish. Modern paintings which were never intended to be varnished can be given a 'matt' varnish containing mainly wax (Cosmolloid 80H in this case). This does not alter the surface appearance yet provides a light coating which will protect the paint and facilitate removal of surface dirt in the future.

Ann Massing